THE
HUMAN
PREDICAMENT

THE
HUMAN
PREDICAMENT

An International Dialogue on the Meaning of Human Behavior

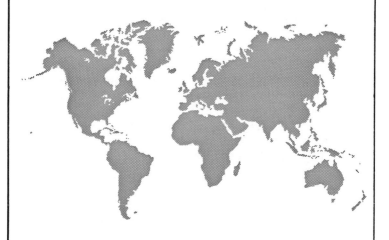

Edited by Dennis V. Razis, M.D.

Prometheus Books

59 John Glenn Drive
Amherst, NewYork 14228-2197

Published 1996 by Prometheus Books

00 99 98 97 96   5 4 3 2 1

Library of Congress Cataloging-in-Publication Data

The human predicament : an international dialogue on the meaning of human
    behavior / edited by Dennis V. Razis.
        p.   cm.
    Includes bibliographical references.
    ISBN 1–57392–085–1 (cloth : alk. paper)
        1. Man. 2. Humanism. 3. Psychology. 4. Philosophy. 5. Science.
I. Razis, Dennis V.
BD450.H863   1996
128—dc20   96–3036
                                                                    CIP

Printed in the United States of America on acid-free paper

To all those who believe

that this is not the best possible world,
that the structure of human societies
must be drastically changed, and
that we must preserve the existence of the Human Species

Contents

7

Contributors

Eftichios Bitsakis, Professor Emeritus of Philosophy, University of Ioannina, Athens, Greece

Bonnie Bullough (deceased), University of Southern California, Northridge, California, United States

Vern L. Bullough, Ph.D., R.N., President, International Humanist and Ethical Union, Distinguished Professor Emeritus, State University of New York, Northridge, California, United States

P. B. Cliteur, Professor of Philosophy, Technical University of Delft, The Netherlands

Jules Dassin, Theater and Film Director, Athens, Greece

José M. R. Delgado, Professor of Neurobiology, Center of Neurobiology Studies, Madrid, Spain

11

Antony G. N. Flew, Professor, Keele University, Reading, England

Emil J. Freireich, M.D., Professor of Medicine, M. D. Anderson Cancer Center, Houston, Texas, United States

William J. M. Hrushesky, M.D., Professor of Medical Oncology, Stratton Veterans Administration Medical Center, Albany, New York, United States

Dušan T. Kanazir, Academician, Serbian Academy of Sciences & Arts, Beograd, Yugoslavia

A. G. Kefalas, Ph.D., Professor of Management, University of Georgia, Athens, Georgia, United States

Vally Koubi, Department of Political Science, University of Georgia, Athens, Georgia, United States

Martha Koukkou, M.D., Professor of Psychophysiology in Psychiatry, EEG-Brain Mapping Laboratory, Hospital of Psychiatry of Bern, Switzerland

Paul Kurtz, Professor Emeritus of Philosophy, State University of New York at Buffalo, Amherst, New York, United States

George P. Larounis, Businessman, Athens, Greece

Dietrich Lehmann, University Hospital of Psychiatry, Zurich, Switzerland

Max Oelschlaeger, Professor of Philosophy and Religion Studies, University of North Texas, United States

Dennis V. Razis, Medical Oncologist, Athens, Greece

Evi Razis, Medical Oncologist, Athens, Greece

Walter Sinnott-Armstrong, Professor of Philosophy, Dartmouth College, Hanover, New Hampshire, United States

Evert Timmer, Medical Epidemiologist, Amsterdam, The Netherlands

H. Visser, Professor of Philosophy and Scientific Humanism, University of Limburg, Maastricht, The Netherlands

Joel Wilbush, D.Phil., M.B., Ch.B., F.R.C.O.G., Adjunct Professor of Medical Anthropology, University of Alberta, Edmonton, Alberta, Canada

P. O. Williams, M.D., F.R.C.P., London, United Kingdom

Martin S. Zand, Ph.D., M.D., Beth Israel Hospital and Harvard Medical School, Boston, Massachusetts, United States

Carla M. Zoethout, Lecturer, Center of Constitutional Law, Erasmus University, Rotterdam, The Netherlands

We owe our profound respect to the memory
of the late Melina Mercouri who, first,
as Greek minister of culture, enthusiastically
supported our movement.
Without Melina's help the Delphi Conference
would not have been realized.

Introduction

This book includes the main papers delivered at the First International Multidisciplinary Conference on "Human Behavior and the Meaning of Modern Humanism" held in Delphi, Greece, June 14–17, 1995. The purpose of this conference was to ponder the human predicament. The participants, representatives of many fields of science and intellection, have searched behind the diversity of their fields for unifying principles concerning humanity. They have also contemplated the new philosophy and ethical rules we need to face a new, emerging world where power progressively passes from nature to humans. Our aim was to contribute to the prevention of meaningless catastrophes and to the eventual justification of the term *"Homo sapiens."*

After an intense, four-day scientific and intellectual inquiry, a consensus, the Delphi Declaration, was reached. The threats to the existence of the human species, by overpopulation, degradation of the environment, and intraspecies wars are related in the Delphi Declaration to the patterns of human behavior. These patterns remain unchanged throughout history. The propensity of humans to belong to a group, a nation, a religion, an ideology, and so on, is the cause for deep differences within the human species, differences that are more important than the similarities and more significant than the differences with other species. This terrible uniqueness of the human species explains the intraspecies wars, the complete lack of a sense of unity as a species, and consequently the lack of a world will. "Anarchy" is the term for the world structure today. The absence of an international government and of global authorities makes humanity completely impotent to make any decision at the species level. The edicts of the United Nations and all other international organizations are purely advisory and routinely ignored. Thus, all major issues facing humanity are left to chance. Humanity has no intelligence at the species level. Yet the major problems we are facing today are global and must be confronted at a planetary level.

The advances in science and biology in the Western world, which started with the scientific revolution in the seventeenth century and the biological revolution in the nineteenth century, continue at an ever-increasing pace. The exponential progress in sciences and biology has resulted in dramatic changes in the world and in ourselves. This progress, however, is dangerously unbalanced—it is a progress mostly in information, not in ideas; there is little progress on the central principles of ethics, social moralities, spiritual awareness, and related values. The differences between the exponential progress in science and the stagnation of ethics might explain the paranoid elements in human behavior and in human history. Human history is characterized by the continuous swing throughout eons from the most terrible monstrosities to the most glorious achievements. The paranoid elements in human behavior are expressed in all levels— the species level, the national level, and the individual level. At the individual level the problem is what is called the "dichotomy of human mind," that is, the mental split between logic and belief, reason and faith, intellect and emotion.

This book approaches human history and human behavior in a novel and innovative way: through holistic consideration of the major problems threatening the existence of the human species and the causative relation of these problems to the patterns of human behavior.

Can we realize the goals of the Delphi Declaration? The Delphi Society, which was derived from the Delphi conference, has been organized for this purpose, that is, to define the ways and plan the action for the realization of our goals. The society will focus mainly on the patterns of human behavior. Understanding human behavior might be our only hope, as this understanding will possibly lead us to practical approaches to the main problems humanity is now facing. Two new concepts related to the patterns of human behavior, a new role for medicine and population health, are developed in this book. These new concepts have practical implications and might act as catalysts for world change.

The human race is deeply divided. This unique characteristic of the human species, associated with the exponential advances in science and biology and the stagnation of ethics and philosophy, might result in a holocaust. To prevent a meaningless global catastrophe, the Delphi Society has the ambition to contribute where all religions and all ideologies throughout history have loudly failed, that is, to define a way that will unite the human species. A bright new hope might thus rise.

Dennis V. Razis, M.D.

Opening Remarks

Welcome to Delphi, this laureled site that even my contemporary Greek friends insist is the center of the earth. You have responded to a call to, no more, no less, define modern humanism, to develop strategies to prevent a global catastrophe, and to establish an international organization dedicated to the survival of the human species. Now, that is an agenda.

But unfazed you have come. You have read of, or participated in, other conferences that issued storm warnings that were ignored and whose scientists were pronounced doomsday freaks. Yet undaunted you have come, perhaps with the spirit, "Let's try once more."

You asked to contemplate modern humanism when before you are the savage images of Sarajevo and Rwanda; when ozone depletion has reached unprecedented levels; when our waters carry disease and AIDS is a galloping nemesis; when on our planet one of five people, one billion people, live in crushing poverty and massive, desperate migrations have already begun; when powerful business organizations find that the way to make greater and greater profits is to cast more and more into joblessness; when the richest impede environmental preservation and the poorest despoil nature in order to exist; and when nothing has changed from Darwin's view that whatever moral code there is, is but a political compromise established by competing centers of power.

Finally, ladies and gentlemen, I believe you are heroes because religions and governments have failed and the only hope is to invest in nongovernmental organizations. Some have already proved themselves; Amnesty International, Greenpeace, the World Wildlife Fund, Save the Children International, and others have earned respect for thought and action. These heroes were not the stargazers or the idealists that Nietzsche may have joked about. Just as you do, they saw that the time is out of joint and somebody has to put it right.

You know it; a single person or a group of people, as from this country, have changed the course of civilization and bettered the human species. Could it not be that you have been chosen, and from this center, this conference at Delphi, an international organization will be born to affirm the survival of this species; to save man from man, this creature man, this genius, this killer, this creator, this destroyer, this benefactor, this evildoer, this modern human. You are asked to define modern humanism. At the end of Eugene O'Neill's play *The Great God Brown,* a police officer looks down at a dead body, takes out a notebook and pencil and asks a witness, "What's his name?" The witness answers, "Man." The officer asks "How do you spell it?" How?

Jules Dassin
Athens, Greece

On behalf of the Organizing Committee I cordially welcome our distinguished guests and friends at Delphi, the center of the earth for the ancient Greeks. Delphi was also the place of the famous temple of Apollo, god of light, music, and of foreseeing the future; the place of the renowned Amphiktyony, which consisted of delegates from all the "nations" of the Hellenes and contributed to wartime and peacetime enterprises, to political and civil controversies, and to intellectual and religious pursuits. Amphiktyony was thus a prefiguration of modern international institutions. It is no wonder that ancient Greeks chose this imposing place for their intellectual, social, spiritual, and religious activities.

Human societies and the human species might be doomed to extinction by their ever-growing population, their destruction of the environment, and modern wars. Is human behavior rightly blamed for these emerging risks of annihilation? Human behavior and human history are characterized by the continuous swing, back and forth, from the most glorious achievements to the most terrible monstrosities. Which are the forces that shape these paranoid patterns of human behavior, paranoid human history, and propel us to our own demise? During our four-day intellectual trip, we will address and focus on these questions.

The existence of the human species is not threatened only by man. Biological evolution, a continuing process that is poorly understood, earmarks *Homo sapiens,* now the dominant species of earth, as a very transitory creature. Of all the species the earth has ever supported, 99.9 percent are now extinct. Can the genius of man stop the evolutionary process and preserve the existence of the human species? At first thought, it seems futile a priori.

Yet man, now the master of earth, is the first and only form of life able to interfere with earth's evolutionary process of life. Actually, in biology power progressively passes from nature to man. Modern genetic biotechnology, gene manipulation, modern science, and nanotechnology give humanity the unprecedented power to change both the world and itself. By changing our genetic information, we can potentially increase our lifespan, change our biological characteristics by making recombinant people, and create new species by "unnatural selection."

However, are we prepared philosophically and ethically to face this fantastic new situation? And is the structure of human societies capable of dealing with it?

There is not yet a philosophical or ethical system, be it humanist or religion-based, able to face the challenges that confront us today and will be multiplied tomorrow. How are we going to answer such questions as: What is the carrying capacity of the earth? What should the ethical rules for culture and science be? How are we going to preserve the threatened existence of the human species? All these questions are left to chance.

The imbalance between the ever-increasing power of science and the stagnation of ethics and philosophy is in my view basically responsible for the apparent human predicament. That is where, again in my view, we should mostly focus.

This multidisciplinary conference will approach the problem of human existence in novel and innovative ways. Our goal is to define the meaning of modern humanism, to develop strategies for the prevention of catastrophes, and to organize an international club, the Delphi Society, dedicated to the preservation of the human species.

Let me close my short remarks by repeating the comments of the United Nations Educational, Scientific and Cultural Organization on the Delphi Conference: "The problem that you are concerned with is evidently of the utmost significance, dwarfing all others. . . ."

Dennis V. Razis, M.D.
President of the Organizing Committee
Athens, Greece

1

The Human Prospect:
Is the Annihilation of the Human Species
a Real and Imminent Possibility?

Max Oelschlaeger

My mission here (to play on words) is impossible. In fifty minutes I am to address this distinguished forum concerning a matter of utmost gravity, a matter shot through and through with *scientific and philosophic uncertainty*, and a matter which is, moreover, generally contentious. The very notion of environmental crisis is actively opposed by a wide array of political, economic, and social forces—which I shall hereafter refer to as the Dominant Social Paradigm.

Thus I run several risks, the first of which is carrying coals to Newcastle. As the president of the Delphi Conference observes, "The idea of the conference is not just to rehash what is so often said in specialized journals and the mass media about . . . [environmental problems]."[1] Insofar as I recite the standard litany of environmental pathologies—depletion of stratospheric ozone, climate warming, overpopulation, and so on—I stand guilty of keenly observing the obvious. Further, notwithstanding a developing consensus within the global scientific community on a variety of ecological perils that threaten not only the future of the human species but a sixth mass extinction of life, all those who counsel the *precautionary principle* run the risk of appearing as environmental doomsayers, even Cassandras. This risk is compounded by the Pygmalion effect: pessimism is too often if not invariably a self-fulfilling prophecy. Yet I am caught between the Scylla of pessimism and the Charybdis of optimism, for if I take an affirmative tack, that global environmental crisis is a tractable problem, then I appear to abandon the traditional "hands off" posture of scholarly objectivity, being immediately caught up in the messy business of intellectual advocacy and stuck in the messy tar of practical affairs.

You are forewarned: I now begin to skate on thin ice. Nothing less, it seems to me, is adequate to historic crisis, and environmental crisis is a historic crisis, for it calls the basic premises, the basic presuppositions upon which culture has been built, into question. The center, as the poet once said, will not hold. We, the human species en masse, are now testing the question put to us by Shakespeare: Is history but sound and fury signifying nothing? With a number of others, I believe that what is required, perhaps more so than anything else, is entertaining an alternative definition of human beingness, while recognizing that the human species is secondarily nidicolous and thus cannot reinvent itself ex nihilo. We come to our maturity and assume our specifically human projects within the womb of culture. But while the cultural past conditions, it does not entirely determine the future.

My analysis is divided into three parts, all of which are inadequate from a specialized intellectual viewpoint. However, my approach trades on the notion that "the specialized viewpoint" is part of the problem, for intellectuals generally are increasingly isolated, so that they know more and more about less and less until they know everything about nothing. I believe that only some cross-disciplinary or transdisciplinary framework will be adequate to the nature of the environmental challenge we face. Our aim at this conference, as Dr. Razis observes,

> is to approach . . . [environmental crisis] from a holistic point of view. . . . Factors to be considered include . . . patterns of human behaviour which have remained unchanged through history and their explanation on a neurophysiological or other basis. The desired result is the definition of Modern Humanism, the development of strategies to prevent a global ecocatastrophe and the establishment of an international society dedicated to the survival of the human species.[2]

The three areas I address are as follows:

First, the lay of the land. Following the lead of a number of profound thinkers, I characterize global environmental crisis apropos of the survival prospects of the human species in terms of *population health*, which in a narrowly human or anthropocentric framework might be termed *public health*.

Second, an assessment of the resources ready to hand. Here I examine the discrepancy between humankind's scientific and technological achievements and the continued dominance of what has been characterized as alpha-ethics. More generally, I assess the Dominant Social Paradigm and its influence on the human prospect.

Third, a prospective, based on the two foregoing sections. Here I pick up what Dr. Razis has elsewhere called "a new role for medicine" and develop this idea in the context of the *metaphoric of health* (health as defined by Spencer as "the perfect adjustment of an organism to its environment," cited in Timmer[3]). Health, reconceptualized as an ecosocial, organismic-ecosystemic concept, can undergird a potent transdisciplinary discourse potentially adequate to the transformation of culture. Such an idea, consistent with Dr.

Razis's letter to the participants in the Delphi Conference, is clearly utopian. At least on first blush. Yet it is arguably a reflexive (explicitly self-conscious) realization of a *new humanism*, predicated in part on the neurophysiological explanation of human behavior (across its entire spectrum, from reproductive to collective, scientific to political).

I

Native range perception inclines the overwhelming majority of humankind to perceive issues of health and survival in personal and relatively short-run terms. Indeed, we are biologically predisposed to do so. Individuals are aware of environmental impacts on human health, if for no other reason than the reports of adverse effects that abound in the popular press. The disaster at Bhopal, India, comes immediately and dramatically to mind, with casualties in the tens of thousands. But such examples clearly do not address the issue of *population health in an ecosystemic framework*. Health is typically conceptualized as a matter of individual well-being and survival rather than as a species-level issue. Hippocratic medicine itself remains focused on individual health, while our concern at the Delphi Conference is with the human species, that is, the question of whether the annihilation of the human species is a real and imminent possibility. When I talk about the prospects for the annihilation of the human species I mean simply the *risk* (which is not precisely quantifiable and subject to uncertainty) that the anthropogenic disruption of natural systems and biogeophysical processes is either exceeding or threatening to exceed the carrying capacity of the earth. Among many, Dr. A. J. McMichael argues that global ecological disruption is the consequence of cultural evolution that, unlike other health risks that posed threats to individuals or groups of individuals, poses the threat of annihilation for the human species.[4]

I appreciate the semantic issues created by the use of such terms as *carrying capacity*. For example, a population biologist might define carrying capacity as the "asymptotic limit reached when density-dependent morality equals fertility," thus implying a fixed limit to carrying capacity for any species in a relatively constant environment, whereas a neoclassical economist views carrying capacity as subject to change due to technological dynamism and regional, national, and international trade. I use the term herein in reference to the total number of human beings that could economically sustain themselves on planet earth consistent with preservation of habitat and maintenance of biodiversity, social justice, human dignity, and democratic process.

At present the ongoing disruption of natural systems and destabilization of biogeophysical processes threatens irrevocable impairment of the primary productivity of planet earth. The term *anthropogenic biosphere* has been suggested as a descriptor for the biosphere, suggesting that humankind is so "closely coupled" with biogeophysical processes that no credible defense can be made of the idea of a "pristine biosphere" beyond human influence.[5] Which is to say that culture, once relatively impotent in relation to nature, now threatens potentially catastrophic and even irreversible change in the order of things. Writing in the *Journal of the Royal Society of Medicine*, Dr. Razis contends that, "It is a real possibility that the human race could be completely annihilated by . . . overpopulation, viral supremacy, and environmental pollution."[6] McMichael argues in *Planetary Overload* that, "In a world of accelerating environmental impact we may have precious little time to embrace the idea of a sustainable biosphere as the necessary, non-negotiable basis of long-term human health."[7]

What is the material motor that drives us toward oblivion? How is it that a relatively insignificant primate species that first emerged on the savannahs of Africa has become, whatever our storied achievements in historical time (as distinct from natural history), the scourge of the planet? I offer here an oversimplification, one that ignores such obvious factors as ideology and politics, yet one that, adequately fleshed out, might stand the test of critical scrutiny. Namely, population.

Consider that our present biological success—human biomass now exceeds that of any other terrestrial life form on the planet with the exception of domesticated herbivores—endangers our future. The renowned evolutionary biologist, Edward O. Wilson, characterizes species *Homo sapiens* as an ecological aberration.

> Human demographic success has brought the world to . . . [the] crisis of biodiversity. Human beings—mammals of the fifty-kilogram weight class and members of a group, the primates, otherwise noted for scarcity—have become a hundred times more numerous than any other land animal of comparable size in the history of life. By every conceivable measure humanity is ecologically abnormal.[8]

Clearly, the sheer mass of humanity figures significantly in the millionfold increase in the collective impact of human beings on planetary processes in the last ten thousand years. Population pressure drives technological dynamism, the evolution of increasingly complex forms of social organization, and the articulation of ever more complicated schemes of philosophical and religious rationalization (or social legitimation). Johnson and Earle argue that in order to

> sustain economic integration beyond the capacity of the biological bonds that underpin the familistic group, it is necessary to extend the individual's sense of "self-interest" to broader social units. *This extension of self is based on symbols.* The evolution of the political economy represents the elaboration of this symbolizing capacity in order to overcome the individualistic, competitive, divi-

sive, centrifugal stresses that continually threaten to defeat efforts to cooperate beyond the family level.[9] [Emphasis added.]

The upshot is that with the Neolithic turn the *subsistence economy*, with the family at the center, quickly gives way to the *political economy*. The role of the family, the basic biological unit of reproduction, quickly diminishes in cultural affairs, especially so in economic affairs. Skipping over (blush!) ten thousand years of history, we arrive at the present cultural configuration, dominated by nation-states and increasingly powerful multinational corporations. The process of economic depersonalization and ecological commodification is virtually complete, whereby *the symbol system* of the so-called free market regulates human behavior, "the 'invisible hand' of the market allocating goods and services without regard for social relationships, ethics, or need, but only according to the buyer's purchasing power and the seller's costs."[10] Nature, variously conceptualized since time immemorial as a living, organic entity (physiomorphism, anthropomorphism, and so on), becomes intraconvertible matter-energy, standing reserve for human appropriation.

The growth dynamic of *Homo sapiens* appears set to continue until either a slow process of withering away concludes or a cataclysmic collapse of the global ecosystem occurs. More people means more demand placed on an already fragile globe through technologies that are themselves ecologically pernicious. As the recent report of the National (United States) Commission on the Environment states,

Over the next fifty years—within the lifetimes of many of us and of all our children—economic activity in the United States is projected to quadruple and global population to double at least. If growth of this magnitude occurs with current industrial processes, agricultural methods, and consumer practices, the results could be both environmentally and economically disastrous.[11]

Whatever the imperfections of the present analysis, and I am sure they are many, the simple reality of numbers alone presents a rather frightening specter. A variety of prognostications, including those of the United Nations, indicate a doubling of the human population by the year 2100. Or sooner! Given the complicated ecological reality of the world, and the ever-increasing human impacts upon that world, such growth projections are truly ominous.

Time will tell what effects the UNCED conference at Rio de Janeiro in 1992, the Cairo Conference on population, and the recent conference in Germany on climate warming might have. My own belief is that they are inadequate, almost mirror reflections of the etiology that drives humankind toward oblivion, and woefully inadequate to the gravity of the challenge. Razis observes that although we might think that human societies would rush toward devising solutions, responses have been "surprisingly apathetic."[12]

Why? Why do we not perceive the threat? That is the question. A variety of answers might be offered. The present disciplinary dogma that rules the intellectual world predisposes most of us to contend that our specialization, be this philosophy or religion, ethics or ecology, economics or engineering, has the one right answer: if only everybody else would listen and then fall into line.

However, since I am already skating on thin ice, let me offer a relatively straightforward bipolar explanation, one that looks both to *evolutionary history* and *cultural context* (and thus ideally escapes the dichotomization of nature and nurture). Evolution predisposes us biologically to react (along with virtually the entirety of the living world) on the basis of immediate survival and short-term gain. Given our evolutionary equipment, such as the opposed thumbs and the neocortex, human history appears to be a foregone conclusion. Arguably, the crucible and the retort are manifest in the smoky fires of our Pleistocene forbears. McMichael observes that, "It is the combination of this instinct for short-term individual gain . . . with human brain-power that, through its consequences, jeopardizes the longer-term needs of the human species. So, to overcome today's environmental problems we will need both understanding and moral fortitude to compensate for this genetically endowed 'predilection for short-term gain.' "[13]

We find the second dimension of an answer to "the question of apathy" through the reflexive consideration of cultural process. As a secondary nidicolous species, we are biologically underdetermined. Cultural anthropologist Clifford Geertz contends that, "Because human behavior is so loosely determined by intrinsic sources of information (the genes themselves)," symbolic systems (like economic and religious discourse) that "lie outside the boundaries of the individual organism" assume a major role in determining human behavior. Sociobiologists have contributed enormously to our understanding of these extraorganismic symbol systems, if in no other way than through the terminology of the meme, to be understood (analogously to the gene in biology) as the bearer of reproductive information for culture. However, while genes and memes are analogous, there are also important differences between them. Geertz argues that genes are models of an observable pattern or order, but that symbol systems (or memes) are not only models *of* but also models *for* observable patterns or orders: "They give meaning, that is, objective conceptual form, to social and psychological reality both by shaping themselves to it and by shaping it to themselves."[14]

We are touching on complexities hopelessly beyond the possibility of resolution in the present essay. My point is that the exosomatic or memetic sources of information that encode human behavior, making possible both the production and reproduction of culture, are (another analogy) like the gene, selfish (although, as Richard Dawkins makes clear, altruistic behavior is possible: indeed, we even have memes that reinforce such behavior). And necessarily so, since human beings do not in their projects have time to continually reinvent themselves. Co-adapted meme complexes, such as the Dominant Social Paradigm, underlie the present world problematic, and they mindlessly, indeed, automatically, reproduce themselves. Thus, it would seem, *Homo sapiens* is caught between a rock and a hard spot, whipsawed by our biological propensity to focus on the short term and our cultural predisposition to perpetuate the forms of the past. On such evidence, the human prospect is dim at best.

What, then, are we to do? Razis argues that, "The prospect of human destruction, by overpopulation, degradation of the environment and atomic wars, cannot be confronted with archaic philosophical, religious, and biological thinking. Such thinking explains the failure of the Rio de Janeiro conference. Any future conferences with the same attitudes will certainly fail."[15]

II

My goal in this section is primarily to plumb the depths of the resources ready to hand, to see what it is that humankind might avail itself of in the face of possible annihilation. If we have adequate resources, then the risk of annihilation is significantly reduced. If, on the other hand, present resources are inadequate, then the risk of annihilation is significantly increased.

You'll pardon me an Americanism: we are like the proverbial pioneer facing an angry grizzly bear with a willow switch. The resources ready to hand, in other words, while they condition the ambit of possibility, are in and of themselves inadequate. I begin with the Dominant Social Paradigm, as reflected in the conventional wisdom that humankind is, as William C. Clark of Harvard University contends, capable of managing planet earth.[16] The Dominant Social Paradigm predisposes us to technological hubris: the belief that we are somehow in control of the planet. I view such an attitude as typifying those of the elites who are officially in charge of responding to planetary ecocrisis. Notwithstanding such statements as the Brundtland Report and the Schmidheiny Report,[17] plans which ostensibly articulate a sustainable future for humankind, the annihilation of the human species is both a real (as distinct from imaginary) and imminent (meaning within a matter of centuries if not decades) possibility. (One temporal key is *timely action.* For example, the conversion to a solar economy will not be easy, will be expensive, and will take a long time, at least fifty years. We must begin now, that is, within the window of possibility.)

Again, I touch on very complicated issues in a fashion that is altogether too brief. Yet the proposals for so-called *sustainable development* are enormously problematic, as numerous analyses have attempted to make clear. Among these difficulties are (a) a belief that the second law of thermodynamics is economically irrelevant,[18] (b) a privileging of Western interests at the expense of developing and Third World nations,[19] (c) a reification of Western man and society as the normative model for the world,[20] (d) a continued belief in cornucopian solutions, especially technological fixes, for any and all ecological problems,[21] and finally, (e) a failure to identify and confront the ideological foundations of the Dominant Social Paradigm.[22] There is considerable evidence that the programmatic proposals for sustainable development are more manifestations of symptoms than prescriptions for solution.

This latter issue, that is, a failure to confront the ideological foundations of the Dominant Social Paradigm, is further complicated by what Dr. Evert Timmer identifies as the problem of alpha-ethics. "The oldest surviving alpha-ethical codes date from roughly twentieth to eighteenth centuries B.C. . . . They reached an early peak in the ten commandments of the Mosaic world view and evolved over the centuries to the corpus of alpha-ethics produced by religious and philosophical thinking." The problem, Timmer continues, is that alpha-ethical codes have lapsed in the face of the modern, scientifically explained and technologically dynamic world in which we live. The problem was quite evident to Kant, as it was to even his predecessors, such as Francis Bacon, who appealed to biblical themes in order to legitimize sociocultural transformation. Thus, Timmer contends, "Theologians and philosophers have no authority in the area of science and have become . . . kings without a kingdom."[23]

Indeed, the problem of social values and scientific research and application is acute, as manifest in the ongoing underinvestment of capital in research addressing social problems and overinvestment of capital in research devoted to the ends of military hardware. In the context of a global ecocrisis, Timmer argues that the need is acute for beta-ethics (a relative version, since on his account an absolute beta-ethics is a contradiction in terms). Beta-ethics opinion would be "directed towards integrating *Homo sapiens* in the optimized ecosystem of the planet as an integral part of the evolution of life on earth. . . . [In effect,] beta-ethics would be the compass used for steering an optimal course between the interests of *Homo sapiens* and the interest of Living Nature as a whole."[24]

Timmer's term, "beta-ethics," might be associated with a variety of other names. He suggests, for example, beta-ethics are in accord with the philosophy of Spinoza, who equated nature and God, conceptualizing them as different faces of a single underlying reality. This argument is very similar to that of the deep ecologists, especially the Norwegian Arne Naess and the American George Sessions. Beta-ethics might also be associated with land ethics, as in Aldo Leopold's notion that any evolutionary advance in ethical theory would have to include nature as morally considerable. On Leopold's account a behavior is correct when it preserves the integrity, stability, and beauty of the land community, of which humankind is just a member and citizen, not the lord and master.[25]

I am largely in agreement with Timmer's diagnosis: the patient, *Homo sapiens*, is unknowingly in grave condition. Like the unseen danger of arteriosclerosis (hardening of the arteries), the unseen danger of culture is hardening of the categories. Healing is necessary, yet the patient continues to invest resources in perpetuating rather than overcoming disease. Timmer also begins to recontextualize ethics within a neurophysiological framework, and it is in that direction I now turn, primarily because alpha-ethics *can be* and *should be* recontextualized neurophysiologically. Indeed, this work has been pursued on a wide variety of fronts by a number of individuals.

Consider, for example, the issue of religion, or god-talk, as it is designated within the framework of general linguistics. The work of evolutionary biologists and sociobiologists has been very important in helping us come to understand religion scientifically. Edward O. Wilson argues that the human capacity to make ethical judgments has been fashioned in the crucible of evolution and remains very much tied with subcortical, limbic structures of the brain.[26] Religious belief itself is rooted in this structure; religion remains, Wilson writes, not only "the most complex and powerful force in the human mind," but "in all probability an ineradicable part of human nature."[27]

On Wilson's account, religion reflects the deep structure of the human animal in three ways. The first level he terms *ecclesiastic*, that is, "rituals and conventions are chosen by religious leaders for their emotional impact under contemporary social conditions."[28] Which is to say that religious myths, rituals, and symbols move people affectively or emotionally in a way that Wilson claims "makes us people and not computers."[29] We are not strictly and invariably rational (calculating) animals; nor should we strive to be. The second level Wilson terms *ecological*, that is, however emotionally powerful, religion is also "tested by the demands of the environment. If religions weaken their societies during warfare, encourage the destruction of the environment, shorten lives, or interfere with procreation they will, regardless of their short-term emotional benefits, initiate their own decline."[30] The third level is *co-evolution*, that is, the reciprocal influence of memetic and genetic evolution on each other. For an evolutionist like Wilson this means that religion has actually shaped human evolution: "Religious practices that consistently enhance survival and procreation of the practitioners will propagate the physiological controls that favor acquisition of the practices during single lifetimes."[31]

Religion, comprehended as symbolic discourse (see Earle and Johnson above), has been and remains a nearly universal phenomenon that helps to direct (organize, guide) human behavior, that is, provide instructions for expression of genetic potentials. Clifford Geertz offers a useful definition of religion as "(1) a system of symbols which acts to (2) establish powerful, pervasive, and long-lasting moods and motivations in men [and women] by (3) formulating conceptions of a general order of existence and (4) clothing these conceptions with such an aura of factuality that (5) the moods and motivations seem uniquely realistic."[32] Which is to say that as we move toward beta-ethics, the recontextualization of alpha-ethics in an expanded framework, including not only neurophysiology but general linguistics and cultural anthropology, leads clearly to the reconsideration of what to many environmentalists has been and remains anathema: religion.[33]

A later session of the conference will address these issues more directly. At this juncture I want to set the stage for section 3 of the paper by further developing a naturalistic perspective on the human species and the further exploration of beta-ethics and modern humanism. The most salient fact, it seems to me, is that we are language animals. Again, this is a complicated subject matter that I rush over in a way that, retrospectively, must be construed as inadequate. I aim only to relate my account to the general line of development I have been pursuing, to the effect that we are clever, big-brained bipeds whose reproductive success has inexorably pushed us in an upward spiral of increasing sociocultural complexity and technological dynamism. The upshot, at this late juncture, is planetary ecocrisis, engendered by our biological success.

A Chinese sage once remarked that the fish is the last to discover that it swims in water. Like the fish, we too are nearly oblivious to the medium that surrounds and sustains us, in which we live and move and have our specifically human being. There can be little doubt at this juncture that language is shot through and through our evolutionary history. Language and brain are arguably coevolutionary.

Neither is it a far reach to think of ecocrisis as itself a consequence of a failed story, that is, a symbolic narrative carefully nurtured and maintained by successive generations of *Euroman*. From the sociolinguistic vantage point that I am mapping here (which is fully consonant with a neurophysiological vantage point, differing only in the degree of reflexivity), language is the prototypical response of human beings to the world: it is the instrument or means of our survival, mapping not only our relations to the world of things (referential and informative language) but also our own intentions and feelings vis à vis the world and each other (intentional and expressive language).[34]

So construed, the possible annihilation of the human species is a consequence of language: we are caught in the grip of a failed story, the Dominant Social Paradigm. Thus, the issue is adaptation through language: as in the proposal for a new role for physicians, only in a way that language and the use of language is continually transparent to those who use it.

But how? That is the question.

III

Medicine should take the initiative for the creation of a new international multidisciplinary scientific organization devoted entirely to the study of ways to prevent the annihilation of the world.
—Dr. Dennis V. Razis

Perhaps the preceding section seems pessimistic, for apparently such resources as we have, our basic biology and our cultural legacy, are more hindrance than help. On the foregoing account perhaps the annihilation of the human species is inevitable: we can close the meeting with an affirmation of Arthur Koestler's hypothesis that *Homo sapiens* is one of nature's mistakes, an experiment in natural selection gone awry.

Still, there is precedent that suggests at least a possibility for adaptive change, or what I would like to call, following the lead of Dr. Jonas Salk, *metabiological evolution*.[35] There is nothing that can be done about human biology per se. Nor is there anything that needs to be done. Is there not in human biology the same potent force that moves all the living world? As José Ortega y Gasset would have it, "The reality of history lies in biological power, in pure vitality, in what there is in man [and woman] of cosmic energy, not identical with, but related to, the energy which agitates the sea, fecundates the beast, causes the tree to flower and the stars to shine."[36]

Ortega's position is not a rigid biological behaviorism, but rather resonates with the ideas that we are a biological species come to reflexive consciousness through language. We are aware that we are situated in an awe-inspiring, ongoing process of cosmic evolution. Think of the implications of the weak anthropic cosmological principle, as Barrow and Tipler counsel.[37] Better yet, think of the awesome birth of vociferation, as Maurice Merleau-Ponty suggests.[38] We are speaking flesh, flesh of the world, whose being is tied to the ongoing processes of the world. Yet our stories, about who we are and where we might be going—that is, subjectivity—as well as our stories about the nature of the world—that is, objectivity—have led us to rend the flesh of the earth.

We can, as Salk suggests, refashion ourselves in our cultural projects. Of course, Dominant Social Paradigms never give way easily; nor can they, for all things cannot be reinvented. The cultural ground which lies beneath our figurative feet cannot be whisked out from under, regardless of the claims of either dystopians or utopians. We can only advance from where we are, such as we are. Nothing can be changed; everything is possible.

Paradigmatic shifts are always announced ex post facto. However, we are in media res, as the very coming together of this assemblage at Delphi, Greece, implies. Indeed, it is in part through our own biological powers, that is, the energy that courses through our bodies and empowers our minds, the sounds that usher forth from our bodies into the world, the words that spill out across pages of typescript, that we act upon the world. And each other.

Where, I sometimes wonder, is Archimedes? He would be useful. But do we need him? For can we not, through our own performative being, begin to redirect, however subtly, the course of events? There is ample evidence that, from time to time, small groups of intellectuals have affected the course of events. Three precedents come to mind: one is Greek philosophy, as epitomized by the tradition of the Lyceum and Academy, and the radical change that occurred in human being as a consequence of Greek rationalism. Almost any sense of modern humanism has been profoundly conditioned by Greek philosophy (and for that matter Christianity, through the influence of Greek rationalism on Paul), a turn of events that itself is framed by a veritable revolution in the technology of communication and the modality of transmissible culture. (On that point E. Havelock's *Preface to Plato* is unexcelled.)

A second precedent is the so-called Elizabethan School of the Night, a diverse grouping of physicians, scientists, philosophers, and politicians that, over roughly a decade, contextualized the Enlightenment philosophy (itself a humanism) of person and society in a way that empowered it, that is, actually configured what was just another set of ideas in ways that allowed these ideas to become socially efficacious (in the broadest sense, incorporating politics, education, economics, psychology, and so on). Again, as with the Greeks, certain of these Enlightenment ideas yet condition, and in some cases, overdetermine, modern humanism.

Finally, I think of the Club of Rome, a group that, primarily through research and publications, such as the famous *The Limits to Growth* (1972) study by Meadows, Meadows, et al., brought ecological issues to the front and center of international attention in a theretofore unexampled way. Although in many ways dissimilar to the previous two examples, there are similarities in that (1) *The Limits to Growth* utilized a new technology, that is, the awesome power of computers, to marshall data in useful ways which challenged "native range perception" by computer-modeling spatio-temporal variables, and (2) the Club of Rome brought into question unquestioned beliefs that dominated social process (roughly, in this case, the notion that through technology humankind could solve any and all issues of environmental exigency).

History, then, offers relevant precedent for the Delphi Conference. Which brings me to Dr. Razis's admonition (see above). Again, I must gloss complicated issues, that is, discourse and societal transformation. But among several steps that might be taken, and certainly at the top of the list of any steps that might be taken by the presently assembled body, is the creation of an international society that envisions a new role for medicine, one that seizes up the threads of the fabric that is health, and reweaves these strands into a discourse adequate to societal transformation, that is, promotes metabiological evolution. For a variety of reasons, envisioning and then acting on a new role for medicine, one organized around the discourse of health, can be understood as essential to the survival of the human species (or reducing the risk of annihilation). I gloss two of them by way of concluding my argument. I begin with the issue of leadership and then conclude with a commentary on effective discourse.

Many have suggested that democratic leaders can only take the people where they will follow. Fewer have recognized the vital importance that leaders have in shaping public opinion and thus public action. And fewer still are capable of recognizing the obligations of leadership and acting upon them. In this time of mass culture, indeed, to be different is to be indecent: the herd mentality threatens us all.

Empirical studies of the formation of environmental attitudes reveal a complicated causal chain, the elucidation of which is beyond immediate reach. The important point is that the work of leaders is vitally important to the *human prospect*, as I have termed it. If the human species is to escape its own success, then leaders must stand forth. Where are these leaders? Where are the groups from which they might come?

Razis suggests that at least some of them might be physicians. Of course, he notes, "Hippocratic medicine is traditionally involved with our survival as individuals or groups. . . . Medicine has not been particularly involved with the health of future communities and with our survival as a species."[39] And there are a number reasons beyond medical tradition, such as political and economic ones, that suggest that few physicians might be willing to assume the mantle of leadership. Yet what group, I ask, is a more likely one from which leaders might come?

Very few groups ever achieve "standing," that is, a position which commands attention. Intellectuals generally lack standing; they are often characterized as "experts nobody wants." But physicians do have standing in Western society, largely because they are caught up with the awesome processes of life and death in ways legitimated by tradition and reinforced by medical technology: they command respect. The affinity of physicians with issues of health, and the experience and concern of every human being on the planet with issues of life and death, offers an intrinsic link to the primary objectives of the Delphi Conference: that is, to define modern humanism, to prevent global ecocatastrophe, to facilitate survival.

Further, issues of health are one way in which modern humanism can be conceptualized as a universal discourse that transcends cultural diversity. Moreover, a holistic point of view is readily facilitated by and articulated through the discourse of health. The kernel of this discourse is that the biogeophysical health of the planet is intrinsically bound with human health and vice versa. Human pathologies, physical ones, such as malnourishment, and spiritual ones, such as greed, engender ecological pathologies, such as the devastation of the Himalayan ecosystem by hungry peasants or the infiltration of salt water into the central valley of California as a consequence of the greed of agribusiness. Similarly, pathological ecosystems, such as (very generally) the rifts in stratospheric ozone, adversely affect human health. Interestingly, the discourse of health is not the monopoly of physicians; health can also be conceptualized as a powerful metaphor that facilitates the crossing of apparently separate semantic (professional) fields, like ecology, medicine, sociology, and philosophy.

It is difficult to conceptualize progress towards a sustainable future, one that escapes our biological and conceptual predisposition to oblivion, unless the institutionally established elites throughout the world—Moscow and Washington, London and Athens, Delhi and Beijing—come to recognize the uncertain nature of the human prospect. The culturally dominant response to ecocrisis, termed the sustainable development paradigm, is internally incoherent.[40] For its stated ecological objectives (to resolve ecopathology) and its economic objectives (to eliminate poverty) are incompatible. The discourse of sustainable development must be challenged.

If *culture is communication*, and apart from communication on a global scale it is difficult to envision the survival of the species, then an alternative paradigm, which many term the sustainability paradigm, must be societally articulated, consistent with ecological and cultural diversity. Such a discourse must be simple enough to be readily communicable yet analytically robust enough to lead the way toward change. (Agenda 21 is, in my opinion, hopelessly complex, perhaps by design. Such a complicated proposal can neither win mass support among the world's citizens nor in fact be implemented.) The discourse of *public health*, I suggest, offers such a possibility.

What are the salient characteristics of effective discourse? Very briefly, these are three (and I am here following the lead of Bruce Lincoln). First, as suggested above, is the issue of standing: can the discourse be heard? effectively propagated? by whom? In part, success or failure is governed by "the ability of its propagators to gain access to and exploit the opportunities inherent within varied channels of communication—formal and informal, established and novel."[41] Culture is communication, for communication is the means of not only the perpetuation of established forms but also of adaptation to novel circumstances. Second is the issue of the persuasiveness of discourse, which is only in part "a function of logical and ideological coherence." And, Lincoln continues, it must be understood that "persuasion does not reside within any discourse per se but is, rather, a measure of audiences' reaction to, and interaction with, the discourse."[42] Third, and finally, "there is the question of whether— and the extent to which—a discourse succeeds in calling forth a following; this ultimately depends on whether a discourse elicits those sentiments out of which new social formations can be constructed."[43]

The discourse of health, I submit, arguably meets these criteria. Physicians have standing. And all human beings are flesh, bound up with the ongoing process of life and death. The discourse of health cannot but help call forth a following.

Conclusion

I return to the subject of risk and uncertainty apropos of the human prospect. Global ecocrisis suggests that our biological (reproductive) success has created a world where we no longer biologically fit. Many among us believe that the human prospect is uncertain. Uncertainty itself, post-Gödel, Heisenberg, Wittgenstein, and Popper (to name just a few), indeed, post-Darwin, seems to be a new category with which we must reckon. (Evolution implies that novelty—unpredicted outcome, chance events—is a fundamental aspect of being as we know it.) Uncertainty necessarily cuts both for and against those who either affirm or dismiss the possibility of the annihilation of the human species.

However, the precautionary principle is an important qualification of uncertainty. For to affirm the judgment that solutions for irrevocable, anthropogenic planetary change can be found within the Dominant Social Paradigm, as in the many proposals for sustainable development, is to commit the *ad ignorantium fallacy*, that is, to affirm that the proposal for sustainable development is true since it cannot be proven false. Moreover, apropos of uncertainty, I wonder if binary logic and the three laws of thought are fully adequate to our epistemic predicament: it is metabiological evolution of which we speak.

In a world of necessity, where outcomes are predetermined, the question concerning the possibility of the annihilation of the human species does not meaningfully arise (other than as a matter of intellectual curiosity): the future is predetermined. Conversely, in a world of infinite possibility, where outcomes are totally undetermined, the question concerning the possibility of the annihilation of the human species does not meaningfully arise (other than as a matter of intellectual curiosity): the future is wholly undetermined and thus beyond human ken. By all available evidence, *Homo sapiens* exists in a middle zone between sheer chance and total necessity, reckoning with a past that conditions future possibilities (in a variety of ways, including our biological nature and cultural legacy) and a future that beckons, yet is powerless to be born of its own accord without our own, reflexive intentionality.

No doubt there are those who, looking at the events that may transpire here, might claim that like the priestesses of the ancient temple, who inhaled the vapors wafting from the mysterious recesses of the earth before uttering their prophesies, so too some mysterious agent has befuddled our minds.

Some "mysterious agent" is, I believe, at work: but it is reason, small "r" reason, a reason that dares to stand in the hermeneutic circle of postmodern interpretation, one that draws fully from the resources of neurophysiology and evolutionary biology, from nonlinear thermodynamics and quantum theory, and from general linguistics and semiotics. *Cogito quia vivo.* On such a basis, the biological possibility that undergirds cultural evolution might be seized. "Individuals with the greatest capacity for such behavior are," according to Jonas Salk, "likely to be among those who most effectively contributed and thus experienced further evolution. The ability of the mind to function in this way must have been selected in the course of evolution."[44]

Notes

1. Dennis V. Razis, "A Letter from the President," *Preliminary Programme: International Multidisciplinary Conference on Human Behaviour and the Meaning of Modern Humanism* (1995).

2. Ibid.

3. Evert Timmer, "Medical Ethics and Evolution," *Journal of the Royal Society of Medicine* 87 (1994): 250–51.

4. A. J. McMichael, *Planetary Overload: Global Environmental Change and the Health of the Human Species* (Cambridge: Cambridge University Press, 1993).

5. Timothy F. H. Allen and Thomas W. Hoekstra, *Toward a Unified Ecology* (New York: Columbia University Press, 1991), pp. 272–74.

6. Dennis V. Razis, "Modern Cassandras and Our Survival as a Species—A New Role for Medicine?" *Journal of the Royal Society of Medicine* (1989).

7. McMichael, *Planetary Overload*, p. 11.

8. Edward O. Wilson, *The Diversity of Life* (Cambridge, Mass.: Belknap Press, 1992), p. 272.

9. Allen W. Johnson and Timothy Earle, *The Evolution of Human Societies: From Foraging Group to Agrarian State* (Stanford, Calif.: Stanford University Press, 1987), p. 322.

10. Ibid., p. 320.

11. *Choosing a Sustainable Future: The Report of the National Commission on the Environment* (Washington, D.C.: Island Press, 1993), p. xiii.

12. Razis, "Modern Cassandras."

13. McMichaels, *Planetary Overload*, p. 10.

14. Clifford Geertz, *The Interpretation of Cultures* (New York: Basic Books, 1973), pp. 92–93.

15. Dennis V. Razis, "A New Role for Medicine," *Journal of the Royal Society of Medicine* 87 (1994): 190–92.

16. William C. Clark, "Managing Planet Earth," *Scientific American* 261, no. 3 (1989): 47–54.

17. The so-called Brundtland Report was published by the World Commission on Environment and Development, *Our Common Future* (New York: Oxford University Press, 1987). Also see Stephan Schmidheiny, *Changing Course: Report of the World Business Council on Sustainable Development* (Cambridge, Mass.: MIT Press, 1990).

18. See Nicholas Georgescu-Roegen, *The Entropy Law and the Economic Process* (Cambridge, Mass.: Harvard University Press, 1971).

19. Vandana Shiva, *Staying Alive: Women, Ecology and Development* (London: Zed Books, 1989).

20. Christopher Manes, "Nature and Silence," in *Postmodern Environmental Ethics*, Max Oelschlaeger, ed. (Albany, N.Y.: State University of New York Press, 1995).

21. John Firor, *The Changing Atmosphere: A Global Challenge* (New Haven, Conn.: Yale University Press, 1990).

22. George Sessions, ed., *Deep Ecology for the 21st Century* (Boston: Shambhala, 1995).

23. Timmer, "Medical Ethics and Evolution," p. 250.

24. Ibid., p. 251.

25. Aldo Leopold, *A Sand County Almanac: With Essays on Conservation from Round River* (San Francisco: Sierra Club Books, 1970).

26. Edward O. Wilson, *Sociobiology: The Abridged Edition* (Cambridge, Mass.: Harvard University Press, 1980), pp. 3–4.

27. Edward O. Wilson, *On Human Nature* (Cambridge, Mass.: Harvard University Press, 1978), p. 169.

28. Ibid., p. 176.

29. Wilson, *The Diversity of Life*, p. 348.

30. Wilson, *On Human Nature*, pp. 176–77.

31. Ibid., p. 177.

32. Geertz, *The Interpretation of Cultures*, p. 90.

33. On this subject see Max Oelschlaeger, *Caring for Creation: An Ecumenical Approach to the Environmental Crisis* (New Haven, Conn.: Yale University Press, 1994).

34. See Derek Bickerton, *Language and Species* (Chicago: University of Chicago Press, 1990); J. N. Hattiangadi, *How Is Language Possible? Philosophical Reflections on the Evolution of Language and Knowledge* (LaSalle, Ill.: Open Court, 1987); and Will Wright, *Wild Knowledge: Science, Language, and Social Life in a Fragile Environment* (Minneapolis: University of Minnesota Press, 1992).

35. Jonas Salk, *Anatomy of Reality: Merging of Intuition and Reason* (New York: Columbia University Press, 1983).

36. José Ortega y Gasset, *The Revolt of the Masses* (New York: W. W. Norton, 1932), p. 34.

37. John D. Barrow and Frank J. Tipler, *The Anthropic Cosmological Principle* (New York: Oxford University Press, 1986).

38. Maurice Merleau-Ponty, *The Visible and the Invisible*, A. Lingis, trans. (Evanston, Ill.: Northwestern University Press, 1968).

39. Razis, "A New Role for Medicine," p. 191.

40. See AnnMari Jansson, Monica Hammer, Carl Folke, and Robert Costanza, eds., *Investing in Natural Capital: The Ecological Economics Approach to Sustainability* (Washington, D.C.: Island Press, 1994).

41. Bruce Lincoln, *Discourse and the Construction of Society: Com-*

parative Studies of Myth, Ritual, and Classification (New York: Oxford University Press, 1989), p. 8.

42. Ibid.
43. Ibid.
44. Salk, *Anatomy of Reality*, p. 115.

2

Wars and Means of Mass Destruction

Vally Koubi

The phenomenon of war is inherent in civilized societies. War is a socially approved institution of organized violence whose evolution has gone hand in hand with that of civilization. Warfare as a human practice became more sophisticated as civilization advanced, particularly as the institutions of politics became more centralized. Wars are always linked to political objectives and are initiated to promote certain national interests. The specific event triggering the eruption of violence may be a surprise or even an accident but the initiation of a conflict serious enough to become a war occurs in a context of prior planning and preparation that can leave no doubt that it has been carefully calculated. Wars begin with conscious and reasoned decisions made by all parties involved that they can achieve more by going to war than by remaining at peace.

The wars of the last two centuries have become increasingly destructive. There are mainly three reasons for this. First is the growth in the capacity and thus the need of nation-states to field ever larger forces. As states became more industrialized and centralized, they acquired the wealth and developed the administrative apparatus to move men on a grand scale. Concomitant with the increase in military potential was the necessity to realize this potential. As soon as one state expanded the forces at its disposal, because of the security dilemma all other states had to follow suit.

The second reason is the gradual "democratization" of war, the expansion of the battlefield and hence the indiscriminate mass killing of noncombatants. Most of the wars of the eighteenth century did impinge upon the citizenry, but mainly financially; few civilians died in them. With the widespread use of conscription in the nineteenth and twentieth centuries, however, more citizens became soldiers. With the advent of industrialization and with the increasing division of labor, the citizens who did not fight remained behind to produce weapons. Now a nation not only had to conquer its enemy's armies, but also destroy the industrial plant that supplied the enemy's weapons. Gradually the total energy of a country was diverted into waging wars. Everyone, citizens and soldiers alike, began participating, fighting, and dying.

The third reason is the steady technological improvement in weaponry. Weapons such as machine guns, submarines, poison gas, and aircraft made it feasible to kill large numbers of people quickly. The rapidity of destruction that is possible with nuclear weapons is only the most recent advance. Keep in mind, however, that the development of new weapons does not seem to have a decisive impact on the number or character of wars which occur. The continuous increase in the destructive power of weapons has affected the way in which wars have been fought but not the occurrence of war itself. The replacement of bow and arrow and armored horsemen by infantry, or the musket by the rifle, had no discernible impact on the willingness of governments to make wars on each other. The development of bomber aircraft, more powerful bombs, or experiments with missiles and nuclear arms did not deter the launching of World War II. The development and use of nuclear weapons in that war has likewise not prevented the frequent waging of war in subsequent years, even against nations equipped with such weapons. The United States and the Soviet Union, although they did not fight directly during the cold war era, came dangerously close to nuclear war in Cuba and Berlin and fought continuously through proxies on three continents. This suggests that governments make use of those weapons appropriate to the purpose they have in mind. Though more powerful weapons may cause governments to behave somewhat more cautiously, especially in their dealings with other governments having similar capabilities, they certainly have not had the effect of banishing warfare by or against the nations that possess them. What they cause is the adoption of different strategies.

Before World War II, military planners concentrated, not on preventing the next general war, but on winning it. They concentrated on victory partly because they believed that the first strike, if properly executed, could be decisive. But they also knew that the side that conquered the other's military forces could in the process protect its own population. The possibility of nuclear retaliation makes this no longer feasible; in a nuclear war neither side can save itself. Nuclear weapons have brought not only overkill but also mutual kill. Moreover, nuclear weapons can kill more people and lay waste to more property much faster than any other armaments. They are weapons of mass destruction.

What would be the impact of a nuclear war on humanity?

One thing can be said with certainty—a full-scale nuclear war would be a catastrophe beyond precedent in human history. Human casualties and the environmental consequences of such a war cannot be foretold in detail. They would depend on the distribution and sizes of the weapons detonated, on the proportion exploded on the surface rather than high enough so their fireballs did not touch the ground, and on civilian shelters. The results would also depend heavily on wind and the season of the year in which the war occurred. Moreover, fundamental gaps in knowledge of how natural ecosystems work make detailed predictions impossible. Still, more than enough is known to paint a general picture of the human casualties and the ecological consequences of a large-scale nuclear war.

For example, the effects of 1,000 one-megaton nuclear bombs— which is a fraction of the existing world nuclear arsenal and which is equivalent to 76,923 Hiroshima bombs—on Europe would be devastating. Over 200 million people will die immediately following the attack. Keep in mind that total casualties in World War I and World War II were seventy million.

Moreover, gas pipelines, oil pipelines, and electricity grids would be fragmented. Without fuel, the entire transportation system would be crippled. Railroad lines would be chopped up. Water supply and sewage facilities would be destroyed beyond repair. Without power to pump water from reservoirs or underground sources, many people would have to depend on surface waters which could be dangerous, contaminated by fallout or chemical pollutants. This would create epidemics and cause further deaths. Antibiotics and other medical supplies would be quickly exhausted. Radiation damage would lower people's resistance to disease. If food were still available in agricultural areas, it could not be processed and shipped, since those facilities are generally in metropolitan areas. Starvation would be widespread. No possible level of preparation or civil defense could significantly ease this disaster.

In addition to long-term ecological results, such as depletion of the ozone, selective destruction of some plants and animals, and the survival of the hardier forms, cancer from radioactive fallout, and so on, a major scientific report in 1983 raised the possibility of "nuclear winter" and global climatic catastrophe. The sky over the entire

Northern Hemisphere could be darkened for weeks or months by a combination of smoke and soot from the enormous fires, debris injected into atmosphere by weapons detonations, and fugitive dust from burned-over areas. Ninety-nine percent of the incoming sunlight might be excluded. Beneath the spreading clouds of smoke and dust, temperature in interior continental areas would plummet within weeks to well below freezing, regardless of the season. The cold weather, severe reduction or elimination of photosynthesis, on top of the widespread burning of croplands and the heavily eroded soil, would make farming virtually impossible. In the longer term, worldwide food shortage could be the greatest threat. Hundreds of million of people would starve. While the extinction of *Homo sapiens* is not a likely consequence of an all-out nuclear war, the end of civilization in the industrialized world of the North is a virtual certainty.

The recent events of the last five to six years—including the dissolution of the Warsaw Pact, the completion of the Strategic Arms Reduction Treaty, and the dissolution of the Soviet Union—have altered perceptions of the nature and risks of the Russian-American relationship and with it the importance of nuclear weapons. The probability of nuclear war between the two superpowers seems now to be extremely low, and hence nuclear weapons appear to be more a legacy of a previous era than a dominant element of today's international relations.

There are, however, some emerging reasons to review critically the assumption that nuclear weapons are becoming largely irrelevant.

If we could be sure that these destructive capabilities would never be used, that the "balance of terror" would be reliably stable, they might be tolerable. But there can be no such assurance. The status of nuclear weapons in the former Soviet Union is in flux. Russia wants to remain an important nuclear power and thus intends to maintain centralized control over the nuclear weapons of the former Soviet Union through the Commonwealth of Independent States.

But worries about what those former nuclear Soviet republics (Ukraine, Kazakhstan, Belarus) will do with those weapons in the future, questions about whether they might lose control of them, and fears about who might eventually get control of them create a whole new set of reasons to wonder about what kinds of nuclear threats might arise in the future. In addition, these weapons could pose risks to stability in the region if those states came into conflict with one another, revived old national hostilities with their neighbors, or simply lack the technical expertise and administrative cohesion to ensure effective control and security of their nuclear weapons. Furthermore, the spread of nuclear weapons to other countries as well as the opportunity it provides for terrorists to gain control of nuclear material or finished weapons could increase the probability of the use of nuclear weapons.

Well before the end of the Cold War, the proliferation of nuclear weapons and advanced conventional weapons, such as ballistic missiles, into the Third World had already become a worldwide worrisome issue. Some twenty-five countries, nine of which are in the Middle East, have acquired or attempted to acquire ballistic missiles. Such missiles could serve as effective delivery systems for nuclear as well as chemical and biological weapons. Given that these missiles are so expensive, they will not be used to deliver conventional weapons. So it should not come as a surprise that most of the states that have acquired or are trying to acquire ballistic missiles are also trying to develop nuclear, chemical, and biological weapons.

Without exaggerating the amount of nuclear proliferation that may take place in the future, it should nevertheless be acknowledged that with the end of the Cold War the incentives for Third World countries to acquire nuclear weapons have probably increased. Nations such as India may aspire to deploy nuclear weapons to lay claim to big-power status in a multipolar world, which claim was not realistic when the two superpowers dominated international politics. Some others may seek to develop nuclear weapons as a means to increase the level of their national security against present (for example, the case of Pakistan against India) or future (for example, South Korea against North Korea) local nuclear powers. Finally, for ambitious regional states, like Iraq and Iran, a nuclear weapons capability, especially one that would hold at risk the territory, interests, or allies of a major power, might be an important way of deterring military action by that power. There are of course technical barriers to nuclear proliferation, but as Iraq has demonstrated, these can be overcome by a regional power that places high priority on acquiring nuclear weapons.

Some may argue that a world of many nuclear weapons states would be as peaceful as the present world. Perhaps it would be even more peaceful. But it might be considerably less peaceful. Since regional states are unlikely to have the resources and/or the technical competence to build secure second-strike forces and command and control systems, they might instead seek to develop a small first-strike nuclear force in an effort to achieve regional military superiority. These small, vulnerable nuclear forces would be technically unstable and would create considerable pressures for preemption in the event of regional crisis. Even a sober leader might see some advantage in ordering a first strike. In other worlds, "prisoners' dilemmas" are likely to arise. And the difference between the capacity for assured destruction and one or two bombs is the difference between stable deterrence and nuclear war.

Given this gloomy picture, the obvious question is, what can the nations do to avoid a human holocaust?

Nuclear proliferation has the status of a global problem, one that requires international cooperation to address. The nation-states of the international system have already devised a series of international rules and procedures designed to check the spread of nuclear weapons. The Nuclear Nonproliferation Treaty (NPT), which was

concluded in 1968, is the centerpiece of these rules. The main purposes of the NPT have been to prevent the spread of nuclear
weapons, safeguard nuclear materials and facilities, make information on peaceful nuclear energy available to nonnuclear states, and
promote nuclear disarmament. Unfortunately, nations choose to sign
the NPT on the basis of their own interests. Considerations of national pride and internal politics influence the nuclear decisions of
each nation in the world. Because of the security dilemma, each
country's decision to get or forego nuclear weapons also depends on
what other countries do, especially their neighbors.

Unfortunately, nuclear disarmament is unlikely because it would
require a radical change in the way international politics is organized. This is not at all likely to take place in our own days. The term
for the way the system of sovereign nations is structured is "anarchy."
Anarchy does not mean chaos but rather the absence of formal order;
that is, the absence of international government or ruling order. The
world's sovereign countries, which belong to the United Nations,
struggle with one another for power; they must look out for their own
interests and cannot appeal to some higher authority to enforce international law and order. For these reasons they have armed forces
and the power to go to war if their national interest dictates it. There
is no global authority to stop them from doing so. No world government exists to guide and regulate their relations with each other.

Even if there were a world government, complete nuclear disarmament might not be possible; such a government would need to
have nuclear weapons to enforce its decisions. But world government is not in the offing. In our days, in fact, the trend is in the opposite direction. The world has seen the multiplication or perhaps
more accurately the division of sovereignty, not its restriction and
consolidation. Almost every national, linguistic, and religious group
now wants its own sovereignty. Many have gained it. Many others
are still in pursuit of it, still fighting for it.

The nations of the world could conceivably renounce nuclear weapons. They could agree to go about their business, including their quarrels with each other, without having these weapons. Nothing of the sort has happened so far, nor is likely to happen in the near future. Renunciation would mean that each nation trusted the others not to have, or to get, nuclear weapons. Complete trust is unlikely, however, when the possibility exists that others could get them, and when no governing authority could prevent them from doing so. The recent failure of the participating NPT nations to reach consensus, and the recent French nuclear testing in the Pacific Ocean, prove this claim.

Moreover, even if every nation promised not to have nuclear weapons, this vow would not make for an entirely nuclear-free world. The knowledge of how to make them would remain. It could not be readily forgotten.

Nuclear disarmament would not only require the abolition of nuclear weapons. It would also require a revolution in human affairs more sweeping than anything that has happened before or is to be expected in the near future. The abolition of all nuclear weapons is extremely difficult to achieve. And if the past contains information about the future, then it is very probable that armaments and wars will continue to shape the future of the human race.

Yet, given the destructive power of nuclear weapons, there may be other ways to avoid nuclear war. Our very survival may depend on a change in political thinking. A number of possibilities have been envisioned. First, a growing transnational awareness of the nuclear danger among the peoples of the world might cause them to demand from their governments the negotiation of multilateral arms control agreements leading to reduction or even abolition of nuclear weapons. The fundamental change in political thinking in this case would involve the possibility that people from several nations could work together on a common problem in a way that bypasses the traditional allegiance of citizen to state. Another possibility could involve the acceptance of the idea of establishing a world government. Of course, this would require a drastic change in prevailing attitudes, but we have already seen developments in the area of international trade—the General Agreement on Tariffs and Trade organization—that contain such elements. Third, a unilateral decision by one nation to disarm or reduce its nuclear armaments might lead to the avoidance of nuclear war without that nation having substantially to surrender its sovereignty. The change in political thinking here lies in the recognition that it may be possible to maintain sovereignty through conventional arms without reliance on nuclear threats. Furthermore, a unilateral decision by one nation to reduce its nuclear armaments may promote trust and induce further reduction by other nations, since in international relations cooperation breeds expectations of cooperation and defection breeds expectations of defection. In any case, the survival of humanity depends on the realization that the proliferation and use of nuclear weapons even in a limited nuclear war may mean the end of civilization and thus nations must learn to cooperate.

3

Controlling the Population Explosion

Bonnie Bullough and Vern L. Bullough

Since Thomas Malthus broached the subject of the dangers of over-population in 1798, we have had an almost continual discussion of the topic, but have not yet solved the basic problem he posed. Malthus's most well-known statement was that food supply increases arithmetically while population grows geometrically. He was very pessimistic about the dangers of population growth, a pessimism accentuated by the fact that he offered no solutions to the problem he posed. He simply saw population growth as inevitable because of the human need to reproduce, sex if you will, and this would ultimately lead to misery and destruction. All he could advise was sexual restraint, but he predicted that efforts to control the sexual instinct would fail and that the ultimate outcome would be population control by wars, famines, and other disasters, those created both by humans and by nature.[1]

The problem is of course much more complex than Malthus visualized it, but he is important for sounding the alarm and catching the attention of the public. He could not visualize all the factors which would complicate the issue of overpopulation, particularly the increased longevity of individuals due to a radical decrease in infant and maternal mortality, and a decline in the mortality rates from epidemics. In addition, the food supply has increased significantly with better use of land and water resources, and improved methods of handling, storing, and distributing food. However, these developments did not make the problem go away because at the same time that these gains were made the population continued to grow. At the beginning of the industrial revolution in the eighteenth century the world population was estimated at 750 million. With increasing urbanization and industrialization growth escalated rapidly, reaching one billion in 1830; two billion in 1930; three billion in 1960; four billion in 1975, and more than five billion by 1990.[2] The latest United Nations figures for the most hopeful scenario places the topping off figure at 7.8 billion by the year 2050.[3] Other scenarios place the topping off figure at a much higher level.

Early Efforts at Family Planning

Although Malthus himself was convinced that nothing would help the situation, there was a group of nineteenth-century reformers who were called Neo-Malthusians and some of this group could be called humanists and free thinkers. They pointed out that the dire predictions need not be inevitable because people could take steps to control conception. People have in fact always had significant capacity to control their numbers and consciously or unconsciously engaged in family planning behaviors.[4] Abstinence, either lifelong or for temporary periods, is a powerful curb to population growth. The American Shakers for all practical purposes wiped themselves out with their vows of celibacy. The Roman Catholic holy orders and clergy function to withdraw certain members of the community from procreation. Late marriage ages as they were practiced in rural Ireland in the nineteenth and twentieth centuries shorten the procreative lifespan. Separation of husbands and wives for long periods of time as in war or long business expeditions can also curtail fertility.

Abortion was often used to limit family size, and favored methods can be cited from the folklore of women and midwives throughout history. Plato advocated population control to ensure the stability of the state. Aristotle advised early abortions (before sense and life have begun in the embryo) if conceptions occurred in excess of the limit fixed for population stability. He considered this a much better approach than the abandonment of babies after they were born.[5]

Ancient peoples also used a variety of herbs to prevent conception or to cause abortions. Of these the most powerful seems to have been silphium, commonly known as giant fennel. It was discovered by Greek colonists who came from Thera in the seventh century B.C.E. to found the city of Cyrene in what is now Lybia. They called it *silphion* and made a fortune exporting it to Greece and Syria. By the first century C.E. it became scarce from overharvesting and by the third or fourth century was extinct. The ancients then turned to related plants such as asafoetida, or other herbs such as Queen Anne's Lace, which was said to be effective as both a contraceptive and an abortifacient.[6]

Prolonged lactation was also an important method for spacing births. Lactation and the stimulus of the infant suckling ordinarily suppresses ovulation and causes amenorrhea. However, it is highly effective as a birth control mechanism only when the total food supply of the infant is breast milk, or when abstinence during lactation is the norm. As modern supplemental feedings for infants have been developed lactation has become a less effective contraceptive. As partial weaning takes place, the menstrual cycle returns in most women who are adequately nourished, and pregnancy is again possible.

One of the earliest unorganized incidents of the use of broad-scale methods of conception control sufficient to affect national fertility was the decline in the French birth rate from the end of the eighteenth century, a decline attributed to the widespread use of *coitus interruptus*.[7] Other areas and other cultures used different techniques and there seems to be an almost universal desire for humans to gain some control over population. In spite of early volunteer successes in limiting population, particularly in Western countries, it has continued to grow in large part because of our growing success in keeping people alive longer. Today it will take concentrated, worldwide effort to limit population growth.

Fertility Rates

The effectiveness of population control methods is measured by the fertility rate, the number of live births for each woman during her lifetime. In today's industrial countries, population remains stable over the long run with a fertility rate of slightly under two, but in the short run even this rate will result in population increase because of the potential of greater longevity and the existence of several generations of a family at the same time. Modern fertility rates in the 1980s reached as high as eight to ten in some countries of the Third World, including Pakistan, Indonesia, and Kenya.

Organized Family Planning

Organized efforts at family planning date primarily from the nineteenth century, as the Neo-Malthusians struggled to overcome the poverty and malnutrition that seemed to be endemic among large families. The major early efforts occurred in the English-speaking countries, and the person who is generally given credit as the first to mount one was the English tailor and free thinker, Francis Place (1771–1854), who published *Illustrations and Proofs of the Principle of Population* in 1822. He urged married couples to use "precautionary" means in order to better plan their families, but he did not go into detail. To remedy this lack of instruction, in 1823 he printed handbills addressed simply "To the Married of Both Sexes," describing a way to avoid pregnancy by inserting a dampened sponge, with a string attached, into the vagina. Later pamphlets by Place as well as by some of his followers added other methods, all involving the female. Place's pamphlets and others of the time were never subject to any legal interference. Place's disciple, Richard Carlile (1790–1854), took up the cause, which became increasingly controversial, in part because Place and Carlile were social reformers as well as advocates of birth control. Carlile was the first man in England to put his name to a book devoted to the subject of birth control, *Every Woman's Book: or What is Love?* (1826).

In the United States the movement for birth control may be said to have begun in 1831 with the publication by Robert Dale Owen (1801–1877) of a booklet entitled *Moral Physiology*. Owen advocated three methods of birth control: coitus interruptus, which he felt was the best, the vaginal sponge, which was not always successful, and the condom made of animal gut, which was very expensive and could be used only once. Far more influential in the task of public education was a Massachusetts physician, Charles Knowlton (1800–1850), who published his *Fruits of Philosophy* in 1832. As he lectured on the topic throughout Massachusetts, Knowlton was repeatedly tried and jailed. One result of these actions was increasing public interest in contraception, and by 1839 Knowlton had sold some ten thousand copies of his book. In his first edition Knowlton had advocated douching, a not particularly effective contraceptive. Fortunately, in subsequent editions of his book he added other and more reliable methods of contraception.

The Eugenics Movement

Giving a further impetus to the more conservative aspects of birth control was the growth of the eugenics movement. The eugenicists, while concerned with the high birth rates among the poor and the illiterate, emphasized the problem of low birthrates among the more "intellectual" upper classes. Eugenics came to be defined as an applied biological science concerned with increasing the proportion of persons of better-than-average endowment in succeeding generations. Thus the eugenicists threw themselves into the campaign for birth control among the poor and illiterate while at the same time urging the "gifted" to produce more children. The word "eugenics" had been coined by Francis Galton (1822–1911), a great believer in heredity who also had many of the prejudices of an upper-class Englishman in regard to social class and race. Galton's hypotheses were given further "academic" respectability by Karl Pearson (1857– 1936), the first holder of the Galton endowed chair of eugenics at the University of London. Pearson believed that the high birth rate of the poor was a threat to civilization, and if members of the "higher" races did not make it their duty to reproduce, they would be supplanted in time by the members of the "lower" races. When put in this harsh light, eugenics gave "scientific" support to those who believed in racial and class superiority. It was just such ideas that Hitler attempted to implement in his solution to the racial problem, which made even the good ideas of the eugenicists suspect. Advocates of population control still labor under the shadow cast by the eugenics movement. There were, however, other advocates, including women.

Women Advocates of Birth Control

Women, including Aletta Jacobs of the Netherlands, Marie Stopes (1880–1958) in Great Britain, and Margaret Sanger in the United States, entered the struggle for birth control at the beginning of the twentieth century. Jacobs was not only the first woman physician in the Netherlands, her birth control clinic, established in 1882, was the first such effort. Stopes, a botanist, established a birth control clinic in London and in 1918 published *Married Love,* which described and explained the sex act for women.[8]

The situation in the United States was complicated by the censoring activities of Anthony Comstock (1844–1915), who had been appointed as a special postal agent in 1873. One of his first successful prosecutions was against a contraceptive pamphlet by Edward Bliss Foote (1829–1906) and the result drove information about contraceptives underground. When Margaret Sanger, a militant socialist and humanist, began to publish a magazine, *The Woman Rebel,* in 1914, Comstock was determined to stop her work. She decided to further defy the laws pertaining to the dissemination of contraceptive information by publishing a small pamphlet, *Family Limitation.* She was arrested and after a preliminary hearing Sanger fled to Europe, where she studied contraceptive methods under Aletta Jacobs in Amsterdam.[9]

When Sanger returned to United States she found new allies among women's rights advocates. They joined with the radical reformers as well as the eugenicists in an uneasy coalition for dissemination of contraceptives. To better reach the public with propaganda and services, Sanger, along with her sister Ethel Byrne, and two social workers, Fania Mindell and Elizabeth Stuyvesant, in 1916 opened a birth control clinic in Brooklyn, patterned after the Dutch model. Although all of the leaders were arrested, the New York Court of Appeals rendered a decision acquitting them, holding that it was legal to disseminate contraceptive information for the "cure and prevention of disease" but failed to specify the disease. Sanger, interpreting unwanted pregnancy as a disease, continued her campaign through this legal loophole, which was not challenged. Sanger and her sponsor, John D. Rockefeller, Jr., were also instrumental in establishing the International Planned Parenthood Federation.

The work of these reformers was facilitated by the development of the process for the vulcanization of rubber. The process had been discovered in the nineteenth century and the first full-length rubber condom was made in 1869. By the beginning of the twentieth century the manufacture of condoms, diaphragms, and cervical caps was possible.[10] Diaphragms were favored by both Jacobs and Sanger.

All of these activities were by individuals and small groups of volunteers. No governments entered into the work of population control during the nineteenth and early part of the twentieth century. Although the International Planned Parenthood Federation carried out projects in many Third World countries, their efforts were not sufficient to stem the tide of population growth, and the population problem escalated until the Malthusian predictions seemed doomed to follow unless drastic steps were taken.

Japan made history in 1948 by becoming the first country to take such a drastic step. Abortions were legalized with a conscious aim of regulating population growth to keep it to a manageable level. The original law legalized abortion only for women whose health might be impaired from the physical or economic standpoint, but within a few years it was broadened to allow abortion upon request. The birth rate quickly dropped from 34.3 in 1947 to 16.0 by 1961. In recent years the number of abortions have dropped somewhat with the improvements in contraceptive technology and the growing wealth of the country, but abortions are still available and selected by many women as the method of choice for controlling pregnancies. The birth rate in Japan remains low, with a virtually stable level of population growth.[11]

Government activities were even more dramatic in China. As a result of ambivalent policies and neglect of the potential for overpopulation, China had reached the level of 1.2 billion persons in 1981. Government officials decided that drastic measures were called for and China became the first country in the world to embark on a deliberate and comprehensive course to reach zero population growth by the year 2000 or as soon after that as possible. To achieve this, the Chinese government called on the people to limit their families to one child. The limitations are enforced by the *danwei*, the collectives that are used to organize the factories, farms, and even the blocks in the cities. In addition to facilitating birth control, abortions, and sterilizations, these groups provide rewards at work and better schooling for the child if the couple has complied with the one-child norm.[12] Though the Chinese government has allowed more exceptions in recent years, family planning was further emphasized in 1993, when the government forbade marriages of persons with hepatitis, venereal disease, or mental illness. The goal is to reduce the number of congenitally disabled persons as well as limit population growth.[13]

Although most countries have used less drastic approaches, birth control has become government policy in more and more countries, although the international volunteer groups are still influential. There is evidence that contraception is having an impact on the problem of overpopulation. As the standard of living increased in Western Europe, the United States, and the other industrialized countries, the fertility rate fell to 2.0, and in some as low as 1.0. The lowest fertility rate in Europe is in Italy (1.3) with the highest rate in Ireland (2.1) and with Greece falling in between (1.6).[14] There is even a beginning decline in population growth in the underdeveloped countries so that the annual growth in the sub-Saharan African countries, which have the highest rates in the world, has started to fall.

Hopes for the Future

The 1994 Cairo conference reviewed the current situation and came up with recommendations for the future. Although the rate of population increase peaked in the late 1960s at just over 2 percent per year and has since fallen to 1.6 percent, there is still a long way to go to reach a stable population. Three major recommendations were made: (1) to improve access to modern contraceptives, (2) to reduce infant and child mortality, and (3) to expand school enrollment for girls and work opportunities for women. This is a changed agenda from previous conferences. Twenty years ago at the first United Nations intergovernmental conference in Bucharest the emphasis was on supporting industrialization with the hope that this would eventually right the problem. This stance was supported by the theory of demographic transition, which argued that when countries first industrialize the improvements in standards of living increase the population, but that when the transition is completed the birth rate falls. This is what happened in Europe, Japan, and North America. However, it has now become clear that this pattern is not inevitable, as demonstrated by persistently high birth rates in industrialized countries such as Brazil and Mexico.[15]

The second United Nations conference, held in Mexico City in 1984, therefore moved its emphasis to increasing access to modern family planning techniques, including oral contraceptives, injectable Depo-Provera, three- and five-year progestin implants, and improved methods for sterilization of both men and women. The 1994 Cairo conference continued to support access to contraception but added the emphasis on children and women. Parents traditionally have been dependent on their children for old-age insurance. Parents need to be confident that their children will survive and support them in their old age in order to be willing to cut the family size to their actual goal instead of overshooting as insurance. This means that healthy children and government- or industry-sponsored old-age insurance are prerequisite for successful family planning programs.[16] Women were emphasized because research indicates that countries that do not allow their girls to be educated have the highest fertility rates.[17]

In our minds, the empowerment of women may be the single most effective means of controlling population. Yet it is the most controversial because as women gain power men fear they will lose power, and there are men in our country and in other countries who are not ready for this to happen. In addition there is need for male cooperation in family limitation, and this in many parts of the world will necessitate new definitions of what it is to be a man and a husband. But social changes cannot simply stop here. In societies where the aging parents are essentially the responsibility of the eldest son, other means of care and protection of the old are necessary. Where working children add to the family coffers, it is important to offer alternatives, and raise the adult worker's wages sufficiently that the family can survive without working children. In a world where even the best contraceptive methods sometimes fail, it is essential to have abortion as a fallback for those who choose not to proceed with a full-term pregnancy. In effect, controlling the population explosion requires greater cooperation between individuals, families, and governments than presently exists.

To do this requires massive education and a redefinition of public morality. Perhaps this can best be done by asking a basic question: What kind of world do we want to live in? Personally we respond that we want a society with great personal freedom, but we also want one where the dangers of famine, epidemic, poverty, and war are radically curtailed if not eliminated. Obviously this is a long-term goal that is theoretically possible, but only if we recognize the limitations on our own freedom that an overcrowded world will bring and in fact is bringing. We must emphasize in our dream of the future world that Draconian measures ultimately will be required unless we can take effective controlling action in our own lifetimes.

What kind of world do we want for our children? Obviously we all want a better one, but from our vantage point there is very little prospect that this will be the case for vast portions of the world's population unless direct actions are taken. We need, as humanists and members of the Delphi Conference, to commit ourselves to the educational campaign, and to emphasize the positive steps that must be taken now to make a better world.

Notes

1. Thomas Malthus, *An Essay on the Principle of Population,* 1798 (reprinted New York: Dutton, 1967).

2. C. P. Green, *The Environment and Population Growth: Decade for Action,* supplement to *Population Reports,* series M, no. 10, vol. 20, 1992.

3. Wade Roush, "Population: The View from Cairo," *Science* 265 (August 1994): 1164–67

4. Josiah Cox Russell, *Late Ancient and Medieval Population Control* (Philadelphia: American Philosophical Society, 1985).

5. John M. Riddle, J. Worth Estes, and Josiah C. Russell, "Ever Since Eve . . . Birth Control in the Ancient World," *Archaeology* (March-April 1994): 29–35.

6. Ibid.

7. E. Van de Walle, "Alone in Europe, The French Fertility Decline Until 1850," *Historical Studies of Changing Fertility,* C. Tilly, ed. (Princeton, N.J.: Princeton University Press, 1978), pp. 257–99.

8. Vern L. Bullough, *Science in the Bedroom: A History of Sex Research* (New York: Basic Books, 1994), pp. 138–40.

9. Margaret Sanger, *An Autobiography* (New York: Dover, 1971).

10. Vern L. Bullough, "A Brief Note on Rubber Technology and Contraception: The Diaphragm and the Condom," *Technology and Culture* 22 (January 1981): 104–11.

11. Lawrence Lader, *Abortion* (Indianapolis, Ind.: Bobbs Merrill, 1966), and "Japan, a Crowded Nation Wants to Increase Its Birthrate," *Science* 167 (February 13, 1970): 960–62.

12. Vern L. Bullough and Bonnie Bullough, "Population Control vs. Freedom in China," *Free Inquiry* (1983–84): 12–15.

13. R. Tempest, "China Denies Plan for Forced Abortions" *Los Angeles Times* (December 30, 1993), p. A6.

14. Elof D. B. Johansson, "Female Contraception: Changing Priorities," *Annals of Medicine* 25 (1993): 139–40.

15. Roush, "Population."

16. Ibid.

17. George Moffett, *Critical Masses: The Global Population Challenge* (Ithaca, N.Y.: Foreign Policy Association, 1994).

4

Managing an Overpopulated World

P. O. Williams

Last summer my wife and I were in Scotland and drove our car across the pass between the lush, cultivated land of Perthshire into the beautiful valley of the river Dee, where the castle of Balmoral is situated in its magnificent estate. The beauty was breathtaking. We saw very few people or animals all day. In Scotland in summer it stays light until late. We returned over the pass at nine P.M. and the road and the surrounding country were covered by a large number of deer. We described the scene when we got back to our hotel and were told that the deer population had become excessive and that three-quarters of them would be culled later in the year.

A few years ago in Calcutta we were staying in the Oberoi Palace Hotel in the center of that city. This hotel is built around a large courtyard. There are no windows looking outward on the ground floor but above that the bedrooms look out on the city. After a good dinner we retired to our bedroom. Looking out of the window we could see families living on the pavement below with all their worldly goods eating the scraps from the hotel dustbins. We were told that the population of Calcutta would double in the next twenty years. No one told us how the resulting situation was going to be handled.

Last month we were reminded that in the war that ended fifty years ago Germany tried to destroy its Jewish population. Every day we see pictures of refugees in camps in various parts of Africa. We read of virus epidemics that kill hundreds of people. We read accounts of thousands of people killed in wars. We hear of the rise of Islamic fundamentalism and the migration of many people from the underdeveloped world to Europe.

I need not go on. The overgrowth of population is already with us. By the year 2020, just half the time since World War II, the world population will be at least 50 percent larger than it is today. So the problem is already with us and will be much more severe in the lifetimes of our children and grandchildren. And let us not forget that no one has yet suggested realistically how we can return to present-day numbers if we once rise to the ten billion population figure which is accepted as inevitable.

The effects of a population growing to this size is already obvious. If we consider the following incomplete list we immediately can see how remedial action can be taken.

Famine. Although the world can produce enough food, it will have to be distributed and subsidized if the majority of those who need it cannot afford the cost. I think we cannot assume that the distribution will be equitable. One billion are starving now.

Water shortage. In many places there will be a shortage of water and arrangements will have to be made to get it to where it is needed.

Housing. Many more houses will be needed and someone will have to provide the materials and the land.

Fuel shortage. Wood is already in short supply and the other fossil fuels will be used up even more rapidly. How do we intend that fuel requirements should be met in the future? Without fuel quite a large part of the world will be uninhabitable in the winter.

Epidemics. Epidemics of disease thrive on overcrowding, lack of sanitation, water shortage, and the breakdown of civil order. How do we prevent and control them?

Civil war. When population growth causes lack of land the subgroups in any society turn against one another through jealousy, race, or religion.

International war. When a country becomes overcrowded it looks to see where it can expand and often invades its neighbors. Japan in the Far East and Germany in Europe are examples from this century. How do we prevent these conflicts?

Religion. Groups of nations will club together to fight for or against an ideology. Islamic and Christian expansion have dominated the world at various times. Can we plan to avoid these wars?

Demoniac war. A country with an atomic bomb can destroy the world and there is a real possibility that some country will start such a tragedy. Iraq nearly did so very recently.

Anti-intellectualism. Intellectuals have rich resources that make those without them jealous. The mindless have destroyed them many times in the past. They have to be protected.

All of these possibilities and many more can occur as a consequence of overpopulation. We can expect them to be more common. Well-thought-out action taken in good time could lessen a lot of these effects.

International action about the population problem seems to concentrate on prevention—education, contraception, the rights and role of women, the effect on the environment, religious ethics, and so on. All of these are of course important themes but none of them will stop the population doubling its present size during the first half of the next century.

So what are we going to do about this enormous and inevitable problem? If we do nothing we know what will happen.

Since we cannot cull the human race (like the deer in Scotland)—although I fear that it will be culled by wars, epidemics, and starvation—we will have to care for it.

One solution is obviously to share the world's resources more evenly. There is, I read, enough food, water, and land for even double the present population. The people of the industrialized world consume more than a reasonable share.

A second solution is to allow free migration so that the citizens of Calcutta can have land in underpopulated regions. Algeria can spread to Europe, Southeast Asia can spread to Australia and Mexico—not to mention that many other nations can go to the vast area of North America. This solution may happen, in part, but I doubt whether it will be through the good will of the receiving countries.

One trouble with all of these solutions is that to look after the majority the minority will have to be damaged and if this occurs the genetic factors that make *Homo sapiens* unique among animal species are in danger of being lost. Uncontrolled growth of population can easily cause the end of civilization.

The major advances created by science and technology in the last two centuries have all occurred in countries rich enough to provide the facilities for education, research, and manufacturing activities by their populations. If we deplete these riches to look after the world's population the advance of knowledge will be held back. We need this new knowledge to replace the exhaustion of our present sources of power, food, and water. If we lose it we will then gradually lose the skills we have acquired. There will be inadequate money for educational establishments with libraries, data banks, and so on. Nor will there be factories to build motor cars, airplanes, and all the other requirements for present-day living. We will have returned to the Dark Ages when the barbarian horde overwhelmed the civilizations of Europe.

Since it is obvious that we have to share we need to plan the best way to do this without destroying the good results that have come from our capacity to harness the resources of the world. We, therefore, have to use our ability to think and plan to create a solution to this, the greatest problem we have ever faced.

The first step for taking any action must be to acquire a real understanding of all facets of the problem. A start can be made by setting up studies of the actions that need to be taken to deal with the topics on my list. We can store food, conserve water and fuel, plan health measures, prepare the physical defense of vulnerable populations, and improve much that we do inefficiently and wastefully today.

This planning can only take place if we set up a suitable mechanism. I believe we should start on a small, piecemeal scale that can be understood by the proverbial "man in the street." We therefore have to evaluate what each nation has to share and what each one needs. We must then develop partnerships between rich and poor nations so that they can help each other. Global and regional organizations should coordinate this information and provide the resources of money, materials, and food to subsidize these international partnerships. The skeleton of knowledge for such a plan exists in many international organizations such as the World Bank, the World Health Organization, the British Commonwealth, and several private foundations, but it does not seem to lead to specific plans of action. These organizations need to focus on this more specific and overwhelming purpose. If international humanism is the vehicle that can carry this new plan, well and good. I wait to hear more about its meaning at this meeting. Certainly we need something to replace our present-day, strife-ridden, political, economic, and ideological melee. But if humanism is not the answer, then let us set up the Society of Delphi, and start a new movement that can take an original view on how to deal with the requirements of an overpopulated world.

What I have tried to do is to suggest a practical course of action rather than just describe the mess in which we find ourselves. I do not hold out much hope of a solution coming from a major world agreement between nations that are so divided on grounds of politics, culture, religion, and wealth. I believe that we should start with small, regional activities that will be understandable to the "man in the street." Whatever comes out of this Delphi conference, I will be profoundly disappointed if it does not create some continuity of action to deal with the practical problems that the world faces today and that will overwhelm us in the next twenty years. We must create a movement to save mankind from reverting once again to the Dark Ages that followed the great flowering of civilization which started in Greece.

5

Cosmos, Geos, Bios, Homos: Multifrequency Chao-Periodic Competitors for Global Impact

William J. M. Hrushesky

Anthropocentricism examined: The anthropocentric world view advocated by classical humanism is egotistically attractive but may deserve reconsideration. There is no doubt that ethics and behavior affect the capacity of man to be happy and prosperous. The effect of human ethics and behavior upon man's capacity to survive, as a species, has, however, to be carefully considered. Effects of human behavior upon the survival of our planet and ecosystem must be even more critically examined. While there is no question that man is a successful organism, it may be useful to put his existence and success within a global spatiotemporal frame of reference to examine how profound that influence can possibly be.

Natural selection and humanity: No successful organism fails to modify its environment and no environment fails to modify the successful organism. Man is no exception to this truism. Cycles of change are the nature of evolution and will not be avoided. From a biological perspective, change is essential and catastrophe represents great opportunity for change. A biologically successful humanity will necessarily alter the world. Some of these alterations will be favorable for continued success and others will be unfavorable, and successful organisms, including man, will successfully adapt. Photosynthesis altered our environment. This change gave rise to an oxygen atmosphere that made man possible. Can we seriously imagine that man can exert a biological impact approaching the development of RNA, DNA, photosynthesis, respiration, or sex upon our earth? Perhaps man is very important after all. This very brief essay simply tries to put the effects of man into global spatiotemporal perspective.

A fundamental question of scale: The spatial scale of the globe is limited; however, the scale of humanity, relative to it, may be of some interest. No more than one hundred billion, and probably closer to twenty billion, *Homo sapiens* have existed in the entire history of the world. It is obvious that these individuals represent a rather small proportion of the global carbon budget compared to other climax organisms such as bacteria or grasses. Another way to consider relative human impact is to examine the relative global consequence of a virus infecting and killing all plankton or of another killing all extant human beings. Another thought experiment might contrast the results of human-induced thermonuclear war with the cosmic impact of an asteroid the size of the moon. Total thermonuclear war has been estimated to kill two hundred million individuals or 4 percent of the present population of the earth, while such an asteroid collision would probably wipe out most if not all living things and all people.

The temporal scale of humanity's global impact may also be useful to consider.

Cosmic forces: The universal expansion noted today estimates the universe to be no more than ten billion to twenty billion years old. If the dynamics of universal birth and death are cyclical, bang-

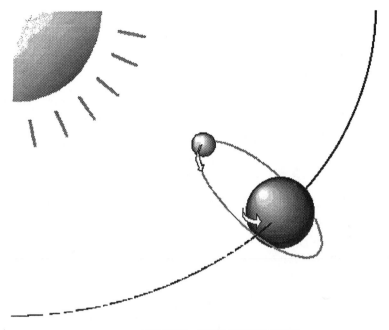

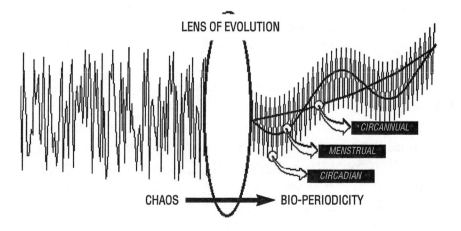

Fig. 1.

expansion-collapse, a twenty-billion- to forty-billion-year fundamental period might be a reasonable estimate. There is global evidence for smaller periodic cosmic cataclysms about every two billion years. There are other cosmic interactions that occur across a very broad range of frequencies. Many of these cosmic interactions have profound physical and biological interactions (seasons, lunar cycles, and circadian rhythms) while the effects of others like background microwave radiation are difficult to perceive (see figure 1).

Geological forces: Global cycles of compaction and rearrangement have existed since the initial planetary accretion. As the planet has cooled and shrunk, the amplitude of these cycles has diminished. Nonetheless, geological rearrangements responsible for plate tectonics, mountain range formation, and vulcanism are still responsible for unarguable global impact. Any estimate of the "kilotonnage" released in the reformation of Santorini, the eruption of Mount Pinatubo, or the explosion of Mount St. Helens does not permit doubt of the global relevance of these infrequent but powerful events. The small earthquake accompanying our Delphi conference, killing two dozen people and destroying a thousand dwellings, should remind us subtly that the geologic power of Nature is real and imminent.

Biological forces: Entirely nonlinear cycles of birth-death-rebirth are tied to cosmological cycles and affected by geological cycles. The Bios has been estimated to be nearly as old as our earth. Flexibility, adaptability, and responsiveness characterize life as a force. This force has had great influence over our environment throughout much of the earth's history. Several stepwise increases in the contribution of life to the overall global environment can clearly be appreciated. It may be useful to think of the impact of these biological events and to compare them to the appearance and success of *Homo sapiens*. Some of these vital advances include the natural selection of amino acids, ribonucleic and deoxyribonucleic acids

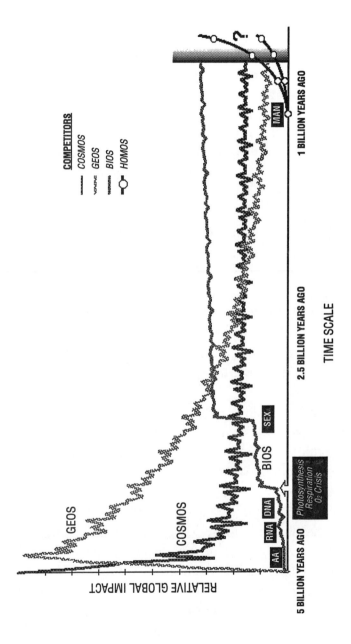

Fig. 2.

(RNA and DNA) as the building blocks of life; the development of the processes of photosynthesis and respiration resulting in an oxygen-containing atmosphere, which in turn enforced the selection of oxygen-producing and oxygen-fueled life forms; and the development of sex, which stabilized and diversified the evolving genomata, which resulted in enhanced survivability by virtue of improved flexibility. How does the erection of man and his development over the last million years compare to these biological events in terms of global impact? Even the most anthropocentric among us may find a growing respect for the relative impact of nonhuman cosmic, geologic, and biologic events in shaping our environment.

Figure 2 depicts the quantity of global impact over time since the "big bang" originating from cosmological, geological, and biological sources. Global impact can be imagined by an environmental integral something like climate. The effect of each component in this overall variance competition is represented by both its vertical height and by the degree of covariance among the competing sources for global impact. Important cosmological, geological, and biological events are depicted.

Immediately following the big bang, cosmological events predominantly affect the environment, which is obviously quite hostile. Cosmo-geological forces predominate during the process of star and planetary accretion. Accretion is followed by a span of very active geologic forces, cyclically compacting and reshaping the globe. Cosmological interactions are intermittently strong; however, the geology of early planetary evolution predominates for many eons. Life forms appear very early following planetary accretion, at least three billion years ago. They falter, exerting little influence until several important steps have evolved. The development of nucleic acid–based "life plans," the evolution of photosynthesis and respiration and sex are responsible for rapid advance of life as a major buffering force in shaping our environment. High-frequency cosmological cycles in climate are modulated substantially by the Bios, relatively early on. This is represented by a convergent covariation of cosmological and biological cycles across several important biological frequencies. These patterns continue to be affected by, historically speaking, low-amplitude chaotic geologic activity.

The time structure of human impact: The appearance and success of human life and its possible influence over the environment occurs in the last second of a twenty-four-hour clock set to universal time. It is possible that this successful life form may exert profound planetary impact. It is, however, from this universal spatiotemporal perspective, a little premature and perhaps a bit presumptuous to be sure of this.

6

The Vitalist Philosophy: A Physician's Point of View

Emil J. Freireich

From the earliest records of human societies, medicine has had a major and highly significant social function. As is most lucidly spelled out in the Hippocratic oath, to which all modern-day physicians subscribe, a physician has as his first and highest ethical principle the value of human life. The physician devotes his entire professional energy to the relief of human suffering and to the prolongation of human life. Over the last century, modern scientific medicine has dramatically changed the human lifespan. It begins with a dramatic reduction in infant mortality, the control of epidemic diseases with the result that human life expectancy at birth has almost doubled in the last century. This is associated with a shift in the human population so that the median age has progressively risen and the most rapidly growing segment of the human population in the Western world are those in the tenth decade of life.

It is clear that the "doomsayer" philosophers of the relationship between the human species and our natural habitat on earth view the "population explosion" as a major contributor to "the destruction of our natural environment." The concept of "overpopulation" and the concept of "diminishing natural resources" fly in the face of the vitalists' philosophical orientation toward valuing human life and human existence.

The human species is as much a part of nature as any other living species. The human species, however, has the ability to interact constructively with other species and with his environment. The increase in population and the progressive increase in the median age of the population or the duration of each individual life contributes experience, skill, and wisdom as a growing characteristic of the human species. When this is combined with technological innovations for communication, speed of travel, and production of natural resources, it is clear that the contribution of medicine to the welfare of the planet is a constructive one; that is, population growth produces the natural environment, which is beneficial to all living species and to the planet itself.

By all objective measures, societies that have an improved quality and quantity of human life are associated with the production of a higher standard of living for all humans. This results from an improving use of the environment for the generation of food. As an example, modern agriculture allows the reduction in the amount of "rain forest" and other natural environments that must be destroyed in order to be committed to food production. In fact, the nations with the highest standard of living devote the lowest proportion of their land to food production.

It is reasonable to assume that the solution to environmental problems is the promulgation of regulations, laws, and treaties that are essentially governmental management of the ecosystems. Yet, in the last twenty-five years it has been demonstrated that the socialist economies of the world have greatly increased the destruction of natural resources and the creation of pollution while at the same time these economies were declining rapidly. In contrast, the Western market economies have experienced not only a healthy economic structure associated with an improved standard of living but there has been progressive reduction in the cost of the natural resources, which indicate that there is an abundance, in fact an overproduction of food, energy sources, and natural products, such as minerals and biologicals, wood products, and so on. This economic health has been associated with a progressive decline in pollution of water and air and a progressive increase in the quality of the natural environment and in the preservation of species that were endangered. The experience of the last twenty-five years strongly suggests that market systems offer effective techniques for managing global environmental and social problems based on the concepts of individual liberty and self-determination.

The residual major social problems relate to the "tragedy of the commons." There are many natural resources, such as the oceans, rain forests, the Arctic areas, and so on, where personal incentives and market incentives will not protect the commons. Here a system of integrating personal self-interest with community necessity and opportunity must be developed. A combination of private ownership and public mandate is clearly a form of global resource management which must be developed to conserve our commonly held resources.

Being a scientist, I am committed to the philosophical method of reasoning, which is called induction. That is, I base my predictions of the future on observations of the present and past. It is clear that when one looks back at the rate of change in our knowledge of our earth and its natural resources the correct prediction is that the human species will continue to improve our natural environment on the blue planet, the planet earth. To maintain an air of optimism in spite of events which might induce me to be pessimistic about the future of man and his environment, I have frequently turned to science fiction writers who have in the past most accurately predicted the events of the future. Virtually all the predictions made by the most creative and innovative science fiction writers of the last century have come to pass in our lifetimes. We now live in an era where the speed at which humans can be moved has increased to the point where it is possible for humans to land on our nearest satellite, the moon, and return to earth. One of the most famous science fiction writers, Arthur C. Clarke, who wrote the novel *2001: A Space Odyssey,* continues to inspire optimism for me and other followers of the vitalist philosophy.

> Since the dawn of time, roughly a hundred billion human beings have walked the planet Earth. . . . By a curious coincidence there are approximately a hundred billion stars in our local universe, the Milky Way. So for every man who has ever lived, in this Universe there shines a star. But every one of those stars is a sun, often far more brilliant and glorious than the small, nearby star we call *the* Sun. And many of those alien suns have planets circling them. So almost certainly there is enough land in the sky to give every member of the human species, back to the first ape-man, his own private, world-sized heaven—or hell.

Suggested Reading

Bailey, Ronald, ed. *The True State of the Planet* (New York: The Free Press, 1995).

Clarke, Arthur C. *2001: A Space Odyssey.* (New York: New American Library, 1968).

Myers, Norman, and Julian L. Simon. *Scarcity or Abundance?* (New York: W. W. Norton, 1994).

O'Rourke, P. J. *All the Trouble in the World* (New York: Atlantic Monthly Press, 1994).

Rubin, Charles T. *The Green Crusade* (New York: The Free Press, 1994).

7

Has Ethics Kept Up with the Development of Science, Technology, and Medicine?

Walter Sinnott-Armstrong

When I was asked to answer the question in my title, it seemed obvious which answer was expected. The question would not be asked unless its answer was supposed to be "No. Ethics is way behind science, technology, and medicine."

This answer is, however, misleading in at least one way. If the basic rules or principles of ethics are universal and timeless, as many philosophers believe, then the basic moral system does *not* either change or need to change. Killing, disabling, and deceiving continue to be morally wrong, at least presumptively, regardless of any technological developments. Technology affects *when* we can save or destroy lives and *how many* lives we can save or destroy, but it does not affect *whether* we morally ought to save lives when we can do so at no great cost, or whether it is morally wrong to destroy lives for no adequate reason.

Even if basic morality really is this constant, however, there are still other ways in which we need to develop our views about what is moral. The same old moral principles need to be applied to new situations as they arise, and technology creates new problems faster than ethicists can figure to how to apply moral principles to those problems. This is one obvious way in which ethics has failed to keep up with science, technology, and medicine.

There is also another deeper and more interesting way in which ethics lags behind technology. Moral judgments depend on many different factors, including both risks and intentions. For example, when I drive my car very fast, even if I am justified in driving so fast, I create a risk of an accident. This risk is a function of both the degree of harm that might occur and the probability of that harm occurring. I might *know* this risk when I drive fast, but I still do not *intend* to have an accident, because an accident is not part of my plan. Thus, intentions are distinct from risks. Now, both intentions and risks are relevant to morality. Nonetheless, I will argue that technology has made certain kinds of risks more important than intentions in our moral lives. This shift has not been recognized either by our common moral beliefs or by our moral theories, so our moral views are unequipped to deal with the most important moral issues raised by technology. To overcome this deficit, we need to refocus our moral views away from intentions and toward risks. These are the claims for which I will argue here.

Modern Life

To begin, we need to ask, "How exactly has modern technology changed our lives?" One obvious answer is that it has given us power to do what we could not do before. This power can be used for good (such as when doctors cure diseases) or for ill (such as when terrorists use plastic explosives). In these cases, the consequences of the technology are intended by the people who use it.

Technology also often breaks down and causes problems by mistake or accident. This aspect of technology can be represented by an everyday example. A few weeks ago, I was writing a paper for another conference. As usual, I was late, but I had almost finished a draft. Then I pushed the wrong key on my computer. The whole file disappeared. I had saved earlier drafts, but I did not know which computer file contained the most recent version, so I did not know what was the best way to get started again.

This incident encapsulates three features of technology that permeate the modern world. First, mistakes are more costly than they used to be. Errors in handwriting affected only single words, but computer errors can destroy weeks of work. Second, mistakes happen more quickly than they used to, which makes major mistakes more likely and more common. I never lost a whole paper when I wrote by hand, but I have lost many computer files in an instant. Third, it is hard to know what to do when a mistake occurs. I never depended on handwriting experts in the ways that I now depend on computer consultants. For these reasons, computers make writing riskier and scarier. I am constantly afraid that my computer will break down or that I will push the wrong key; and I think that many other people share such fears.

These risks and fears are not peculiar to computers; they are shared by other technological developments. Moreover, other advances in technology introduce risks of different degrees and kinds. When I lose a computer file by mistake, I hurt only *myself*. These risks have little to do with morality or ethics, since morality and ethics concern one person's relations to *other* people. In contrast with my computer, many other technologies cannot be used without imposing risks not only on oneself but also on other people. To take another everyday example, it is very unlikely that I will hurt anyone badly if I walk to work. But, if I drive a car, I might run into another driver or a pedestrian; and this risk goes up in crowded cities. Thus, such technological developments introduce new moral issues about when such risks are justified.

These moral issues are serious not only because the risked harms are greater but also because some technologies increase the *number* of people who are at risk. The clearest example is probably new weapons of war. Before the modern world, the most effective soldiers could kill tens of other soldiers, but today even a mediocre soldier can kill thousands or even millions of soldiers and civilians by pushing a single button. Many of these deaths will not be intended even in successful attacks, since large weapons are so indiscriminate; and mistakes will also cause many more unintended deaths than ever before. Just consider the many soldiers who have been killed by friendly fire in recent wars.

Similarly, in medicine, powerful drugs and new equipment can save lives and improve the quality of life, but they can also kill or cause great pain and disability. One infamous case is that of thalidomide. Doctors prescribed this drug as a treatment for morning sickness, which causes nausea and vomiting in millions of pregnant women. Thalidomide did alleviate this condition. It was discovered too late, however, that thalidomide also caused severe birth defects with which thousands of people still have to cope.

Again, consider biotechnology. Scientists can create life forms to eat up oil spills or to eat pests that ruin crops. But, if these new organisms get out of control, they could destroy an entire oil field, crop, or even ecosystem. The probability of these horrors is extremely small, but, since the potential damage is so great, these technologies make even shipping and agriculture risky.

Scientific research is no exception. The genome project is trying to compile tremendous amounts of information about the human genome in the hope of detecting, predicting, and curing many genetic diseases. But, if the information about an individual's genes gets into the wrong hands, it could be used to harm that individual by denying him insurance or a job.

In all of these ways and many more, technology adds to the risks that we impose on each other. Of course, I am not saying that *all* risk is bad. We cannot accomplish anything without some risk. My point is also not that there were *no* risks before technology. Even cave dwellers faced risks from wild animals. I am not even sure that there is a higher degree of risk *overall* today. Before technology, people probably faced many more risks from disease and other natural dangers. Technology has reduced such natural risks. Even when one risk is created by a technology, that technology often reduces other risks; and the risk that one technology creates can often be reduced by other technologies (such as air bags on cars). All of this makes it very difficult to compare the overall risks before and after technology. Nonetheless, when technology does raise new moral problems, those moral problems are often due to the fact that one person cannot use a technology without creating risks of certain kinds of accidents and mistakes that would harm many other people.

The Ethics of Intentions

These new risks pose profound challenges to traditional moral beliefs and theories. The main challenge that I will discuss can be explained by contrasting two broad approaches to morality.

The first is an *ethics of intentions*. On this view, moral judgments are solely or primarily about what agents intend to do or want to do or try to do. An agent can intend or want to do something even when the agent has no real chance of doing it; and an agent can create a real risk even when the agent does not at all intend or want to create that risk. Thus, intentions are mental states. Moreover, even if the agent knows that an act will cause a risk or a harm, the agent does not intend or want that risk or harm if the risk or harm is not part of the agent's plan. Thus, more than just belief about the future is required for the mental state of intention. An ethics of intentions focuses on such mental states because it is these parts of the minds of agents that are supposed to show whether the agents are good people. The main or only goal of moral theory is then to determine which intentions or persons are good or bad, or virtuous or vicious. Harms and risks to other people are seen as important only insofar as they raise the issue of which person is to blame.

In contrast, an *ethics of risks* focuses less on agents or their minds and more on actions. The morally right action is then determined by the consequences or risks that the action creates for other people. The relevant risks might be limited to those that can be or ought to be foreseen, but still the actual mental state of the agent is seen as less important to morality, so that acts can be morally wrong even when their agents are neither bad nor vicious nor even blameworthy.

Of course, morality is complex, so any adequate moral theory must say something about a variety of moral judgments that depend on a variety of factors, including both intentions and risks. Nonetheless, different moral views emphasize different factors in different areas. It is such a difference in emphasis that separates an ethics of intentions from an ethics of risks.

Although each of these approaches is coherent and has some attractions, one of them—the ethics of intentions—has dominated the history of moral theory. In this wonderful Greek setting, it should hardly be necessary to mention that Socrates, Plato, and Aristotle started serious moral philosophy. All three of these great Greek philosophers focused on moral virtue as a state of character that is revealed in an agent's intentions. This beginning deeply influenced future developments. St. Thomas Aquinas and the Catholic tradition attached primary importance to intentions in such doctrines as double effect, according to which it is harder to justify causing harms that are intended than to justify harms that are merely foreseen but not intended. The great Protestant moral philosopher, Immanuel Kant, also insisted that the right act has no moral worth at all unless it is done from the right motive, and he formulated his categorical imperative so that it applied to maxims of action (which are much like intentions) rather than to actions themselves. More recently, many modern ethicists have called for a return to virtue ethics; and even some utilitarians have moved to motive-utilitarianism, which judges an action by the consequences of its motive or intention. All of these views lie within the ethics of intentions, because they all take moral judgments to be primarily about mental states and agents.

This general approach to ethics does seem plausible in many contexts. When we choose which individuals to admire or to trust, and which to befriend or to love, it does seem to make a big difference whether they harm us intentionally or unintentionally, and whether they are vicious or virtuous. When my wife hurts me, I want to know whether she did it on purpose or by accident. If the main point of ethics is to judge people in such contexts, then an ethics of intentions might seem to be on the right track. An ethics of intentions will also seem attractive to those who think that our minds or souls are more valuable than our bodies, since an ethics of intentions focuses on that mental essence.

Against the Ethics of Intentions

Nonetheless, despite its popularity and apparent plausibility, I will argue that the ethics of intentions is inadequate in our modern world, especially when applied to acts that use technology on a large scale. Here I will give three reasons.

The first is that modern technology has increased the importance of risks and decreased the importance of intentions (both absolutely and relatively). Consider the examples above. A doctor who prescribed thalidomide might have disabled many people, but this doctor's only intention was to help their mothers. A biologist who develops a new organism to eat pests might ruin a whole ecosystem, but his or her only intention is to help farmers. A scientist at work on the human genome project might intend only to provide knowledge and to help cure diseases, but her research might end up harming the very people that she wants to help, as well as many other people far into the future. These agents are not bad as people, and their intentions are also not bad.[1] But that does *not* show that their acts are morally permissible. In order to determine whether their acts are morally right or wrong, we still need to consider the risks. After all, it barely matters to someone with a severe birth defect that the doctors who developed thalidomide and prescribed it to his mother did not intend to hurt him or that they were good people. Thus, the main issues in such decisions get distorted by an ethics that attaches too much importance to intentions.

A second, related reason to reject an ethics of intentions is that exclusive focus on intentions can lead to wrong decisions in some cases. For example, during the cold war, the United States and other nuclear powers had to choose whether to continue to aim their nuclear weapons at cities or to retarget their weapons at the silos that housed their opponent's nuclear weapons. City-targeting was often criticized on the basis of an ethics of intentions. It was argued that (1) it would be immoral to fire nuclear weapons at an opponent's cities even after being attacked by that opponent's nuclear weapons; but (2) it is morally wrong to intend to do what it would be morally wrong to do; and (3) targeting cities involves an intention to use nuclear weapons against cities if attacked; so (4) it is morally wrong to target cities.

This argument suffers from some technical defects,[2] but here I just want to point out how dangerous it can be. Targeting silos seems to increase the risks for both sides. First, a country's leaders are more likely to think that a first strike is worth the risk, if they think that they do not have as much to lose because the attacked country will retaliate only against their silos. Second, silo-targeting fuels the arms race, because opponents will need to build more and more weapons in order to be assured of enough weapons to retaliate in case of attack, since an attack on their silos will destroy many of the weapons that they need to retaliate. Third, silo-targeting creates a mentality of "use them or lose them," for, if a country believes that its opponents have begun to attack or are about to attack their silos, then they will need to fire those weapons very quickly in order to prevent their weapons from being destroyed, thereby leaving them helpless. In response, critics of targeting cities deny that these risks are so large. Still, even if these probabilities are small, they provide strong reasons not to target silos, because the lives of so many people are at stake. But none of these risks are intended, so they are overlooked or deemphasized by an ethics of intentions. That means that someone operating with an ethics of intentions is more likely to switch targeting from cities to silos, even if this switch does increase the risks of nuclear war, including the risks to the very city dwellers for whom the critics were so concerned. That is counterproductive.

Another example, which is even more controversial, concerns abortion and contraception as means of population control. These measures are often opposed on the basis of the doctrine of double effect, because they involve intentional harm to a fetus or to a fertilized egg. However, if contraception and abortion really are important parts of the most effective ways to slow the population explosion, which threatens not only the quality of our lives but also our very survival, then we need to focus less on the intentions of people who use contraception or abortion and more on the risks to all of us if we do not solve the population problem.

My third reason to reject an ethics of intentions is that many intentions become much less clear as technology advances. For one thing, people act more often in larger groups or institutions, and it is notoriously hard to say what a group's intentions are. A country's military strategy or population policy usually results from deals and compromises among competing groups, each of which includes individuals with different and even conflicting intentions; and then it is not at all clear that the country as a whole has any specific intention. Those who enforce the resulting policy also often have very different intentions than the policymakers.

Even when individuals act apart from groups, their intentions are more often unclear in the modern world. Consider a doctor treating a terminally ill patient in extreme pain. In order to relieve the pain, the doctor must give higher and higher doses of morphine. As the dose goes up, so does the risk that the patient will die from an overdose. At a certain point, the amount of morphine that is necessary to relieve the pain also creates a high risk of killing the patient. The doctor administers the dose anyway, because it will relieve the pain one way or the other, and the patient finally dies from an overdose. In this case, did the doctor *intend* to kill the patient? It's just not clear. The doctor did intentionally administer a dose that the doctor knew would be likely to kill the patient, but the doctor's goal was not to kill the patient, although death was one means to the doctor's goal, which was to relieve pain. In such cases, a person's intentions are unclear, so the ethics of intentions is not much use. And modern technology has created more and more cases of this kind. This is yet another reason why modern technology has rendered the ethics of intentions obsolete.

An Ethics of Risks

But what should replace the ethics of intentions? My answer is: an ethics of risks. We need to determine when it is morally permissible to impose a risk on one set of people in order to prevent a different risk to a different set of people (or possibly to the same set of people). We can explore this issue by looking at small-scale moral problems in everyday life as well as large-scale problems faced by governments and other institutions. We could also ask when rational, impartial people would agree on public policies of allowing certain kinds of trade-offs. We can use these reflections to formulate principles governing trade-offs among risks.[3]

Very little work has been done in this area. Moral philosophers have tended to argue against simplistic versions of utilitarianism, which is the view that an act is morally right if and only if it creates the greatest balance of good over bad, regardless of distribution. I am still not sure that such utilitarianism is wrong, when formulated properly,[4] but the point I want to make here is just that we need moral principles governing risk creation and distribution in order to face the challenges of the modern world.

On a more practical level, other steps would also be useful. We need to figure out how to redirect risks toward the people who cause them, so as to induce those people to stop causing so many risks for others. We also need to redirect risks at those who benefit from those risks, so that others will not have to shoulder an unfair share of the burden. And we need to educate people to make them more aware of and more sensitive to the risks that they cause.

All of this is, admittedly, vague. I wish that I could specify the correct moral principles governing risks, as well as the best practical and pedagogical solutions to these problems, but that work remains to be done. That is why ethics has not kept up with the development of science, technology, and medicine.

Responses to Objections

This call to replace an ethics of intentions with an ethics of risks is bound to run into several objections. The most common objection will probably be that, even if risks are more important in many areas of modern life, intentions are still more important in other areas. I have focused on unintended harms, but the modern world is also filled with intended harms, including those caused in wars and by terrorists. These intended harms are also increased by technology. Moreover, on a smaller scale, we still depend on each other in our everyday lives, so we need to form friendships with other individuals. In order to decide whom to befriend, we need to know what kind of people we are dealing with, so we need to know their intentions and their characters.

I do not deny any of this. I am not saying that intentions and character do not matter at all ever. Of course, wars and terrorism are terrible, and friendships do still matter. My point is just that modern technology has created many situations where strangers as well as friends unintentionally impose great risks on us.

When people stayed in small groups, their neighbors could harm them, but they could not hurt as many people at once, and it was rarer for one person to harm another unintentionally, especially if these people were strangers. Consequently, if you surrounded yourself with friends and good people who would not harm you intentionally, then you were relatively safe. This is the world that produced our moral intuitions and beliefs, so it should not be surprising that many people's immediate moral beliefs even today place a premium on intentions. These people will have reservations about an ethics of risks.

But the world has changed. Even a person surrounded by many friends is subject to unintended risks, from computer breakdowns to medical errors to ecological disasters. In response to this new world, ethics needs to grow up. If ethics is ever to catch up with the development of science, technology, and medicine, ethics needs to refocus its attention so as to deal with the problems that have been created by science, technology, and medicine. My thesis is that this requires an ethics of risks. But whether or not this particular direction is right, it is clear that ethics has a long way to go.[5]

Notes

1. This is less obvious in the case of war, since soldiers often intend harm to enemy soldiers, but modern warfare is distinctive in the great number of civilian deaths that are not intended but are at most foreseen or are even just accidental.

2. See my "The Wrongful Intentions Principle," *Philosophical Papers* 20 (May 1991): 11–24.

3. For some discussion of some such principles, see my "Risks, National Defense, and Nuclear Deterrence," *Public Affairs Quarterly* 6 (July 1992): 345–62.

4. A proper formulation needs to count freedom, death, and other goods and harms in addition to pleasure and pain. I argue for part of a variation on utilitarianism in "An Argument for Consequentialism" in *Ethics,* vol. 6 of *Philosophical Perspectives* (1992): 399–421. However, my argument there needs to be reformulated in terms of risks, as James Dreier pointed out to me. See his review in *Nous* 28 (December 1994): 522–25. Another reason why I now talk about an ethics of risks instead of an ethics of consequences is that a failed attempt at murder is immoral because it creates risks even if it has no bad consequences at all.

5. For very helpful comments, I thank Celia Chen, Bernard Gert, Amy Hollywood, Jim Moor, Eric Steinhart, and many people at the Delphi conference.

8

Ethics and Biological Evolution

Dennis V. Razis

Ethics is a manmade concept referring to rules concerning good and evil. It has belonged to the area of religion and philosophy since the dawn of history.[1] Socrates was the first to seek to define this term and his maxim "Virtue is knowledge" became famous. He was followed by Aristotle, who believed that ethics was a science unto itself. The Stoics divided philosophy into three different branches: logic, physics, and ethics. This separation of philosophy lasted to the Renaissance and beyond and was accepted by Kant, the philosopher who profoundly influenced the shaping of modern ethics.[2]

What is the modern definition of ethics? Ethics is the systematic study of the nature of the value concept, "good," "bad," "ought," "right," "wrong," and so on, and the general principles which justify us in applying them to anything.[3] The next question is of course what is the definition of good and so on and what makes an action right or wrong. Man's behavior has been governed by the answers given to this query. These answers vary widely at different times and at different places—diversity in this field is proverbial. As Shakespeare put it in *Hamlet,* "There is nothing either good or bad, but thinking makes it so."[4]

Ethics is nevertheless one of the forces shaping the life of human societies, though is not by any means one of the most powerful or dominant forces. Where is ethics derived from? Thracymachos in Plato's *Republic* states that, "Moral rules brought benefit to the governing group or individual in each State," anticipating thus the Marxists' analysis of political power and bourgeois morality. Ethical rules derive from the nature of man, and his needs and ethical systems contribute to the group's survival and to keep order and peace and to satisfy social needs.[5]

The question of what is good is obviously related to what we ought to do and the next question is whether we can accept a priori any universal laws according to which we should act independently of their consequences. The differences, however, within the human species are more vital than the similarities and greater than the differences with other species.[6] This terrible uniqueness of man explains the mutual repellence in humans, the intraspecies wars and the complete lack of a sense of unity as a species and, consequently, lack of world will. Thus, at first thought, universality of morality seems impossible, as seems impossible an internationally accepted definition of ethics.

Yet, in our time the possibility of annihilation of human species by overpopulation, the degradation of the environment, and the modern wars, seem real. This might force us to accept the universality of certain ethical rules related to the survival of human species and to the survival of this planet's ecosystem.[7]

Life on earth is a process continuously evolving. The primitive forms of life appeared 3.5 billion years ago, and *Homo sapiens* 0.5 million years ago. During this half million years, one of the most determinative events in biological evolution occurred, that is, the explosive evolution of the human neocortex in so short a time, unprecedented in evolutionary history.[8] The neocortex made man the only creature able to think and to formulate "world views," that is, systems of ideas about the universe, the solar system, and the planet earth; it also made man the only being able to interfere with biological evolution.[9]

How did man use the power endowed to him by the neocortex? Man for the greatest period of his existence (98 percent) lived in tribes as a hunter. Ten thousand to twelve thousand years ago agriculture was discovered and then everything changed; man stopped moving from place to place, organized societies, improved his nutrition, and increased his lifespan. The discovery of agriculture is the first milestone in human history. Some thousand years passed and then suddenly, as if sprung from nowhere, around the sixth century B.C.E., philosophers from Melitus, Elea, and Samos, started discussing the origin of evolution of the universe, searching for the ultimate principles underlying all diversity. The heroic age of Greek science and culture lasted from 600 to 400 B.C.E., and during the three hundred golden Greek years, accumulated growth of knowledge was achieved for the first time in human history. The Greek years were followed by centuries of hibernation until the "intellectual and information crisis" in the Western world. This crisis involved the revolution in the physical sciences that started with Newton in the seventeenth century and reached a climax with Einstein in the twentieth century, and the revolution in biology that began with Darwin in the nineteenth century and Watson and Crick in the twentieth century. Human history can be thus summarized in a simplified way as follows: 98 percent of his existence, man lived in tribes as a hunter; this was followed by three determinative milestones: the discovery of agriculture ten thousand to twelve thousand years ago, the three hundred golden years of Greece from 600 to 400 B.C.E., and the last three hundred years in the Western world.

Nothing more impressive or more significant has ever occurred on earth than the progress achieved in the Western world during the last two hundred to three hundred years. The curves of progress in science, technology, destructive power, communication, specialized knowledge, and so on, during the last three hundred years are not just exponential, but rocketlike.

The population curve, however, is also exponential and rocketlike. The explosive growth of the human species is the result of reducing mortality without adjusting reproduction and for this medicine is mainly responsible.[10] It was achieved by the use in biology of applied sciences for the benefit of man. Application of sciences for the benefit of one species implies that it must be detrimental for other species and this has far-reaching consequences.[11] Nevertheless, in closed ecosystems population explosions end abruptly in a catastrophe for the exploding system. *Homo sapiens* is rapidly approaching such a situation in the closed ecosystem of planet earth. If no adjustments are made the demise of *Homo sapiens* is probably imminent.[12]

But how did we reach the overpopulation impasse? In a broad biological sense, the order and laws of modern man are based on concepts dating back to periods when man lived in tribes in virtually unlimited areas. These basic concepts are nowadays nonbiological and have caused the population explosion and the disorganization of the ecosystem of this planet. If we are going to survive the overpopulation crisis, the ancient Greek anthropocentric worldview, "Man is the measure of all things" (Protagoras) must be now adapted to an *evolution worldview*, as proposed by Evert Timmer.[13] Biological evolution worldview must direct applied sciences toward integrating *Homo sapiens* in the optimized ecosystem of the planet as an integral part of the evolution of life on earth. This would steer an optimal course between the interests of *Homo sapiens* and the interests of living nature as a whole. It would accord with the worldview of Spinoza, who tried to equate Nature with God.

To realize this biological evolution worldview, we need a multidisciplinary approach. Medicine is important because it is largely responsible for the overpopulation and degradation of the ecosystem. Furthermore, medicine must now play a new role, much more important than keeping us, as individual or groups, alive and healthy. Medicine, at the population level, should be primarily involved with bringing and keeping reproduction under control and optimizing the ecosystem of the earth.[14] To achieve this goal it must study and understand the patterns of human behavior, which remain unchanged throughout history. Without understanding and trying to explain human behavior, probably on a neurophysiological basis, we will never be able to grasp our destiny.[15]

Human behavior is determined to a great extent by the propensity of the individual to devote himself to and identify himself with a social group, a religion, an ideology, a nation, and so on, and consider all other groups as hostile. The results of this terrible uniqueness of man is intraspecies warfare, lack of sense of unity as a species, and consequently lack of world will.

It is very impressive that in ethics we are not better today than in any time before in human history. Actually the curve of ethics, social moralities, spiritual awareness, and related values, has remained completely flat throughout the centuries. This fundamental difference between the two evolutionary curves, that is, the flat curve of ethics and the exponential, rocketlike curve of the sciences, might explain the paranoid elements in human history, which swings back and forth throughout the eons from the most glorious achievements to the most terrible monstrosities.[16]

"In wisdom has Thou made them all" is only partly true and we should be by now mature enough to understand and accept it. There is a paranoid element in human behavior and in human history and we cannot wait for spontaneous mutations to correct it. Nature cannot save us. It is for medicine and other disciplines to study this paranoid element and attempt to find ways to "cure" it. This is our most important task.[17]

Notes

1. D. V. Razis, "Ethics and the Universality of Morality," *Quality Assurance in Health Care* 2 (1990): 369–73.

2. "History of Ethics" and "Ethics Comparative," *Encyclopaedia Britannica,* vol. 8 (London: William Benton, 1971), pp. 762–80 and 156–62.

3. "Ethics Comparative," *Encyclopaedia Britannica.*

4. E. Timmer, "Medical Ethics and Evolution," *Journal of the Royal Society of Medicine* 87 (1994): 250–52.

5. Razis, "Ethics."

6. A. Koestler, *The Ghost in the Machine,* vol. 17, Danube ed. (London: Hutchinson, 1971), pp. 297–312.

7. D. V. Razis, "A New Role for Medicine," *Journal of the Royal Society of Medicine* 87 (1994): 190–92.

8. A. Koestler, *The Ghost in the Machine,* vol. 16, pp. 267–96, and D. V. Razis, "Modern Cassandras and Our Survival as a Species—A New Role for Medicine?" *Journal of the Royal Society of Medicine* 82 (1989): 575–76.

9. Timmer, "Medical Ethics."

10. Razis, "Modern Cassandras," and Timmer, "Medical Ethics."

11. Timmer, "Medical Ethics."

12. N. Keyfitz, "Are There Ecological Limits to Population?" *Proceedings of the National Academy of Science of the USA* 90 (1993): 6895–99, and J. Wilbush, "Impact Management, Worst Scenario: Possible Technological Strategic Options," *Technology Analysis and Strategic Management* 2 (1990): 27–38.

13. Timmer, "Medical Ethics."

14. Razis, "A New Role," and Timmer, "Medical Ethics."

15. Razis, "A New Role" and "Modern Cassandras."

16. P. D. Maclean, "Contrasting Functions of Limbic and Neocortical Systems of the Brain and Their Relevance to Psychophysiological Aspects of Medicine," *American Journal of Medicine* 25 (1958): 611–26, and Razis, "A New Role" and "Modern Cassandras."

17. Razis, "Modern Cassandras."

9

Medical Ethics and Evolution[*]

Evert Timmer

Health and ill-health are relative concepts, like good and evil: they can be made absolute only if an ideal situation is assumed, like heaven, nirvana, utopia. Herbert Spencer (1820–1903) defined health as a relative concept: "Health is the perfect adjustment of an organism to its environment." In 1946 the World Health Organization defined health as an absolute concept: "Health is a state of physical, mental and social well-being and not merely the absence of disease or infirmity." The WHO definition lacks a biological basis and has proved impracticable.

Ethics may be defined as rules concerning good and evil but it is a manmade concept. As Shakespeare (1564–1616) put it in *Hamlet*: "There is nothing either good or bad, but thinking makes it so."

---

*This paper was published in the *Journal of the Royal Society of Medicine* 87 (1994): 250–52, and is reproduced by the kind permission of the journal.

Ethics has belonged to the areas of religion and philosophy since the dawn of history and absolute ethics has proved to be an impossibility. There are many relative ethics, which in this editorial are called alpha-ethics (in analogy to the phrase alpha-scholarship). Pure science is completely nonethical, hence the nickname "amoral scientists." Likewise living nature is also completely nonethical: she opposes maximum production to maximum destruction and eating to being eaten. Heterotrophic life can exist only at the sacrifice of other life and man belongs to the most brutal form of heterotrophic life that has ever lived on earth. This character of living nature has been expressed by many, for example, by Shakespeare in *Hamlet* ("To be or not to be"); by Darwin (1809–1882) in *The Origin of Species* ("struggle for existence"); and by Spencer (1820–1903) in *Principles of Biology* ("survival of the fittest"). The introduction of alpha-ethics into the area of applied science is like a contradiction in terms, for in practice it means the application of science for the benefit of man. In this editorial, "application of science for the benefit of man" will be termed "beta-ethics."

Ethics is viewed here in the light of evolution of life on earth. Modern biologists accept that in the universe a process of continuous evolution is going on and that the evolution of life on earth is a fact, although not yet fully explained. Some milestones in the evolution of life on earth are of importance to this editorial. They are approximately dated by science as follows: the appearance of primitive forms of life 3.5 billion years ago; of primates 7 million years ago; of hominids 3.5 million years ago; and of *Homo sapiens* 0.5 million years ago. When compared with the 3.5 billion years of life on earth, the 3.5 million years from hominids to *Homo sapiens* is equivalent to about one minute compared to a day. In this metaphoric minute a crucial phase in the evolution of life on earth took place, namely the explosive evolution of the human cerebrum or, more specifically, of the neocortex. In neurophysiology, the neocortex is seen as the anatomical substratum of the megabrain which makes thinking possible. The importance of thinking was expressed by Descartes (1596– 1650): *Cogito, ergo sum* ("I think, therefore I am"). Neocortex, megabrain, thinking, makes *Homo sapiens* the only species capable of formulating a "worldview." Here the phrase "worldview" is used as the equivalent to *Weltanschauung* in German, meaning systems of ideas about the universe, the solar system, and the earth.

Worldviews evolved from prehistoric animist-polytheist worldviews to the wealth of religious and philosophical worldviews of the modern era, with their riches of ceremonies, arts, and literature. These are characterized by what Protestant-Christian theology termed the *sensus numinis* (the awareness of a godlike supreme power).[1] Monotheist worldviews may be seen as the highest stages of this evolution; they arose in the Middle East, roughly in the twentieth to eighteenth centuries B.C.E., and came to a peak in the Mosaic worldview (thirteenth century B.C.E., catchword Moses). The influence of the Mosaic worldview on Western thinking during the next thirty centuries can hardly be exaggerated. Two revolutions caused its loss of supremacy: the scientific revolution (seventeenth century, catchword Newton; twentieth century, catchword Einstein); and the biological revolution (nineteenth century, catchword Darwin; twentieth century, catchword Watson and Crick). *Homo sapiens* are now going through a period which dawned with the Enlightenment in the eighteenth century, for these worldviews are now being replaced by biological evolutionary worldviews.

Ethical codes are also subject to evolution. The oldest surviving alpha-ethical codes date from roughly the twentieth to eighteenth centuries B.C.E. (eighteenth century B.C.E., catchword Hammurabi). They reached an early peak in the Ten Commandments of the Mosaic worldview and evolved over the centuries to the corpus of alpha-ethics produced by religious and philosophical thinking. The scientific revolution brought about an incompatibility between alpha-ethics and science. Kant (1724–1804) proposed a demarcation between the area of religion, philosophy, and alpha-ethics and the area of science, and the incompatibility was again expressed by Wittgenstein (1889–1951): "Ethics, in so far as it springs from the desire to say something about the ultimate meaning of life, the absolute good, the absolute valuable, can be no science. What it says does not add to our knowledge in any sense."[2] The incompatibility resulted in the present-day situation, where theologians and philosophers have no authority in the area of science and have become *Herrscher ohne Reich* (kings without a kingdom).

Beta-ethics is an awkward situation, since as the total amount of life on planet earth is limited, the application of science for the benefit of one species implies that it must be to the detriment of other species. This has far-reaching consequences. Man is the first form of life to be able to interfere with the evolutionary process of life on earth and he has done so without realizing the consequences and without being called to render account. He has transformed this planet into a mass-rearing factory of humans. In a broad biological view, the order and laws of modern man are based on concepts dating back to periods when man lived in tribes in virtually unlimited areas. These basic concepts nowadays are nonbiological and have caused the population explosion, the disorganization of the ecosystem of the planet, and the reduction of the pool of genetic resources of living nature. The human population explosion (5.5 billion now, doubling time thirty-five years) is becoming a cancer attacking the living nature of the planet. The dynamics of the rise and decline of population explosions, from microbes to mammals, are now fully understood, including the special case of closed ecosystems where explosions abruptly end in a catastrophe for the exploding species. *Homo sapiens* are rapidly approaching such a situation in the closed ecosystem of planet earth. If no adjustments are made, the demise of *Homo sapiens* is imminent and man will become one of the misfits of evolution on earth. Expert biologists have already worked out their anticipated scenarios of the imminent catastrophe,[3] but expert economists may see things rather differently.[4] For the time being, biologists are doomed to the role of Cassandra.[5] Only after a revision of the basic concepts will biology be able to play her role in the management of the planet, including a new role for medicine.[6]

Beta-ethics deserves careful thought. From a general biological evolutionary worldview *Homo sapiens,* pretenders to the "crown of creation," are the most brutal, voracious, and murderous of all the species which have evolved on earth. Man preaching ethics is like the devil preaching the gospel. Man is an interested party and therefore not in a suitable situation to conceive absolute beta-ethics. If, however, an anthropocentric biological evolutionary worldview were adopted, relative beta-ethics could come within range, for then applied science could be directed toward integrating *Homo sapiens* into the optimized ecosystem of the planet as an integral part of the evolution of life on earth. In such a worldview, the evolution of life on earth itself would constitute the godlike supreme power, *sensus numinis.* This would accord with the worldview of Spinoza (1632–1677), who tried to equate nature with God. Beta-ethics would be the compass used for steering an optimal course between the interests of *Homo sapiens* and the interests of living nature as a whole. It would need the rise of a neo-Moses to lead the exodus from the riches of traditional worldviews to the riches of evolutionary biological worldviews. The definition of beta-ethics, in accordance with Herbert Spencer's definition, could, for instance, read: beta-ethics is the application of science for the benefit of the species *Homo sapiens* as an integral part of the evolution of life on earth and respecting the interests of living nature as a whole.

Medical ethics nowadays has proved incapable of coping with modern applied biology. The "Corpus Hippocratum" (fourth century B.C.E.) is generally considered to be the cradle of modern Western

medicine and the Hippocratic oath, sworn by the Greek gods, is generally seen as the basis of medical ethics. The oath is both a code of conduct for the medical profession and a unilateral contract between doctor and individual patient. Its main principle is acting $ε
π$ $ωφελείη καμνόντων$ (for the benefit of patients) and it specifies doing no harm, no deadly poison, no abortion, no vice, no love-making with patients, and confidentiality. It is only appropriate to modern Western medicine to a limited extent. There are two main reasons for this: (1) the discovery that the bulk of traditional diseases are, in fact, part of the struggle for existence at the microbiological and parasitological level (nineteenth century, catchword Pasteur); and (2) the explosive development of molecular biology (twentieth century, catchword Watson and Crick). These two facts are fundamentally changing Western medicine. Metaphorically, doctors are undergoing a metamorphosis from knights fighting hostile species for the benefit of individual patients into bioengineers managing the mass-rearing factory of *Homo sapiens*. The board of directors prefer quantity to quality and the doctor-engineers interpret the main principle of the oath "acting for the benefit of patients" as "acting to prolong the life of patients." This means that Western medical practice no longer always acts for the benefit of the *individual* patient. However, there is more, for in relation to the population and the ecosystem the directives have caused antibiological effects that foster and maintain defects in the human genetic material and lead to a population explosion which, with urbanization and regression, could lead to *Homo sapiens* evolving into the lower level of insect states. They are also largely responsible for the disorganization of the ecosystem of the planet. Abortion, eugenics, euthanasia, and a spate of bioengineering activities are fast becoming part and parcel of medical practice. The accompanying medical-ethical problems have spawned a stream of publications[7] and the conflict between cure and health care demands a different kind of ethics.[8]

The appointment of alpha-ethics scholars to medical faculties cannot solve the actual impasse of medical ethics. The solution will have to come from beta-ethics, to be formulated by beta-ethics scientists searching for "a new role for medicine."[9] From an anthropocentric-biological standpoint, medicine is a branch of applied biology and its beta-ethics should accord with Herbert Spencer's definition of health. It would, however, have to be applied on two levels. At the level of the population and the ecosystem, health care would have biological directives with a primary aim of restoring the genetic material to health, bringing reproduction under control, optimizing the ecosystem, and integrating *Homo sapiens* into the optimized ecosystem of the planet. At the level of the individual, curative treatment would have to serve a different purpose than at present. Therefore it must be for the *benefit* of the *individual patient* under the terms of a bilateral contract between doctor and patient, with decisions to be taken jointly.

In terms of the opening words of the Hippocratic oath: then Asklepios will be rejuvenated as a reborn young god, daughter Panakeia will be freed from servitude to the chemical industry, and daughter Hygeia will be recalled from banishment to the island of microbiology. They will join forces for integrating *Homo sapiens* into the ecosystem of the planet as an integral part of the evolution of life on earth.

Notes

1. R. Otto, *Das Gefühl des Überweltlichen (sensus numinis)*, 5th and 6th eds. (München: C. H. Beck'sche Verlagsbuchhandlung, 1932), first published 1924.

2. Anonymous, "Wittgenstein's Lecture on Ethics," *Philosophical Review* 74 (1965): 12.

3. P. R. Ehrlich and A. H. Ehrlich, *The Population Explosion* (New York: Simon and Schuster, 1990).

4. N. Keyfitz, "Are There Ecological Limits to Population?" *Proceedings of the National Academy of Science of the USA* 90 (1993): 6895–99.

5. D. V. Razis, "Modern Cassandras and Our Survival as a Species—A New Role for Medicine?" *Journal of the Royal Society of Medicine* 82 (1989): 575–76.

6. Razis, "Modern Cassandras," and "A New Role for Medicine," *Journal of the Royal Society of Medicine* 87 (1994): 190–92.

7. A. S. Duncan, G. R. Dunstan, R. B. Welbourn, and J. A. Rivers, eds., *Dictionary of Medical Ethics* (London: Logman & Todd, 1977), and W. E. Fayerweather, J. Higginson, and T. L. Beauchamp, eds., "Ethics in Epidemiology," *Journal of Clinical Epidemiology* 44, supp. 1 (1991): i–ix, 1–151. These two publications have been chosen from the stream of publications because of their encyclopedic approach.

8. B. G. Charlton, "Public Health Medicine—A Different Kind of Ethics?" *Journal of the Royal Society of Medicine* 86 (1993): 194–95.

9. Razis, "Modern Cassandras," and "A New Role for Medicine."

10

Ethics for a Planetary Society

Paul Kurtz

Our planetary habitat is rapidly changing. Scientific, technological, economic, political and social changes are transforming the globe. We are all becoming, whether we like it or not, part of an interdependent world.[1]

To cope with these changes, there is a compelling need to enunciate a new humanistic planetary ethic. It should be apparent that if we are to succeed in this important endeavor, we need to transcend the ancient religious, ethnic, and national loyalties that have set us apart. We must endeavor to build cooperatively a genuine world community. May I be so bold as to suggest some of the guidelines for this humanistic ethic.

The Trees of Knowledge and Life

There are two contrasting approaches to ethics in the world today. The first, religious morality, attempts to deduce moral rules from

God's commandments as found in the Bible, the Koran, the Book of Mormon, or other sacred texts. Here the chief duty is obedience to commandments that are usually taken as absolutes. Religious piety precedes moral conscience.

In the Old Testament, Jehovah forbids Adam and Eve to eat the fruit of the Tree of Knowledge of Good and Evil. They disobey him and are expelled from the Garden of Eden. Jehovah expresses his displeasure and his fear that they might next be tempted to eat the forbidden fruit of another tree in the garden, the Tree of Life. The cardinal Muslim virtue is to *submit* to the will of Allah.

There is a second historic tradition, however, whose primary imperative is to base ethical choices on autonomous rational and scientific grounds and on eating the forbidden fruit of the Tree of Knowledge of Good and Evil and the Tree of Life. This tradition begins with the philosophers of Greece and Rome—Socrates, Aristotle, Hypatia, Epicurus, and Epictetus—and the Chinese sage Confucius. It was expressed during the Renaissance by Erasmus, Spinoza, and others, and many philosophers, such as Immanuel Kant, John Stuart Mill, and John Dewey, seek to develop ethics based on rational foundations.

This deep humanist cultural stream of civilization runs side by side with Judaic-Christian-Muslim tradition. The ethics of humanism is an authentic approach to moral principles and ethical values, and it has contributed immeasurably to human culture. It is especially relevant to the present world.

The Common Moral Decencies

The question is constantly asked: How can one be moral without religious foundations? What are the grounds on which the ethics of humanism rest? Let me outline some of the main features of the ethics of humanism.

First, there is a set of what I call the "common moral decencies," which are shared by both theists and nontheists alike and are the bedrock of moral conduct. Indeed, they are transcultural in their range and have their roots in common human needs. They grow out of the evolutionary struggle for survival and may even have some sociobiological basis, though they may be lacking in some individuals or societies since their emergence depends upon certain preconditions of moral and social development.

Nevertheless, the common moral decencies are so basic to the survival of any human community that meaningful coexistence cannot occur if they are consistently flouted. They are handed down through the generations and are recognized throughout the world by friends and lovers, colleagues and coworkers, strangers and aliens alike as basic rules of social intercourse. They are the foundation of moral education and should be taught in the schools. They express the elementary virtues of courtesy, politeness, and empathy so essential for living together; indeed, they are the very basis of civilized life itself.

First are the decencies that involve personal *integrity*: these include *telling the truth*, not lying or being deceitful; being *sincere*, candid, frank, and free of hypocrisy; *keeping one's promises*, honoring pledges, living up to agreements; and being *honest*, avoiding fraud or skullduggery.

Second is *trustworthiness*. We should be *loyal* to our lovers, friends, relatives, and coworkers, and we should be *dependable*, reliable, and responsible.

Third are the decencies of *benevolence*, which involve manifesting *good will* and noble intentions toward other human beings and having a positive concern for them. It means the *lack of malice* (nonmalfeasance), avoiding doing harm to other persons or their property. We should not kill or rob, inflict physical violence or injury, or be cruel, abusive, or vengeful. In the sexual domain it means that we should not force our sexual passions on others and should seek *mutual consent* between adults. It means that we have an obligation to be *beneficent*, that is, kind, sympathetic, compassionate. We should lend a helping hand to those in distress and try to decrease their pain and suffering and contribute positively to their welfare. Jesus perhaps best exemplifies the principles of benevolence.

Fourth is the principle of *fairness*. We should show *gratitude* and appreciation for those who are deserving of it. A civilized community will hold people *accountable* for their deeds, insisting that those who wrong others do not go completely unpunished and perhaps must make reparations to the aggrieved; thus, this also involves the principle of *justice* and equality in society. *Tolerance* is also a basic moral decency: We should allow other individuals the right to their beliefs, values, and styles of life, even though they may differ from our own. We may not agree with them, but all individuals are entitled to their convictions as long as they do not harm others or prevent them from exercising their rights. We should try to *cooperate* with others, seeking to negotiate differences peacefully without resorting to hatred or violence.

These common moral decencies express prima facie general principles and rules. Though individuals or nations may deviate from practicing them, they nonetheless provide general parameters by which to guide our conduct. They are not absolute and may conflict; we may have to establish priorities between them. They need not be divinely ordained to have moral force, but are tested by their consequences in practice. Morally developed human beings accept these principles and attempt to live by them because they understand that some personal moral sacrifices may be necessary to avoid conflict in living and working together. Practical moral wisdom thus recognizes the obligatory nature of responsible conduct.

In the Old Testament Abraham's faith is tested when God commands him to sacrifice his only son, Isaac, whom he dearly loves.

Abraham is fully prepared to obey, but at the last moment God stays his hand. Is it wrong for a father to kill his son? A developed moral conscience understands that it is. But is it wrong simply because Jehovah declares it to be wrong? No. I submit that there is an autonomous moral conscience that develops in human experience, grows out of our nature as social beings, and comprehends that murder is wrong, whether or not God declares it to be wrong. We should be highly suspicious of the moral development of one who believes that murder is wrong *only* because God commands it. Indeed, I believe that we attributed this moral decree to God because it is we who apprehended it to be wrong.

Ethical Excellences

The common moral decencies refer to how we relate to others. But there are a number of values that we should strive toward in our personal lives, and I submit that we also need to impart to the young an appreciation for what I call the *ethical excellences*. I believe that there are standards of ethical development, exquisite qualities of high merit and achievement. Indeed, in some individuals nobility shines through; there are, according to the Greek philosopher Aristotle, certain virtues or excellences that morally developed people exemplify. These states of character are based upon the golden mean and provide some balance in life. I think that these classical excellences or virtues need to be updated for the present age. What are they?

First, the excellence of *autonomy*, or self-reliance. By that I mean our ability to take control of our own lives; to accept responsibility for our own feelings, our interpersonal relationships, and our careers, how we live and learn, the values and goods we cherish. Such people are self-directed and self-governing. Their autonomy is an affirmation of their freedom. Unfortunately, some people find freedom a burden and thus are willing to forfeit their right to self-determination to others—to parents, spouses, or even totalitarian despots or authoritarian gurus. A free person recognizes that he or she has only one life to live and that how it will be lived is ultimately his or her choice. This does not deny that we live with others and share values and ideals, but basic to the ethics of democracy is an appreciation for the autonomy of individual choice.

Second, *intelligence* and reason are high on the scale of values. To achieve the good life we need to develop our cognitive skills, not merely technical expertise or skilled virtuosity, but good judgment about how to make wiser choices. Unfortunately, many critics of humanism demean human intelligence and believe that we cannot solve our problems. They are willing to abdicate their rational autonomy to others. Reason may not succeed in solving all problems—sometimes we must choose the lesser of many evils—but it is the most reliable method we have for making moral choices.

Third is the need for *self-discipline* in regard to one's passions and desires. We must satisfy our desires, passions, and needs in moderation, under the guidance of rational choice, recognizing the harmful consequences that imprudent choices can have upon ourselves and others.

Fourth, some *self-respect* is vital to psychological balance. Self-hatred can destroy the personality. We need to develop some appreciation for who we are as individuals and a realistic sense of our own identities, for a lack of self-esteem can make one feel truly worthless, which is neither healthy for the individual nor helpful to society at large.

Fifth, and high on the scale of values, is *creativity*. This is closely related to autonomy and self-respect, for independent persons have some confidence in their own powers and are willing to express their unique talents. The uncreative person is usually a conformist, unwilling to break new ground, timid and fearful of new departures. A creative person is willing to be innovative and has a zest for life that involves adventure and discovery.

Sixth, we need to develop *high motivation,* a willingness to enter into life and undertake new plans and projects. A motivated person finds life interesting and exciting. One problem for many people is that they find life and their jobs boring. Unfortunately, they are merely masking their lack of intensity and of commitment to high aspirations and values.

Seventh, we should adopt an *affirmative and positive attitude toward life.* We need some measure of optimism that what we do will matter. Although we may suffer failures and defeats, we must believe that we shall overcome and succeed despite adversity.

Eighth, an affirmative person is capable of some *joie de vivre,* or joyful living, an appreciation for the full range of human pleasures—from the so-called bodily pleasures such as food and sex to the most ennobling and creative of aesthetic, spiritual, intellectual, and moral pleasures.

Ninth, if we wish to live well then of course we should be rationally concerned about our *health* as a precondition of everything else. To maintain good health we should avoid smoking and drugs, drink only in moderation, seek to reduce stress in our lives, and strive to get proper nutrition, adequate exercise, and sufficient rest.

All of these excellences clearly point to a *summa bonum.* The intrinsic value humanists seek to achieve is *eudaemonia*: happiness or well-being. I prefer the word *exuberance* or *excelsior* to describe such a state of living, because I believe it is an active, not a passive, process. I believe that the end or goal of life is to live fully and creatively, sharing with others the many opportunities for joyful experience. The meaning of life is not to be discovered only after death in some hidden, mysterious realm; on the contrary, it can be found by eating the succulent fruit of the Tree of Life and by living in the here and now as fully and creatively as we can.

Yet the humanist is often condemned by religionists for focusing on happiness as a goal. For some salvational theologies this life has no meaning—it is only a preparation for the next. But this is an escapist theory, for even if immortality exists, that is no reason to denigrate life in the here and now. The important point that is often forgotten is that whether we find life meaningful depends in large part on what we give to it. Life presents us with opportunities and possibilities, and whether or not we tap these depends on our capacity for autonomy and creative affirmation.

There are those who maintain that the ethics of humanism, since it focuses on joyful, creative living, is corrupting and demeaning and may lead to libertarian licentiousness and hedonism in which "anything goes." For them, morality is repression, the body is despised, sexual expression for reasons other than procreation is sinful, and the world is a tragic vale of tears. They believe that they are incapable of solving their own problems or obtaining happiness on earth by their own efforts, and create they myth of solace to help them escape from the trials and tribulations of mortal injustice. They are laden with guilt and a sense of sin and try to assuage this by preferring comfort to truth.

This point of view is extremely pessimistic, for it often demeans and denigrates our intelligence and our capacity for high achievement. In its excessive form it is profoundly antihuman, even pathological. It masks a deep fear of one's own capacities to live autonomously, and it expresses a lack of self-respect and even shows self-hatred.

The Need for Creative Ethical Thinking

Thus far I have focused on two areas of ethics: (1) the common moral decencies, and (2) the ethics of personal excellence. The ethics of humanism is anything but self-centered or egoistic; it involves a deep appreciation for the needs of other human beings, as well as a recognition that no person is an island and that among our highest joys are those we share with others. Indeed, the common moral decencies point to the need to develop the excellences of integrity, truthfulness, beneficence, and fairness—and these excellences directly concern our relationships with others. The ethics of humanism prizes strength of character. I believe that most members of our society can accept the principles and values I have enumerated and that we do share more common ground than is usually appreciated. But we live in a period of rapid technological and social change in which we are constantly confronted by new ambiguities and new problems. The quest for absolute certainty is impossible to satisfy. We cannot simply draw upon the moral wisdom of past generations; we must be prepared for some revision of our traditional moral outlook. We need to adapt to the new challenges that confront us and develop new principles and values appropriate to the twenty-first century and beyond. The age-old morality contains many tested principles, but much of it—particularly our religious morality—was developed by early nomadic agricultural societies. It is difficult to apply these ancient moral codes to the highly technical, postindustrial society in which we now live. How, for example, shall we deal with the problems of medical ethics engendered by new technologies that can keep people alive far beyond the time when there is some significant quality of life? How shall we deal with organ transplants, given the widespread need and limited supply? How will society be able to support the growing number of nonworking elderly? These issues pose new moral dilemmas with which a classical biblical religion, for example, is unable to cope. These situations simply did not exist for previous generations; this is the age of space travel, the computer-information revolution, biogenetic engineering. Dramatic new scientific and technological breakthroughs provide enormous opportunities for human betterment, but they also raise moral dilemmas concerning possible dangers and abuses.

We cannot cope by retreating to the absolutes of the past; fresh thinking in the future is essential. Critical intelligence is the most reliable tool we have—it is not perfect, but nothing is when dealing with moral dilemmas.

This position is often attacked by those who do not understand the nature of moral deliberation. They condemn it as "situation ethics"—but the point of situational reasoning is that we often encounter new contexts in human experience unlike anything that has been faced in the past, and we need to bring to bear creative inquiry to deal with them. If there is any excellence that society should develop it is the need for pooled ethical wisdom and social intelligence. Instead of resorting to shrill denunciations, we should be willing to engage in cooperative rational dialogue and develop, where needed, new values and principles appropriate to the emerging world. This is also the primary quality of mind we should seek to impart to our children: to think not only about facts, but about moral principles and values as well.

There are many moral philosophers today who are engaged in creative ethical thinking, and they have come up with new moral guidelines. In the field of medical ethics, for instance, the principle of informed consent is a basic general moral principle that is applicable to health care; that is, patients have rights and their consent is required concerning the nature and extent of their treatment.

This brings me to another point, which is particularly relevant to those who cherish an open, pluralistic, and democratic society. It regards the importance of the principle of privacy in ethics. That is, a free society should grant adult individuals some autonomy and responsibility for their own lives, especially in regard to those areas that concern intimate beliefs and values. Society should not unduly interfere with the free exercise of these rights.

Responsibilities to the Planetary Society

The moral imperative today is to expand the horizons of our ethical concerns from our parochial interests to the planetary society. Each of us as an individual has obligations and responsibilities to ourselves, to our immediate family and friends, to our coworkers and colleagues, to the community in which we live, and to our nation as a whole—but I would also add that we have a responsibility to the broader community of humankind. The moral systems of the past have been rather chauvinistic, focused on preserving our own race, ethnic group, religion, or nation over others. We need to break out of that narrow focus, for it is abundantly clear that we are now living in an interdependent world, and that what happens in one part often reverberates in every other part.

We need to develop a new *planetary ethics* in which each of us fully recognizes our responsibility to every other member of the human species. The classical religions, in the best sense, have recognized the brotherhood of human beings. In the worst sense, they have disputed as to which faith should be ascendant. Our ethical concern today and in the future must be transnational in scope and philosophy, and the arts and sciences cannot be limited by narrow religious, political, or ideological barriers. We need to develop a new ethical awareness that transcends the divisiveness and intolerance of the arbitrary barriers of the past. Intercommunication, travel, the free exchange of ideas, and the intermingling of peoples will no doubt accelerate in the future. We want a democratic world in which individual human freedoms and rights are everywhere respected. The ethical imperatives implicit in this task should be apparent to all who are concerned with preserving and enhancing the human species on this planet, not only for our time but for future generations.

Ethnic Chauvinism

Unfortunately, there are two powerful, often contradictory forces that are at work in the world today for and against the planetary society. There is, for example, the continuing demand of national and ethnic minorities for the right to determine their own destinies. On the other hand, there are many positive tendencies emerging, contributing to the building of a planetary society.

The movement for ethnic self-determination may be viewed in some contexts as progressive, especially where it seeks to liberate minorities from oppression and provides some basis for democratic self-government. But it also can foment intense conflict. The turmoil in various parts of the world illustrates the powerful attraction of ethnic loyalties. Witness the breakup of the former Soviet Union and Yugoslavia into separate national republics; the split in Belgium between the Flemish- and French-speaking populations; and the division in Canada between the Quebecois and Anglo Canadians. One may feel that the movement for autonomy has some justice; but at the same time, it may engender extreme hatred and even bloodshed—as between Croatians, Bosnian Muslims, and Serbians, Afrikaners and black South Africans, Palestinians and Jews, Armenians and Azerbaijanis, and as in the brutal genocidal warfare between Hutus and Tutsis in Rwanda. In Europe there is an outcry, particularly in Germany, Austria, and France, against recent immigrants and demands that they be expelled.

The term *ethnicity* encompasses a wide range of meanings. It is derived from the Greek term *ethnikos,* or *ethnos,* meaning "nation" or "people." It refers to a collective group within a society or region perceived by its members as having a common ancestry and sharing an historic past or cultural tradition. This may be based on kinship and race, religion, or geographical location. It includes a consciousness of ethnic identity. Often it is based on religious differences.

Ethnicity has historically taken various destructive forms. Its most horrible expressions have occurred in wars of invasion and genocide—the battle to the death over racial, national, and religious differences. Rome's obliteration of Carthage graphically illustrates this. Historically, blacks were enslaved by their colonial masters, and Jews were persecuted by anti-Semites. Nazism was the most vulgar expression of racial hatred. Hitler glorified the Aryan race as "superior" to other racial stocks, in order to justify his extermination of those he considered to be "inferior." There seems to be a powerful impulse in human behavior to identify with one's own kind, a longing for "roots," and an all-too-easy abhorrence of aliens. No nation is immune to racial, religious, or ethnic fervor, and any nation can be overcome by ethnic animosities.

Planetary humanism is committed to the preservation and realization of *all* human beings. It allows for no discrimination because of ethnicity, national origin, religion, race, gender, religion, or creed. All human beings are equal in dignity and value. All possess the same rights, including the right to exist.

There are diverse national heritages in the family of humankind, each of which is entitled to some place in the sun. These represent a wide range of cultural expressions, in language and literature, music and the arts, culinary and social customs. No one group is entitled to dominate or deny cultural freedom to others.

Many people find their own ethnic networks gratifying. People cherish belonging to some close-knit community. But at the same time there is an urgent need to transcend parochial differences and recognize shared values and interests with all human beings. This is the distinctive humanist message in the contemporary world, for it seeks to take us beyond narrow, chauvinistic, and intolerant prejudices to a new ethical plateau.

Homo sapiens is descended from a common genotype. The division into separate ethnic, racial, religious, and national enclaves is

recent in the history of the species. It is a function of isolated breed-
ing populations and the influence of particular social, economic, political, cultural, and geographical conditions. Relatively few peoples
in the past have lived in isolation; there have always been incursions
from "outsiders." If the Eskimos of Alaska and the aborigines of
Australia lived relatively cut off for centuries, in other parts of the
world there were constant periods of intermingling and assimilation.
China was able to absorb its invading hordes, and Rome built an empire from Britain to Palestine.

The world today is in rapid transition. Human civilization for the
first time in history has become truly global. Thus, sharp distinctions
between Western and Eastern, Asian and African civilization are no
longer tenable. We all participate in a world civilization. We all are
heirs to a common scientific, philosophical, economic, and artistic
heritage. Travel and intercommunication are so widespread that we
are becoming, though some may protest, co-citizens of the newly
emerging planetary society—if not directly, then at least symboli-
cally. The information revolution allows us to communicate through
cyberspace beyond frontiers and boundaries. Whatever happens in
one corner of the globe is of significance everywhere.

The real heroes of this new global society are those who identify
with the world community. So-called pure racial, national, or ethnic
stocks are diminishing everywhere. New societies of people of
mixed blood are being created overnight, particularly in the "New
World." In North and South America especially, new ethnicities are
developing from the intermarriage of Hispanics and Anglos, blacks
and whites, Europeans and Asians. America for over 350 years has
been open to waves of immigration. On the frontier there was a constant blending of Scotch-Irish, German-Polish, Norwegian-Spanish,
Indian-Anglo, Italian-British, and so on.

People of mixed blood, in one sense, are the harbingers of a new
planetary ethnicity. Racists and nationalists hate intermarriage and

have condemned it bitterly as "mongrelization." They seek to forbid it—witness historically the strict religious prohibitions against the marriage of Gentile and Jew, Protestant and Catholic, and Muslim and Hindu. Laws against miscegenation in the past had been applied with a vengeance. But a strong case can be made that intermarriage contributes immeasurably to the diversity and richness of the human family, as does interracial and interethnic adoption.

In Europe, particularly since World War II, many Caucasians are opposed to the presence in their midst of significant Muslim, Hindu, Arab, and African minorities. There are vituperative demands for an end to immigration by Monsieur Le Pen in France, for example. Skinheads threaten innocent immigrants. Granted that an open-door immigration policy places strains on social services, especially in a recessionary climate; nonetheless, every effort must be made to build bridges beyond narrow, nationalistic hatreds. This is humanism in practice.

Human Rights

The beginnings of a new global ethic are now evident by the issuance and adoption of universal declarations of human rights, which enunciate the rights of *all* human beings. These affirm the following:[2]

1. All persons are born equal in dignity and value.

2. They are entitled to rights and freedoms without any distinction of sex, race, language, religion, politics, creed, national or social origin, property, or birth.

3. The right to personal security and self-protection.

4. The fundamental right to personal liberty. This includes: (a) freedom from involuntary servitude or slavery, (b) freedom from harassment, (c) freedom of thought and conscience, (d) freedom of speech and expression, and (e) moral freedom to express one's values and pursue one's lifestyle so long as it does not harm others or prevent others from exercising their rights.

5. The right to privacy, which means that the rights of others should be respected regarding: (a) confidentiality, (b) the control of one's own body, (c) sexual preference and orientation, (d) life stance, (e) reproductive freedom, (f) birth control, (g) health care based on informed consent, and (h) the desire to die with dignity.

6. The right to intellectual and cultural freedom, including (a) the freedom to inquire and to engage in research, (b) the right to adequate education, (c) the right to cultural enrichment, and (d) the right to publish and express one's views.

7. The right to adequate health care.

8. Freedom from want, which means that society should guarantee (a) the right to work, (b) the satisfaction of basic needs when individuals are unable to provide for themselves, (c) care for the elderly, (d) care for the handicapped, and (e) the right to adequate leisure and relaxation.

9. Economic freedom, including (a) the right to own property, (b) the right to organize, and (c) protection from fraud.

10. Moral equality, which entails equal opportunity and equal access.

11. Equal protection under the law, which is vital in a free society: (a) the right to a fair trial, (b) the right to protection from arbitrary arrest or unusual punishment, and (c) the right to humane treatment.

12. The right to democratic participation in government, which includes a full range of civil liberties: (a) the right to vote, (b) the legal right of opposition, (c) the right of assembly and association, and (d) the right to hold religious beliefs or not to hold such beliefs.

13. The rights of marriage and the family: (a) the right to marry or cohabitate, (b) the right to divorce, (c) family planning, (d) the right to bear and raise children, and (e) child care.

14. The right of children to be protected from abuse and physical or cultural deprivation.

Principles to Develop a World Community

Humanistic ethics seeks to foster the development of a genuine world community. If we are to achieve this, the following principles should apply:[3]

1. Moral codes that prevail today are often rooted in ancient parochial and tribal loyalties. Absolutistic moral systems emerged from the values of the rural and nomadic societies of the past; they provide little useful guidance for our post-modern world. We need to draw on the best moral wisdom of the past, but we also need to develop a new, revisionary ethic that employs rational methods of inquiry appropriate to the world of the future, an ethic that respects the dignity and freedom of each person but that also expresses a larger concern for humanity as a whole. *The basic imperative faced by humankind today is the need to develop a worldwide ethical awareness of our mutual interdependence and a willingness to modify time-hardened attitudes that prevent such a consensus.*

2. Science and technology continue to advance rapidly, providing new ways to reduce famine, poverty, and disease and to improve the standards of living for all members of the human family. The great imperative is to extend the benefits of the scientific revolution to every person on earth. We disagree with those fearful voices seeking to censor science and thus limit future discoveries that could have great benefits for humankind. Biogenetic and neurobiological engineering hold enormous promise; yet such research is extremely controversial. New reproductive technology calls for new legal and ethical thinking to protect the rights of the people involved and avoid commercial exploitation. Critics warn that we might be opening a Pandora's box. Proponents reply that although we must be alert to possible abuses, each new scientific advance in history has had its prophets of doom.

The frontiers of space exploration continue to beckon humankind. We have hurled satellites to the moon, to the planets, and even beyond our solar system. Scientists tell us that it is technologically feasible to build space colonies and to mine other planets. The possible adventures in space that await us are truly Promethean in dimension. Computers and other electronic media facilitate instantaneous communication to all corners of the planet. Yet in many countries the mass media or organs of propaganda often abdicate their responsibilities by feeding the public a diet of banalities.

We face a common challenge to develop scientific education on a global scale and an appreciation for critical intelligence and reason as a way to solve human problems and enhance human welfare.

3. The awesome danger of thermonuclear war is held in check only by the fear of "mutually assured destruction." Fortunately, the great powers have entered into an era of negotiation for the reduction of nuclear arms, which is welcomed by men and women of good will. Still, these negotiations are no substitute for a broader diplomacy that promotes more fundamental understanding and cooperation. We have not yet learned how to control warfare, for there does not exist any supranational sovereignty with sufficient power to keep the peace between nation-states. We submit that it is imperative that such a sovereignty be created. The United Nations has made valiant attempts to develop transnational political institutions—but so far with limited success. We recognize that in this quest for a world community, we will need to guard against the emergence of an all-powerful nondemocratic global state. We believe, however, that *it is necessary to create on a global scale new democratic and pluralistic institutions that protect the rights and freedoms of all people.* As a first step, humankind needs to establish a system of world law and to endow the World Court with enough moral force that its jurisdiction is recognized as binding by all the nation-states of the world.

4. The disparities in economic wealth between various portions of the globe widen. Economic development in the Third World is now virtually stagnant. Massive deficits, runaway inflation, and un-

controlled population growth place a heavy burden on fragile economies and threaten to bankrupt the world's monetary system. We believe, however, that the more affluent nations have a moral obligation to increase technological and economic assistance so that their less-developed neighbors may become more self-sufficient. We need to work out some equitable forms of taxation on a world-wide basis to help make this a reality.

5. Economic relations today are such that many corporations are multinational in scope, and some of these have been successful in promoting intercultural tolerance. All regions of the globe—socialist and nonsocialist alike—are dependent upon the continued flow of world trade to survive. Interest rates, deficits, capital investments, currency and stock market fluctuations, commodity prices, and import quotas in any one nation can influence trade on a global scale. The loss of industries in some countries and the consequent rise in unemployment are a direct function of the ability to be productive and to compete effectively for international markets.

The governments of the separate nations nevertheless continue to prepare their budgets in haughty isolation and primarily in terms of national self-interest. Full-scale cooperation among countries is still limited, and competitive rivalries rule the day. *A new global economic system based on economic cooperation and international solidarity needs to emerge.*

6. The vitality of democratic societies over authoritarian or totalitarian regimes has been vividly demonstrated. Democratic institutions make possible higher standards of living and provide more opportunities for creativity and freedom than their alternatives. Genuine political democracy still eludes much of the world; unfortunately, many countries are ruled by dictatorial or authoritarian elites that deny their citizens basic human rights. *We need to firmly defend the ideals of political democracy on a worldwide basis, and to encourage further extensions of democracy.*

7. Each of the regions of the world cherishes its own historical ethnic traditions and wishes to preserve its national identity. We should appreciate the richness and diversity of cultures, the values of pluralism and polyethnicity. Yet *we urgently need to enlarge our common ground. We should encourage the intermingling of peoples in every way we can.* Continuing scientific, artistic, and cultural exchanges are vital. The right to travel across national borders should be defended as a human right. Intermarriage can help unify the world more solidly than can conventional politics and those who intermarry should not be considered pariahs of society but rather harbingers of the new world of tomorrow.

8. We all inhabit the same globe; we have a vital stake in helping to preserve its ecology. The contamination of the atmosphere, damage to the ozone layer, deforestation, the pollution of the oceans, the increase in acid rain, the greenhouse effect, and the destruction of other species on this planet adversely affect us all. *We urge the establishment of international environmental monitoring agencies and recommend the development of appropriate standards for the disposal of industrial waste and for the control of toxic emissions.* The time has come to call the alarm before the global ecological system deteriorates further. *We have a clear duty to future generations to curtail excessive population growth, to maintain a healthy environment, and to preserve the earth's precious resources.*

The overriding need is to develop a new global ethic—one that seeks to preserve and enhance individual human freedom and emphasizes our commitment to the world community. Although we must recognize our obligations and responsibilities to the local communities, states, and nations of which we are citizens, we also need to develop a new sense of identity with the planetary society of the future. . . .

Implicit in this is the recognition that each of us has responsibilities to the world community, for each of us is (a) a member of the human species, (b) a resident of the planet earth, and (c) an integral part of the world community.

It would be appropriate for the citizens of each nation or region of the world to add the following affirmation to their pledges of loyalty:

"I pledge allegiance to the planetary society, of which we are all a part. I recognize that all persons are equal in dignity and value. I defend human rights and cherish human freedom. I vow to honor and protect the global ecology for ourselves and for generations yet unborn."

Notes

1. The materials in this paper are based on Paul Kurtz, *Forbidden Fruit: The Ethics of Humanism* (Amherst, N.Y.: Prometheus Books, 1988), and Paul Kurtz, Levi Fragell, and Rob Tielman, eds., *Building a World Community: Humanism in the Twenty-First Century* (Amherst, N.Y.: Prometheus Books, 1989).

2. These are drawn from "A Declaration of Interdependence: A New Global Ethics," in Paul Kurtz, Levi Fragell, and Rob Tielman, eds., *Building a World Community*. This declaration was adopted by both the Academy of Humanism and the International Humanist and Ethical Union.

3. These are also drawn from "A Declaration of Interdependence."

11

Ethics for Avoiding Global Catastrophe: Lessons from Medicine

Martin S. Zand

W e have come to Delphi to discuss two fundamental questions. Why has the ethical behavior of our species lagged so far behind its technological progress? And how can we work to assure our species' survival?[1] The juxtaposition of these two queries clearly implies a linkage. If only our species were to behave according to a more advanced ethical code, the odds of human survival would improve, the odds of extinction would diminish.

Let me be clear, it is not an external catastrophe that we are speaking of, a worldwide plague or the impact of a massive comet. No, we seek to avoid the most difficult of plagues, that of self-annihilation: wars of mass destruction, starvation from overpopulation, and large-scale environmental poisoning, to name a few. Toward this end, we ask: What conduct is good, right, and obligatory if we are to prevent the annihilation of our species? We seek an ethics for self-preservation.

I would like to discuss some of the ethical lessons learned by physicians grappling with similar questions. More than any other profession, medicine has had to confront the collision between new technology and old human behavior. Physicians treat the victims of warfare, bring to light industrial poisoning, and attempt to halt emerging pathogens. We see the results of self-inflicted injury: cigarette smoking, alcohol abuse, and suicide. We treat the consequences of deliberate human cruelty: rape, torture, and mutilation. Finally, we confront the repercussions of our own success: patients sustained with artificial life support beyond the point of recovery, the use of expensive technology while children go unvaccinated, and the extension of technology into the ethically controversial areas of euthanasia and fetal tissue harvesting.

For physicians practicing in this "midworld" between individuals, technology, and society, there is no daily decision without an ethical underpinning. When prescribing antibiotics we must consider that widespread use of these drugs creates resistant bacteria. Recommending elective surgery begs the issue of how to allocate health care resources. And the use of cancer chemotherapy forces us to balance suffering and hope.

Thus, physicians have learned much about the relationship of ethical and technological development. We have considered the ability of ethical behavior to prevent personal, group, and global catastrophe.[2] And finally, we have thought much about the frequent discrepancy between ethical knowledge and personal action. It is these specific areas that I will address.

Human Ethics and Technological Progress

Let me begin by considering the question: Why has the ethical behavior of our species lagged behind its technological progress? The answer from the experience of medicine is that new technology takes time to reveal its effects and its ethical dilemmas. There are few medical technologies which do not have the potential for unintended harm, and our inability to predict these effects a priori is striking. Thus, we have found that virtually all ethical dilemmas, and principles, arise a posteriori to technological advancement. I am, no doubt, stating the obvious. For example, before artificial ventilators existed, there was no need for an ethical framework to discuss disconnecting the ventilator of a brain-dead patient.[3]

I believe the situation in medicine mirrors that of our general experience with technology and ethics. I contend that ethical progress will *always* lag behind technological advancement. For example, the international ethics of biological warfare arose only after the development of biological weapons. But does this mean that we are doomed to horrific errors before we develop a new ethics for each technology? Are there any ethical principles which might guide our actions in the absence of situation-specific ethics?

The first answer from medicine is in the form of an ethical principle: "Above all, do no harm."[4] The admonition clearly prohibits the intentional and deceptive use of technology known to be harmful. But more significantly, it is an ethic of self-restraint. Simply because a new technology or treatment exists does not mean that we should use it! This is not technological nihilism, but rather a positive obligation to deliberately consider the side effects and ethical consequences of any technology, nascent or established.[5] Thus, physicians introduce new technologies cautiously and with suspicion. Throughout, we are cognizant of our limits: that our judgments may be flawed, our theories and facts inadequate. We ask whether each new technology will lead to more benefits than harm for our patients.

The second lesson is the absolute necessity of an ongoing ethical dialogue. Because ethical dilemmas arise a posteriori to new technology, our ethical knowledge must be constantly revised. Physicians have aspired to make such daily dialogue a venerated professional standard. I suggest each of us must do the same, making ethical dialogue an integral part of our lives, that we may be better prepared to deal with the consequences of new technology.

Can Ethical Behavior Avert
Self-Destructive Catastrophes?

Next I turn to the question: Can ethical behavior avert self-destructive catastrophes? Let me be quite clear that by catastrophe I mean the severest result: personal or species annihilation. For obvious reasons, this question is of central importance. If the answer is yes, we need to know under what conditions. If the answer is no, we must look elsewhere for solutions to assure our individual and our species' survival.

Over the past few centuries, medicine has been forced to acknowledge man's increasing capacity to inflict injury on his own species. Each technological advance is a Janus: nuclear energy and nuclear war, mass production and mass pollution. Human behavior, however, has remained largely unchanged. As a species, we are still driven by hope for infinite resources and seemingly unlimited greed for sectarian domination. Often our experience in medicine is that when individuals are threatened with death from an *external* source, they will use all available resources to fight for life. In contrast, when the threat of death is *internal*, from self-destructive behavior, this drive for life appears blunted. As Freud suggested, there seems to be a *thanatos* impulse present in man, directed toward the extinction of life.[6]

What is medicine's response to such self- or species-annihilating catastrophes? Primarily, we treat the victims. Secondly, we try to prevent catastrophe, especially the self-inflicted. This is an ethical obligation, but an effective response requires the knowledge, expertise, and technology of medicine. And here is the critical lesson: *ethical behavior is necessary to respond to a catastrophe, but it is not suf-ficient to avert or treat one.* Thus, ethics may impel us to prevent global starvation from overpopulation, but our efforts will be absolutely inadequate without a knowledge of reproductive biology, agriculture, demographics, and regional beliefs about reproduction.

The Problem of Knowledge and Right Action

Lastly, I address the ancient problem that knowledge often does not lead to right action. Physicians encounter this aspect of human behavior daily. We have long recognized the necessity of education in preventing catastrophe. Accordingly, physicians have assumed an ethical obligation to teach others about deterrence. We have the sense that if only our patients act on our advice, if only they recognize the self-destructive nature of their actions, catastrophe could be avoided. But often, knowledge does not lead to prevention.

The problem of knowledge and right action is, as others here have noted, a crucial issue for our species.[7] Socrates argued that a man who acted wrongly could not have true knowledge.[8] If this were correct, the problem of right action could be solved by education; simply giving people the right knowledge should lead right to action. As we know, the situation is much more complex. Physicians often see patients who are given explicit knowledge of the consequences of their actions, and yet persist on a path of self-annihilation. Despite advances in psychiatry and psychology, we are still far from a good understanding of this behavior, and even farther from effective treatments. Here is where medicine often fails.

Therefore, I suggest that we need to develop the field of ethical epistemology. We must study *how* we know what is right, and *why* we act, or abstain from acting, on this knowledge. Perhaps then we will be closer to a true knowledge of how to avert global catastrophes.

Conclusions

The evolution of technology in medicine has mirrored that of society in general. I hope that I have offered some useful insights from the experience of physicians. Some have suggested that ethical development and human behavior have lagged behind technological advances, and that this disparity may lead to global catastrophe as technology is used for interspecies warfare or as unrestrained industrial growth ravages the environment. In contrast, the experience of physicians suggests that when confronted with the collision of technological advancement and human behavior, our species is capable of recognizing ethical dilemmas and formulating new ethics to guide our actions. It gives us optimism that a committed community is capable of sustaining a vibrant dialogue about what actions are good, right, and obligatory when the goal is to prevent catastrophe. But knowledge does not always lead to right action. And toward this end, we must develop an epistemology of ethics, that we might better understand the gap between ethical knowledge and ethical behavior.

Acknowledgments

I would like to thank Dr. Dennis Razis for planting the seeds which led to this talk, and Ellen Ingram for her critical reading of the manuscript. This paper was partially supported by a grant from the Department of Medicine, Beth Israel Hospital, Boston.

Notes

1. D. V. Razis, "Modern Cassandras and Our Survival as a Species— A New Role for Medicine?" *Journal of the Royal Society of Medicine* 82 (1989): 575–76, and "A New Role for Medicine," *Journal of the Royal Society of Medicine* 87 (1994): 190–92.

2. T. L. Beauchamp and J. F. Childress, *Principles of Biomedical Ethics*, 4th ed. (New York: Oxford University Press, 1994).

3. President's Commission for Ethical Problems in Medicine, *Defining Death* (Washington, D.C.: United States Government Printing Office, 1981).

4. L. Edelstein, "The Hippocratic Oath: Text, Translation, and Interpretation," in *Ancient Medicine*, O. Temkin and C. Lillian Temkin, eds. (Baltimore: Johns Hopkins University Press, 1967), pp. 3–63, and A. R. Jonsen, "Do No Harm: Axiom of Medical Ethics," in *Philosophical and Medical Ethics: Its Nature and Significance*, S. F. Spicker and H. T. Engelhardt, eds. (Dordrecht, The Netherlands: D. Reidel, 1977), pp. 27–41.

5. E. Kübler-Ross, *On Death and Dying* (New York: MacMillan Publishing, 1969).

6. S. Freud, "The Libido Theory and Narcissism," in *Introductory Lectures on Psychoanalysis*, J. Strachey, ed. (London: W. W. Norton, 1920), pp. 414–15.

7. Aristotle, "Ethica Nicomachea," in *The Basic Works of Aristotle*, R. McKeon, ed. (New York: Random House, 1941), book 10, ch. 9, pp. 1108–1109.

8. Plato, "Meno," in *Plato: The Collected Dialogues*, E. Hamilton and H. Cairns, eds. (Princeton, N.J.: Princeton University Press, 1980), pp. 353–84.

12

On Human Nature

Eftichios Bitsakis

Human history is the history of class struggles. Contrary to the speculative anthropology, this aphorism emphasizes the barbarous and tragic aspect of human endeavor. How to explain this fact? Is there an immutable human nature? Are egoism, aggressiveness, and barbarous and paranoiac practices the result of some biological elements inscribed in our brain? However, class exploitation, wars, and class struggles are not the only features of history. Inseparable from them are intelligence, creativity, art, science, sensibility, emotion, affectivity, love, altruism. Human nature appears as a field of contradictory attributes and potentialities. Consequently, is it permissible to conceive of human nature as something without internal contradictions? As an invariable factor of history?

Marx emphasized that the starting point of his analytical method was not the man, taken *in abstracto,* but the economically given social period.[1] For the author of *Capital* the anatomy of the man is the key for the anatomy of the monkey. Concerning our question: it is impossible to explain human relations uniquely on the basis of the biological characteristics of the human species. According to Marx (and to Aristotle), man is in the strict sense a *zoon politikon.* Not only a social animal, but an animal which can become an individual only in society. Let us try then to bring to light the dialectic between the biological and the social: How in our biological nature existed the hidden potentialities of the social, and how social life modified human nature. How the alienating social relations of capitalism actualized the most negative potentialities of human beings and at the same time actuated the most positive elements of human essence.

Science proved the philosophical premise of ancient and modern materialism, namely, that man is a natural being. This is not a trivial truth. And as a scientific datum it is today accepted at least by scientists against a dominant idealistic conception, the origin of which is to be found in the Pythagorean, Platonic, and Cartesian dualism. In fact, we know today that the emergence of the human species was the culminating point of the long biological process of phylogenesis, that anthropogenesis and noogenesis presupposed the potentialities of the primates and at the same time marked the emergence of new realities and new qualities of social character, not reducible to the biological level. Physiology, biochemistry, neurology, molecular biology, and genetics from one side, the whole history of the evolution of life from the other, demonstrated the unity of the human with the inferior animal species. There is not a dichotomy between man and the rest of the animal kingdom. However, human nature is not reducible to its biological characteristics. Accordingly, it is impossible to explain social relations on the basis of biology and of an individualistically oriented psychology!

Man is the unique terrestrial animal capable of conceptual thinking. He can think about things in the absence of things. By this way, concepts become independent of their material and social counterpart. They become relatively autonomous. This liberty is a necessary condition for science, as well as for art, ideology, and the creation of the imaginary creatures—gods, demons, and the like, with whom man furnished the universe of his imagination—in a few words, for the creation of the universe of ideology, the active factor of history.

The material substratum is a necessary condition for psychical and intellectual life. Neurology is necessary but not sufficient to understand the internal self and conceptual thinking. Modern reductionism is not only epistemologically inadequate, it has direct political and philosophical implications. Concerning our problem, it is a vulgar antihumanism: reducing the whole of the intellectual and psychical life to material structures genetically determined, it constitutes an epistemological obstacle to the scientific understanding of human nature and behavior. For mechanistic reductionism, our barbarous past and present are the result of a genetically determined and, consequently, immutable nature.[2]

However, monstrosities and paranoia are not, as already emphasized, the unique characteristics of our species. Affectivity, love, altruism, creativity are also elements of the human behavior. Higher animals have also a psychical life. In their case, psychical life is genetically determined. In the case of man, on the contrary, it is an original reality not reducible to its material substratum. In order to understand this specifically human reality, we must bring to light the intrinsic unity of the biological and the psychical without superposing them in a mechanical way—without neglecting the originality of the psyche.

Man is a genetically social being. We know today that the attachment of the child to his mother and to the persons of his milieu corresponds to an innate need. Wallon, on the base of his observations, maintained that the child is a genetically and biologically social being.[3] Also, today we know that our sense organs, our nervous system, and our brain were developed during the long period of phylogenesis and especially of anthropogenesis in interaction with the natural and social environment, as a result of the activity of our species. Sense organs and the brain mediate the relations of humans with their environment. Organs of sensations and of conceptual thinking, they secure the survival of individuals and of our species. "The human brain, and specifically the neocortex," Professor Koukkou writes,

> is the organ which generates and coordinates all dimensions and aspects of human experience. . . . Human brain is a knowledge producing system and this knowledge is created by the cooperatively, synthetically and holistically functioning neurons of the neocortex. These are the functions with which humans produce in their brains retrievable symbolic representations of the outcome of the interactions with their physical and social environment.

Behavior is initially always purposeful and well adaptive. Consequently, humans are born with well-functioning operations. And Professor Koukkou concludes, "Our destructive behavior is not due to some inherited evil in us or to some evil around us which we have to fight." Consequently, "our destructive behavior is not our fate and is neither inevitable nor unalterable."[4]

Our brain and other corporeal organs serve the survival of human species. Consequently, the biological is a positive and normal factor of social life. Paranoia, individual or collective (aggression, wars, and other monstrosities) is a social phenomenon, possible but not inevitable. As such it is not inscribed in our genetic program. Wars and the like are "deviations" from the normal function of our intellect, and yet they serve concrete interests, justified by politics and ideology.

Here I must quote from the "Seville Statement on Violence," drafted by an international committee of twenty internationally known scholars at the Sixth International Colloquium on Brain and Aggression held at the University of Seville, Spain, in May 1986:

War is biologically possible but not inevitable, as evidenced by its variation in occurrence and nature over time and space. There are cultures which have not engaged in wars for centuries, and there are cultures which have engaged in war frequently at some time and not at others.

It is *scientifically incorrect* to say that war or any other violent behavior is genetically programmed into our human nature. While genes are involved at all levels of nervous system function, they provide a developmental potential that can be actualized only in conjunction with the ecological and social environment. While individuals vary in their predispositions to be affected by their experience, it is the interaction between their genetic endowment and conditions of nurturance that determines their personalities. Except for rare pathologies, the genes do not produce individuals necessarily predisposed to violence. Neither do they determine the opposite. While genes are co-involved in establishing our behavioral capacities, they do not by themselves specify the outcome. . . .

It is *scientifically incorrect* to say that humans have a "violent brain." While we do have the neural apparatus to act violently, it is not automatically activated by internal or external stimuli. Like higher primates and unlike other animals, our higher neural processes filter such stimuli before they can be acted upon. How we act is shaped by how we have been conditioned and socialized. There is nothing in our neurophysiology that compels us to react violently.

It is *scientifically incorrect* to say that war is caused by "instinct" or any single motivation. . . .

We conclude that biology does not condemn humanity to war, and that humanity can be freed from the bondage of biological pessimism and empowered with confidence to undertake the transformative tasks needed in this International Year of Peace and in the years to come.[5]

Consequently, aggression, wars, and egoism are not the manifestation of biological-hereditary factors. The biological pessimism of reductionism does not have a scientific foundation. However, history, with its violence, wars, exploitation, slavery, and the like, and the present, with its "meta-modern" brutality, do not permit any naive social optimism. But now, in order to explain the monstrosities of the past as well as of the present, we must pass from the individual to the social level.

It is difficult and dangerous to try to pass from the individual to the social level. Two diametrically opposite errors are possible in that case: (1) to explain social relations on the basis of the attributes of individuals, and (2) to forget the reality of the concrete man; to consider social relations as independent of the acting subjects; to accept that subjects are overdetermined by social relations and that history is "history without subject." (In fact, contemporary "theoretical antihumanism" considers individuals as simple "supports of the social relations.")

Let us now try to understand the barbarous aspects of history and to give an answer to our initial question with the help of the dialectic between the individual and the social.

It is well known that collaboration, mutual assistance, and the whole of the culture of tribal societies were the mediated consequences of the conditions prevailing in this phase of human history (common possession of the soil, tribal organization, and the like). Marx analyzed the unity between the individual and his tribe in the case of Indian societies, in opposition to the antagonistic relations and the individualism prevailing in capitalist societies. Some of the positive potentialities of the human being were actualized in these societies. However, superstitions, cruelty, and a totality of barbarous practices, the cause of which is to be found in the ignorance of the laws of nature and the corresponding mythical worldviews and not in some genetic faults in the brain of primitive man, coexisted with solidarity, pride, and affectivity. Solidarity and altruism coexisted with a latent individualism. With the development of productive forces, private property became possible. The latent individualism now took actual and monstrous forms. Wealth, egoism, vanity, and cruelty became the dominant characteristics of the rising aristocracy. Out of the ruins of the tribal society emerged, as Engels notes, the new, slave-owner society, with its internal class contradictions, its barbarous practices, the violence of the state, and the wars.

Private property was not, in the beginning, the product of alienated labor. In the new, class societies, alienation was, according to Marx, the result of a triptych: private property, division of labor, and commodity-money. Alienation has two, interrelated aspects: (1) alienation from the means of production and from the products of labor, which become commodities and stand in the face of the worker as alien and incomprehensible realities, and (2) alienation as an ensemble of positive elements of human nature and of human essence existing in the previous, tribal societies, that has disappeared or degenerated. Exploitation, slavery, wars, an ensemble of monstrosities, were the products of the new social relations.

One would be inclined to think that with the development of the productive forces and the new social wealth, the unity of the tribal society would be maintained and strengthened in the new, better material conditions. However individualism was already a potentiality of human nature. The final result was the disintegration of the primitive communities. The unity of the ideological superstructure of the tribal societies reflected the internal unity of this form of human symbiosis. The contradictions of the class societies were now reflected in the new legal, political, and ideological superstructure. Ideology, as the mystified conception of reality, justified and sanctified the new social reality: class exploitation, wars, and state violence. Men were now the victims of their own ideas. The mystified conception of the social reality became the source of new, barbarous practices.

In our modern societies commodity production is generalized. Everything becomes now a commodity: the soil, the labor force, knowledge, art, the human imagination. The worker becomes a tool for the production of surplus value. The new division of labor is, according to Marx, the assassination of the people. Every progress in science and technology becomes a calamity for the working class. The objectification of human potentialities during the productive process became a process of alienation. Antagonism became the dominant characteristic between nations, classes, and individuals at the practical and the institutional level. (See, for example, the treaty of Maastricht.) *Homo hominis lupus.* What was already a reality in the dawn of capitalism became the dominant social relation in our "post-modern" era.[6]

On the basis of the preceding analysis, one can maintain that the prevailing and monstrous antagonisms of our societies are not the consequence of a metaphysically conceived human nature but the necessary consequences of the internal contradictions of the capitalist mode of production. These contradictions are imposed as external blind forces to the active individuals. In this ruthless milieu, the most negative potentialities of the historically modulated human nature are now actualized. In fact, the antagonistic social relations reinforce egoism, aggression, individualism, and so on. On the other hand, wealth, exhibition, vanity, became the dominant values of our societies. Solidarity and peace, the fundamental values of Christianity and of Marxism, are now considered historically outdated, utopian values. War became an effective means for the appropriation of natural resources and markets (examples: the Gulf War and the war in Yugoslavia).

However, as already emphasized, aggression and violence are not characteristics inherent in our hereditary substance. Latent individualism was not a negative or a paranoiac feature of the primitive man. It was a normal element of the relations of unity and differentiation between the group and the individual. Every system, physical, chemical, biological, and so on, strives to conserve its identity. This is normal. The monstrous individualism of the capitalist societies is a social, not a biological phenomenon—it is an actualization of one of the potentialities of human nature. And the massive crimes of Nazis, of the U.S. army in Vietnam, of the Russians in Chechnya, and the like, are not the result of a certain paranoia. They are the "rational" outcome of the antagonisms in which people and leaders are entangled, and at the same time of the ideological, mystified conception of the world, the distortion of the consciousness by the mass media and the forces generated by the totality of these contradictions.

Human nature and human essence were profoundly affected by modern social relations. The already existing danger of extermination of the human species is not the consequence of a genetic fault of our chromosomes. It is not explained by the personal qualities of our political leaders. It is the consequence of the fact that people, classes, and states are entangled in an ensemble of contradictions and are driven by forces objectively independent of their volition. The anarchy of capitalist production on the other hand, entails the exhaustion of the natural resources and the destruction of the environment. The need for raw materials, energy, and markets, provokes local wars. A global destructive war is not today excluded. At this moment the question: Will humanity be able to control the course of history and to survive? is objectively posed.

On the basis of the preceding facts we can now try to define the concepts of human nature and of human essence. These concepts are identified by many authors. In fact, they are intrinsically related, but not identical. Then, how to define human nature?

Ancient idealism of the Socratic-Platonic tradition elaborated an ahistorical-metaphysical conception of human nature. For Christian theology man is a sinful being, entangled in the contradiction between necessity and free choice. The Enlightenment, on the contrary, tried, in its more rational moments, to conceive man as a natural and social being. However, the anthropology of the Enlightenment was, in most cases, tributary to Christian metaphysics. More than that: the man of the rising capitalist society has been considered as the final product of history; man was identified with the bourgeois man. Correspondingly, as Marx remarks, a definite form of social relations was considered as the immutable laws of history, conceived *in abstracto*. Kant, for example, despite his dialectical intuitions, conceived man *sub speciae oeternitatis* and tried to found an ethics on a priori, ahistorical principles. Hegel, on the other hand, considered liberty as the essence of man, essence to be realized in the process of the Absolute Spirit to self-consciousness. He was contemplating, by this way, an end of history.

Reason was considered by the Enlightenment as one of the fundamental attributes of human nature. However, logos, liberty, law, justice, all these ahistorical concepts and attributes of human nature characteristic of bourgeois humanism were the ideological product of a "mauvaise abstraction." They were the ideological justification of bourgeois society. The Romantic reaction against the omnipotence of Reason and the flaws of the rising industrial society, in spite of its progressive-utopian moments, was unable to discern a way out of the narrow horizon of capitalism.

Contrary to the Enlightenment and the Marxist tradition, some contemporary currents, as is well known, rejected the concepts of human nature, of human essence and humanism, as deprived of theoretical content. For structuralism, for example, history is a process without subject. Subject is a simple vehicle of social relations. Althusser, also, in his structuralized Marxism, rejected the concepts of human nature and of humanism, and professed a militant antihumanism. For the different currents of positivism, finally, statements about values are pseudostatements void of theoretical content.

After all, I will try to define human nature as the totality of the relatively invariant and mutually determined elements, attributes, relations, and potentialities of the human being in a given moment of history. Such a definition accepts the existence of relatively invariant, as well as of changing elements of human nature. It tries to grasp not only the biological but also, and above all, the social and political determinations of the human being. In the frame of this conception human nature becomes an historical category. Therefore man is considered not as an immutable being but as a field of contradictory potentialities which can be actualized in favorable external conditions.

What is invariable and what is mutable in human nature? Let us examine first the biological aspect of the question. It is well known that we possess a number of invariant biological elements: a number of chromosomes and stability of the hereditary substance, an historically constituted but now essentially invariable physiology, stable chains of biochemical processes, an invariant nervous system, a brain with stable structures and functions, and so on. On the other hand, it would be possible to define the so-called instincts (hunger, love, self-preservation, and the like) as the manifestation of psychosomatic mechanisms having a biochemical support, mechanisms activated under given circumstances. However, even the invariability of diachronic elements of human biological nature is not absolute. The genetic code, for example, is affected by the physical environment. Our brain evolved in mutual determination with labor and social life. The evolution of cortex is not simply a product of biology. It is a presupposition and a result of the collective social life and of work in particular. Even the instincts entail differentiated cognitive adaptations to exterior data.[7] Ontogenesis does not reproduce really phylogenesis, as Zazzo maintains. According to Wallon, there is not destiny. The biological and the social are necessary conditions, but only conditions.[8]

The psychosomatic unity of man is a scientific datum today, of a crucial ontological impact. Our feelings have a somatic-physiological and biochemical substratum. A sudden and great joy, for example, can kill you, because of the excessive production of adrenaline. Love, also, has a biochemical-hormonic support. Fear releases biochemical processes and strain provokes somatic maladies. The brain, our "thinking body," is the material support of our intellect. (Thought, "spirit," are not exterior to brain; they are not a substance dwelling in our brain; they are the "product" of the function of the brain in given social conditions.) Our idiosyncrasy is determined by biological peculiarities and at the same time it can be modified by the education and the social activity of the individual. Our dispositions, potentialities, and propensities depend on corporeal but also on social determinants.

Psychosomatic unity means the existence of biological as well as social determinations of the individual. Biological reductionism, on the contrary, as I have emphasized it, tries to explain everything in biological terms. Behaviorism, in particular, is a very known specimen of mechanistic ideology. To understand and to define human nature and human history, it is necessary to grasp both, the corporeal-biological and the social dimension of the human being.

However, man is, above all, a social being. At the same time he constitutes a relatively autonomous totality in the frame of a given society. The so-called instincts (autopreservation, love, and so on) are not an anthropological obstacle to the socialization of man. On the contrary, they played a positive role in the frame of tribal society. Latent individualism, on the other hand, was not the manifestation of a paranoiac element inscribed in the genetic code of the primitive man. Moreover, it was a source of creativity, of dignity, pride, and courage. The ungenerous individualism of our "civilized" societies is the consequence of the antagonistic social relations and of the unique value of capitalism: private property. In our society, as Hobbes conceived it in the aube of capitalism, *bellum omnium contra omnis* is the dominant relation. Consequently, "paranoia" is a social phenomenon.

The biological is the material substratum of the intellect and more generally the personality, with its idiosyncratic singularities. During historical development, experience, knowledge, capacities, art, culture, and so on were accumulated and constituted the common heritage of humanity. Progress was now essentially social, not biological. However, progress was a contradictory process, because it was based on class exploitation, wars, and the like. During this process, the biological itself was, to a certain degree, socialized. As Jacob puts it, the behavior of the individual is modified because of the increase of social experience. With the possibilities of response to the stimulus, the degree of liberty of the organism increases. The number of possible responses increases to such a degree that it is possible to speak of free will.[9] Consequently, free will is not a metaphysical gift from a transcendental being. It is not inscribed in the most profound structures of matter—in quantum particles—as modern mysticism professes. Free will and liberty are the signs of a relative liberation from the objective necessity gained by labor and knowledge.

Two one-sided conceptions of man, as already noted, were formulated by philosophers: (1) Social relations are independent of individuals, considered as simple supports of them. A fatalistic conception of history is the implication of this conception. (2) Human nature is considered *in abstracto,* independently of the social relations. Idealism is the main propagator of this point of view. However, individuals are determined directly, or via complicated mediations, by the existing social reality. Yet they are not the passive support but the active and conscious nucleus of the historical becoming. It is impossible to explain social relations by taking as a starting point the single individual. Social relations transcend the aspirations, the illusions, and the praxis of individuals. They act as objective forces and determine the ideas, the praxis, the essence, and the nature of individuals. At the same time, it is impossible to understand history if we do not take into consideration the historically constituted individual. To take an analogy from physics, the laws of thermodynamics are not reducible to the properties of the atoms or of the molecules of a statistical ensemble. However, atoms and molecules are the material supports of the laws of thermodynamics. These laws transcend atomic or molecular properties and at the same time they depend on these properties via existing mediations between the microscopic and the statistical level. The same is valid for chemical reactions and more generally for the collective properties of statistical ensembles. In a similar way, social laws are not reducible to the biological or other properties of the single individual. But in the social case the mediations, the objective contradictions, the role of ideology, and so on, make the understanding of the relevant phenomena much more difficult.

Consequently, the source of the internal relations of the individual are to be found, via complicated mediations, outside of him: in society. Society constitutes the external base of the personality, *"sa propre essence excentrée,"* its objectified potential, on the basis of which and by the internalization of which man becomes "man." The social rapports determine the historical forms of individuality. They are the necessary forms for the activity of the individuals to be realized. The study of personality begins with the study of the ensemble of social relations.[10] The category of biography is also an historical category. This aphorism holds for the biological aspect of man as well.

To sum up: Human nature is constituted of a number of biological and psychological, relatively invariant elements, and at the same time of a number of more variable characters which reflect mediated, social relations. Human nature is an historical category. In a given society, as already emphasized, human nature is a field of contradictory potentialities. Which of them will be actualized depends on social reality. The historicity of human nature corresponds to the historical forms of society, without being a passive and linear reflection of them. Consequently there is not, in principle, an anthropological obstacle for a society free from class exploitation, violence, and war.

And now concerning human essence. The debate concerning the category of the essence has, as is well known, the same age as philosophy. For metaphysical essentialism the essence of a thing exists objectively, as a reality in itself, unaffected in space and time. Nominalism considered essence as a conceptual instrument, deprived of any objective existence. For Aristotle, contrary to Plato, essence exists in the singulars, as a form specific in matter. Hegel tried to formulate the dialectic between essence and appearance. Marx rejected the metaphysical conception of essence but conserved this category giving it a new sense.[11]

It would be possible to define essence as "the ensemble of the necessary and invariant properties of a reality." Another definition would be the following: "Essence is the ensemble of the rapports constituting a given reality, taken in their becoming."[12] The preceding definitions are more suitable for material realities. Karl Marx, breaking with the speculative-ahistorical anthropology, gave a new sense in the category of human essence: "Human essence is not an abstraction inherent in the single individual. In its reality it is the ensemble of the social relations."[13] Against the dominant essentialism (essence: immutable, ahistorical category) Marx grasped the historicity and the foundation of human essence. In this way he dissociated his anthropology from the dominant metaphysical tradition, which makes human essence, conceived *in abstracto,* the foundation of politics, history, and ideology.

Individuals, for Marx, are products of history. It is impossible, Sève writes, to found the science of individuals on a base different from the science of history. Correspondingly, it is impossible to found the science of history without founding at the same time the theory of the historical production of the individuals. In this way Marx shifts the field of his analysis from human essence to social relations.[14] This inversion of the standpoint of abstract humanism permits the passage to a concrete conception of the individual, henceforth realized in his real essence: social relations.

I emphasized the existence of relatively invariant elements of human nature. And if, without being unaware of their intrinsic correlation, we do not identify human nature with human essence, then it would be possible to define essence as the totality of the psychical and spiritual content of the life of the individual, as well as of the dominant characteristics of man, as they are actualized in the course of history. Essence becomes then an historical category related, above all, to the spiritual, moral, and cultural contents of the human being. It is then evident that essence varies in relation to the external, social conditions and the totality of the biography of the individual. And it is also evident that because of alienation, in the double sense described above, the essence of man in contemporary capitalist societies evaporates in direct relation with the destruction of social relations, of the cultural tradition and the normal relations with nature. However this historical process is not, necessarily, irreversible.

Until now I have tried to analyze some of the crucial moments of the historical process of hominization and the contradictory character of this process. On the basis of the preceding analysis one could arrive at a naive, optimistic conception of history. This optimism is not absent in the Marxist philosophical tradition. Even Marx overestimated the positive potentialities of human nature, and vulgar Marxism in our century conceived history as a glorious process to end up in a perfect communist society. Yet history is here, with its barbarity, horrors, and tragedies. However, we are not living the end of history. The planetary antagonisms of our century will result in the destruction of our species or in a society based on a freely adopted collective form of organization.

The future does not depend on our chromosomes. It depends on the possibility of the human species to create an ensemble of new social relations conforming with its most positive potentialities. This possibility is not a priori excluded. Socialism is objectively necessary for the survival of the human species. In reality, it is one of the possibilities of our society.

Notes

1. K. Marx, "Marginal Notes on the Treatise of Political Economy of Adolphe Wagner." Compare K. Marx, *Le Capital* (Paris: Editions Sociales, 1973), 1, 3, p. 249.

2. On the above questions see J. Piaget, *Psychologie et Epistemologie* (Paris: Gonthier, 1970), and *Biologie et Connaissance* (Paris: Gallimard, 1967); A. Leontiev, *Le Développement du Psychisme* (Paris: Editions Sociales, 1976); L. S. Vygotski, *Pensée et Langage* (Paris: Editions Sociales, 1985); H. Wallon, *La Vie Mentale* (Paris: Editions Sociales, 1982); R. Zazzo, *Psychologie et Marxisme* (Paris: Denöel-Gonthier, 1975); and Tran Dui Thao, *Investigations into the Origin of Language and Consciousness* (Dordrecht, The Netherlands: Reidel Publishing Co., 1984), and *Phenomenology and Dialectical Materialism* (Dordrecht, The Netherlands: Reidel Publishing Co., 1986).

3. R. Zazzo, *Psychologie et Marxisme*, p. 29.

4. M. Koukkou-Lehmann, "Models of Human Brain Functions and Paranoid Elements in Human History," *Delphi Conference Report*, June 1995.

5. *American Psychologist*, October 1990, p. 1167.

6. K. Marx, *Le Capital*, passim.

7. J. Piaget, *Biologie et Connaissance*, pp. 377–78.

8. R. Zazzo, *Psychologie et Marxisme*, p. 49.

9. F. Jacob, *La Logique du Vivant* (Paris: Gallimard, 1970), p. 338.

10. L. Sève, in *Je, Sur l'Individualité* (Paris: Editions Sociales, 1987), pp. 224–26, and *Marxisme et Théorie de la Personnalité* (Paris: Editions Sociales, 1974), passim.

11. G. Labica, ed., *Dictionnaire Critique du Marxisme* (Paris: P.U.F., 1982).

12. Ibid.

13. K. Marx, "Sixth Thesis on Feuerbach."

14. L. Sève, *Marxisme et Théorie de la Personnalité,* passim.

13

On the Knowledge of Nonexistence

Evi Razis

We are gathered here in an intellectual endeavor attempting to interpret human behavior and then, if possible, to establish ways to adjust this behavior so that our species will not self-destruct. Although each one of us will attempt to identify unifying principles amongst men as members of a species, we may fail to consider the individual in every man—the lonely, agonizing, Sysiphian forces within each one of us. And though our knowledge of animals is mostly at a species level, our experience with the human species is clearly individualistic in nature, so I would like to consider what forces move each human as an individual. Then, using relatively basic sociological concepts, the behavior of the species as a whole could possibly be deduced.

Whatever the neurophysiological mechanisms that allow it, whatever the evolutionary steps that preceded it, one thing seems to differentiate the human species from others—the ability to experi-

167

ence agony over death. We certainly do not know for a fact that animals are incapable of such "angst," but there is at least indirect evidence that though animals make sure they survive, they don't attempt to come to terms with the temporariness of their existence, at least when they are not threatened.

Be that as it may, I would like for the purposes of my talk to assume that our species is the only one so far that agonizes over death. I propose that both progress and destruction caused by men is explainable as behavior propelled by an attempt to gain power over one's own existence.

From the beginning of time there were attempts to find peace by turning to a great power—God. Later on came philosophy and art—other approaches to the same great issue. Understanding the meaning of existence seemed like a way to at least come to terms with it intellectually. After all, our own *nonexistence* is a purely theoretical concept to all of us. The evolution of science was an even more promising step toward such intellectual concurrence. The systematic study of things that "are" was filled with the hope that, if everything were objectively proven and understood, then more power and control could be gained over it—life could be in our hands, it could be prolonged, death could be averted. So far all these approaches have failed to ease the angst in most men.

Meanwhile, powerlessness over one's own existence can be compensated in our ephemeral life by power over other humans, control of our micro-environment, obsessive preoccupation with fanatical groups, the creation of timeless works of art, or just simple anxiety about the next day. An example of such a coping reaction are the Egyptian pyramids, where magnificent graves were built and equipped with all the necessities of what was perceived as continuation of life. Another interesting example is that the perfectly functioning replica of man, one that man created—the robot—has no existential angst.

It is certain that our existence here, as we perceive it now, is only momentary, but "coping" mechanisms, like the ones I have just mentioned, make this realization a bit more tolerable. When the sneaky questions of existence poison our thought, most turn their face away—some turn to God or art or philosophy.

The knowledge of nonexistence as we come to experience it, our ability to conceive, even subconsciously, of *nothingness* as something real, leads to absurd, pointless behavior, and the products of such behavior can be (and have been) admirable or abominable.

In summary, I would propose that the agonizing knowledge of nonexistence at the individual level can explain admirable or abominable aspects of human behavior at the level of species.

14

Chao-Periodic Patterns in the Achievement of Understanding

William J. M. Hrushesky

Complex interactive systems (human nature and behavior) self-organize according to nonlinear rules. These dynamical rules must be defined if human nature and behavior are to be understood, predicted (probablistically), or modified (probablistically). Science has not been rigorously applied to these important problems. Furthermore, serious imbalances in modern science must be addressed before adequate methodologies can be developed to enhance our genuine understanding and to provide us with a scientific basis for "modern humanism."

Societal Roots of Antiscience

At an apparent zenith, science is perceived to be failing to adequately address the major problems of humanity such as individual and societal aggression, uncontrolled population expansion, and resultant increased utilization of poorly renewable natural resources. Is this perception accurate? If it is, why is this so?; and if it is not, why is this the societal impression?

This distrust of science, technology, and scientists has venerable literary and historical roots. Mary Shelley's *Frankenstein* brought many common fears into focus. Her book, appearing during "the golden age of English medicine," reflected profound distrust of scientists that grew directly from the public perception of great advances which were poorly understood. George Orwell's *Animal Farm* and *1984* change the focus of distrust from fear and suspicion of the individual scientific accomplishment to fear of apparently inevitable and chilling societal oppression born directly out of technological capabilities applied for the accumulation of power at the expense of beauty, liberty, and humanism.

We must admit as citizens, or as scientists, that many important problems have not been solved politically or scientifically. We must further admit that certain of these real human problems appear to be worsening. These admissions bolster the unrest and dissatisfaction that is an essential component of human nature. Since it has been assumed by society (and put forward aggressively by many scientists) that one of the byproducts if not purposes of science is to solve human problems, people seem to make a "reverse causality" assumption. They assume that, since science is at a zenith and since their problems are not solved and are apparently worsening, that, therefore, science has failed. This illogical connection is embellished further in the common conclusion that if science is advancing rapidly, coincident with the worsening of many serious human problems, that this indicates that the advance of science is, in fact, responsible for the worsening of these problems. These loose trains of coincident reasoning are faulty but may, nonetheless, represent some of why antiscience is so prevalent today.

Scientific Disinterest

In fact, scientists have not been attracted to these messy problems of humanity. Science has, therefore, not been rigorously applied to them. Scientific understanding of human problems is poorer than is generally believed. Any scientist with even a small amount of talent, objectivity, and self-confidence finds the unknown lying surprisingly close to a thin veneer of apparent understanding. Scientific methodology is, in principle, clearly up to the task of addressing these, as all other problems. So that while it is true that our understanding of humanity and its major problems is rudimentary, it is also true that our ability to gain understanding about them is genuine. Put another way, there is nothing in the nature of the problems of humanity to indicate that they cannot be approached and improved or even eventually solved using scientific methodology.

Scientific Competence and Priority

Current science may not be competent to tackle these sorts of problems. Perhaps the wrong science has been developed. This is, to me, a very real possibility. We have spent the better part of a century understanding the physical universe better for the express purpose of developing the most efficient weapons of mass destruction. This perspective is not totally consistent with the goals of addressing problems of human ethics and behavior. Clearly the priorities of science have been and remain at odds with the priorities of individuals and societies. It may not be fair for society to judge the success or failure of science designed to kill massively or to make investors rich in terms of humanism.

Scientific Balance

There is another more subtle reason. Science has apparently failed, I believe, because it has become unbalanced and thereby has isolated and alienated itself from humanity and its problems. Before going further with this idea, however, a brief glossary is essential:

Science is an organized means of more accurately describing and thereby cumulatively understanding the universe. A scientific discovery is a more accurate observation.

Fact/datum/information is the unit of what is observed. These units are generally obtained reductively; that is, by either mentally or physically taking things apart.

Idea is the conceptual context into which the data are received and processed. Ideas are developed inductively by observing and generalizing the apparent rules by which things work.

Knowledge is accurate information placed within a genuinely useful context.

Understanding is mature and balanced interactive information/idea, capable of accurately explaining past events and accurately predicting future events (or their probability, given the reality of the nature of complex nonlinear systems).

Golden and Dark Ages

Any superficial assessment of the growth of understanding must allow that the rate of this growth has been inconstant (nonlinear in mathematical terms, episodic or rhythmic in ordinary terms). The golden age of Pericles was followed by a profoundly dark age. Pax Romana was followed swiftly by the decline and fall. The Renaissance closed with a cruel and oppressive inquisition. The recent golden age of science has, I believe, been followed by a shadowy information age.

Golden Examples from Medicine

Revolution has occurred periodically for millennia across the cultural faces of medicine. Some have focused upon a single therapy, perfected and applied it more and more broadly until its use attained ceremonial and even religious significance. Others have provided broad frameworks from which physiology and the balance between health and disease could be better understood.

The recognition of contagion, the generalization of the idea of natural selection, and the understanding of heritability have each had revolutionary biomedical consequences. Each of these revolutionary concepts has had more than a century to impact medicine.

The early nineteenth-century epidemiologic recognition of contagion through isolation of the Broadstreet pump as the point source for an epidemic of cholera was closely followed by the experiment of Semmelweis proving that puerperal sepsis was transmitted from the autopsy room to the labor and delivery suite (on the unwashed hands of medical students); each led to Koch's development of microbiology. The full range of therapies for microbiologic diseases from Ehrlich's Salvarsan through Domagk's sulfa and Fleming's penicillin as well as the subsequent understanding of immune networks flow directly from the Broadstreet pump and the Vienna obstetric wards.

The impact of the generalization of Darwin's concept of natural selection in biomedicine has included the recognition of the tendency of selective pressures to mold patterns of subcellular and cellular function, to organize tissue and organ function, and to integrate individuals, societies, and ecosystems. Temperospatial gradients responsible for embryologic development, cellular and tissue differentiation; the establishment, erasure, and renewal of specific immune network response; the continuous interactive renewal, updating, and remodeling of neurologic structure and function associated with learning, forgetting, and relearning; as well as the selection of bacterial or cellular drug resistance; or the development, emergence, and predominance of effectively metastatic clones can each be understood better by the application of the concepts of evolution and selection.

The development of an appreciation for, a deepening understanding of, and most recently the technical mastery over heritability is leading medicine into the next millennium. This revolution, beginning with Mendel's observations, accelerated by Haldane's elegant descriptions and predictions, broadened by McClintock's experimentation, and given substance by Jacob and Monod and Watson and Crick, now serves as the basis for a pharmacopeia of unimagined power and specificity.

Limitations of Reductive Science

Since Mendel's induction of the unseen internal script of life we have been racing headlong into the abyss of reductionism. We have begun to reach the core of this attractive black hole with the impending definition of the entire human genome and the genomata of many of our cousins in life. The ensuing, rather concrete, definition of problems by identifying abnormalities of omission, duplication, or misrepresentation within the primary structure of a gene, its message, or its product is truly satisfying. This approach will continue to result in many important advances. It will, however, never lead us to the fullest understanding of life. For this we must embrace its secondary, tertiary, and quaternary structures.

The amino acid sequence of a protein determines to a limited extent the other entities with which it will interact. The secondary or tertiary folding of that protein, in response to the local neighborhood in which it finds itself, is likewise only a part of the story. The probablistic time structure (biodynamics) of what is where . . . when . . .

is of absolutely critical relevance to the determination of these interactions. Biological time structure is defined by nonlinear rules responsible for complex rhythmic integration of all living systems. Nonlinearity is demanded for its inherent stability and also because it has clear thermodynamic advantage. These rules are not stochastic. They are chao-periodic because they have been impacted within living organisms by the geophysical site of their evolution. Understanding life cannot be approached in the most meaningful way outside the living organism. Accurate depiction of the temporal organization of vital function is completely dependent upon intact central, peripheral, and cellular time-keeping mechanisms. This symphony, both its melody and its beat, are nonsense outside the organism. Life's tempo or resonance structure changes markedly upon removal from the organism, usually becoming less thoroughly ordered and reverting to higher frequency ranges or, when mortally disturbed, to linearity.

Understanding How Systems Work Requires Observing Them Intact

The broader essence of integrative biology includes, but is not limited to, chronobiology. The experiments of the chronobiologist are dependent upon being able to stimulate spatially defined subsystems of the living organism or cell at recognizable points in its internal time structure. Studies of reproducible biological variations within the organism's circadian and/or fertility cycle are cases in point for the necessity of whole, live, animal research to complement classical reductionist investigation.

We will never really find out how the mind works or the immune networks function unless we study them within the living system. Nonlinear models, which are interactive and multifrequency, best describe and will most accurately predict biology. The most effective and accurate models will consider the strong tendency toward organization at and around certain specific geophysically originated frequencies. Integrative biology is absolutely essential to the future of biologic knowledge and therefore that future is dependent upon the continued development and application of nonlinear mathematics to live animal research. Cellular and molecular reductionism will continue to aid our search for knowledge. During the next hundred years, however, in my view, understanding induced from detailed, precisely quantitative, minimally invasive, multilevel observation of the intact living organism will be essential.

The Unbalancing of Science

Science, an organized way of increasing our cumulative understanding of the universe, employs two general plans for turning information into knowledge and knowledge into understanding. Reduction helps us figure out how things work by taking them apart, looking at the pieces from different points of view, seeing how the pieces interact, perturbing those pieces and observing the effects upon the system. When we take a mechanical clock apart we can inspect each of its gears, gain understanding of how energy is gradually transferred from its spring, and how this predictably propels its hands. The understanding generated is wholly a mechanical one. No understanding of time results. Analogously, we will not find out how the mind works, why human beings behave as they do, or how to influence that behavior unless we study these things within the living system.

Induction uses observation, perception, and logic to describe rules by which things seem to interact. Time is induced to be a concept relating to the number of events that occur between other recognizable events. This concept can result in the construction of a clock with a spring, gears, and hands, or as easily one employing flowing water, sand, or atomic decay; or one that employs natural events from sunsets to heartbeats. The idea of time can then be applied not simply to measuring it but also toward a deeper understanding of all life forms and all life processes within each of these creatures.

The understanding gained from each of these approaches to science is interdependent but has become unbalanced. Routine scientific pursuits have become more reductive. The information generated by this process is expanding exponentially, and the need for synthesis of this information has outstripped the inductive capacities of late-twentieth-century science. If the growing need to integrate reductive facts into a genuine understanding is not attended to, society will turn against this unbalanced science. The ratio of reductive and inductive science must be more thoughtfully balanced.

Ancient and medieval science was dominated by induced models of the universe which relied upon little or no data. Dogma based upon complex logical extension of very few observed facts resulted in very inaccurate understanding of the nature of our universe. With the Renaissance, rationalism eventually dominated science and scientists from Galileo to Newton to Darwin employed careful and accurate observation and experimentation within the context of flexible, nondogmatic, induced models. This balanced science resulted in a flowering of knowledge and the greatest rate of growth of genuine understanding in the history of science. The second half of the twentieth century has been dominated by the dogma that information is the goal of science. We call this the *information age*. We build *information superhighways*. Science is again unbalanced. Reductionism has become a religion and the relative rate of growth of both knowledge and understanding has diminished. Society rebelled against the dogmatic world of idea without data. Society will rebel against a world of data without the framework of idea in which to place these endless data. This rebellion will be expensive for scientists and society. Only scientific integration of idea and information can prevent the impending and justifiable societal wrath (see figure 1).

Science and Modern Humanism

Science is an essential component of modern humanism. We must make understanding human behavior a top scientific priority. We must more fully develop methods that can elucidate human motives and explain behaviors more clearly. These methods must be more highly inductive. The tools essential to increasing our understanding

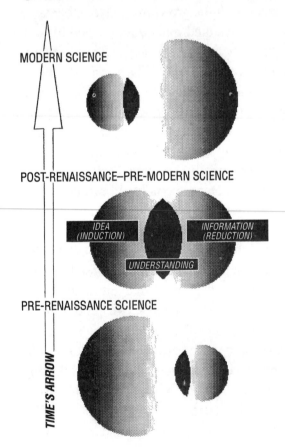

Fig. 1. The rate of change of a process is that most clearly sensed by a biological system, an individual, an ecosystem, or a society. This figure uses two spheres to depict the relationship between the rate of growth of idea and information within three arbitrarily defined epochs in the history of Western science. Both idea and information are essential for understanding (that volume defined by the intersection of these two spheres). Regardless of the "absolute quantity" of idea or information, the perceived adequacy of understanding relates totally to the balance between the growth rate of each of these essential components. A persistent relative imbalance of these in either direction adumbrates revolution.

of human nature must be nonlinear and the relevant data must be obtained nondestructively.

Nature includes us; there is nothing outside Nature; there is nothing unnatural. Everything that we do affects every part of the universe. Discovering the rules by which our genes and brain interact with the environment is a part of Nature that is discoverable. As modern humanists we must get on with the critical scientific task of understanding our human behavior.

Summary

Hopefully, this brief essay has explored the basis for periodicity of golden and dark ages. It may have demonstrated that the essence of a "golden age" is a critical dynamic balance between the processes of induction and reduction, and the rate of growth of their respective products, idea and information. Dark ages are characterized by dynamic dysequilibria of either of two varieties: the unconstrained growth of groundless idea (dogma); or the explosive growth of meaningless information. We are currently in a shadowy dynamic dysequilibrium of the latter variety. A golden age occurs when the rate of growth of idea and information remain within range of one another (either growing in tandem or in rapid alternation). When this happens information is transformed into knowledge which can provide understanding. Growing understanding is felt by society and sculpts science to a human scale with a trusting demeanor, an honest face, and soothing tone. Dysequilibria, of either possible variety, make science hideous, threatening, and dangerous.

15

Information Technology and the Sense of Unity in Humanity

H. Visser

Scientific humanism is the ethical view that the human condition can and should be improved by scientific research and the proper use of scientific knowledge. Formulated this way, it follows that there have been scientific humanists since Greek antiquity. Hippocrates, the founder of profane, scientific medicine, formulated his "golden rules" according to which the physician should proceed for the benefit of his patients, abstaining from whatever is deleterious and mischievous.[1] Centuries later, at the beginning of the Scientific Age, Francis Bacon generalized this idea to the whole of scientific knowledge, and, perhaps, to the whole of humanity, when he characterized the last end of knowledge as the benificence of man.[2]

In the eighteenth century, the Encyclopedists led by Diderot and D'Alembert followed Bacon, but they emphasized more the role of technical knowledge, though it seems that they still separated the sciences from the arts and crafts.[3] Despite their *rapprochement* in Europe during the nineteenth century,[4] the traditional terminological distinction, as if two different disciplines are involved, has not stimulated scientific humanists to include considerations of technology into their programs. The almost exclusive emphasis on the scientific attitude[5] prevents them from recognizing the possible positive role of modern technology for the future of mankind. As a result, scientific humanists seem to support unconsciously antitechnological trends in contemporary culture. At best they share the answers given by the sociologist George A. Lundberg in his once famous book *Can Science Save Us?*[6] Some of Lundberg's well-articulated arguments are here presented. They serve as a frame of reference for indicating ways in which modern technology may be used to alleviate some of the social problems of our time. That is, the question of whether science can save us will be shifted to the question of whether technology can save us.

Can Science Save Us?

The central problem of the Delphi meeting is the question whether such events as war and peace, environmental destructions and population explosion can be prevented.[7] Again and again, humanists have asked such questions and their answers were more than once supported by the idea that the means for solving social problems would be provided by an elaborated social science. Just as in the eighteenth century Condorcet and in the nineteenth century Comte and Clifford based their hope on the development of the social and political sciences on the basis of a scientific approach, George Lundberg in the twentieth century believed that human relations will improve when we undertake a serious scientific study of how to improve them.[8] On the supposition that all behavior, human and animal, is as regular and predictable as the behavior of the inanimate world, Lundberg argued that it would be possible to solve social problems by scientific means.

In Lundberg's time, as now, overpopulation was seen as one of the most serious of the world's problems; it was regarded as more dangerous than nuclear war, and considered together with great concern about "the millions who know want in the midst of abundance" and other "millions who die from preventable diseases."[9] Today, ethnic wars have brought misery to hundreds of thousands of people, not only in Africa, but also in Europe. According to scientific humanism, avoidable misfortune must be prevented, and human beings are considered responsible for not preventing avoidable misfortune; it is also held that the boundary between what *can* and what *cannot* be prevented is not fixed, so that a better insight into nature, human beings, and society should be furthered. Therefore, Lundberg's plea for the advancement of scientific research should be supported in the light of the threats to human beings or even to the entire human species. In other words, there is nothing wrong with the view that the scientific approach is a necessary condition for gaining a better insight into the factors which determine the possibility of disaster, which is in its turn a necessary condition for finding the means of prevention. Only by asking clear questions, formulating tentative answers on the basis of assumptions, and making observations and reporting them, in order to revise the assumptions, can people hope to make progress.

However, Lundberg's optimism as to the possibilities of *his* science of human relations cannot be shared; his idea that there is a "social weather" that can be predicted with high probability, just as meteorologists predict sunshine and storm, seems to be a misplaced metaphor. Moreover, the contemporary scientific controversy about the influence of the emission of carbon dioxide on the putative global warming shows that even natural scientists often do not agree about the theories, models, or recording of observations on which the predictions are based. Therefore Lundberg's assumption that he could predict "the will and the choice of men by exactly the same techniques" that are used "to predict natural phenomena"[10] is astonishingly naive. It ignores the fact that there are actions for which individual human beings may be held morally responsible, namely those actions which are not wholly determined by "external circumstances," though they are responsible only for the choice which was left them.[11] Free will is not a statistical phenomenon.

Yet the prospects of a scientific humanism for the prevention of the indignities that are put upon human beings by human beings are not wholly chimerical. Ironically, these prospects are due to developments which were not foreseen, let alone predicted by Lundberg . . .

It is true that Lundberg here and there displayed insight into the importance of relevant phenomena. Despite his predictability axiom, he admitted that, "When the alternate possible courses have been laid before a community and the costs and consequences of each have been pointed out"—in short, when different *scenarios* are presented—"there will still be differences of opinion as to which course we should pursue."[12] One of the social problems of all times is that it can be extremely difficult to reach consensus about, or at least acceptance of, a particular course of action, instead of forcing a solution by resorting to war. But it is questionable whether any method and technique of securing agreement on important questions can be developed, contrary to what Lundberg believed.

The problem with scientific humanism, as conceived by Lundberg, is that there is too large a distance between the scientific method and "real life." At best they are linked on one point: the improvement of education. But it is remarkable that most of what Lundberg and other sociologists have to say on education does not come out above the level of untested generalities. Moreover, he was only concerned with the teaching of scientific method, and this looks rather unworldly.

A more serious shortcoming of the Lundbergian scientific approach to human affairs is the almost complete lack of attention to modern technology. Nowhere is it realized that the "scientific method" is not as such applicable to technological research and development, if it is applicable at all. Still worse is the negligence of the fundamental differences between science and technology. Though modern technology is partially dependent on science—just as science has been technology-based for a long time—technology has such characteristics that it might be a better candidate for "saving us," controversial though such an assertion appears.

Can Technology Save Us?

In 1994, a Dutch sociologist and former politician, who in 1995 is director of one of the Dutch public broadcasting corporations, caused a stir when he stated that, "It is infinitely better to solve or to diminish social problems by technological innovation than by imperatives and prohibitions for citizens"! The strongest rejection came from a social philosopher who argued that solutions to social problems with the help of modern technology would "reduce" society to "connections that are only suited to a technological system." He feared a reduction of human beings to "technological products," in other words, they would be regarded as cyborgs. What he had in mind was the example of the regulation of the behavior of, say, car drivers, with velocity limiters . . .

This kind of criticism is as old as automation; in the words of Margaret Mead, in a seminal paper: "Technical devices are pictured as robbing people of privacy, reducing them to cyphers, and subjecting them to decisions made by computers."[13] Apart from its historical and theoretical incorrectness, for computers do not make decisions, only human beings can decide to rely on the outcome of computer calculations, the argument misjudges the many possibilities of modern information technology. Moreover there is no a priori evidence that automation will make society less human. It is equally well possible to take an optimistic stand, as Margaret Mead dared to do: "Is it more or less humane for mothers and daughters, separated by hundreds of miles, to be able to telephone each other cheaply? Is it more or less humane to provide a bed-ridden patient with a self-regulating bed?"[14]

The essential point is that technological innovation is not an autonomous process, but a concatenation of choice moments, from the first deliberation and policy formation, through use of tools and systems, to the actual manufacture and use of technical products. In fact, every decision has ethical dimensions, and eventually the engineers are culpable for the consequences. This is another reason why technological processes should not be regarded merely as categories of scientific processes. They differ, in the words of the late Colin Cherry, in their histories, their social values, their responsibilities, their methods, and their goals.[15]

The proposal to solve or diminish social problems by technological innovation should be seen in this light. Of course, decision-makers can try to straitjacket human beings by technological means, but who would defend such an approach from a humanistic point of view? Why not try to use technological means in order to strengthen, consolidate, or restore human values as much as possible? Humanists can contribute to such a program, at least by discussing creative possibilities.

In fact, there is already a discussion on the possible advantages of information technology: some participants welcome a worldwide electronic communication network, not only for exchanging, say, technical and medical information between specialists anywhere in Europe or for the use of people asking for help in say, Zambia, but also as a means for reaching a better understanding between human beings, and eventually for creating and reinforcing everywhere a sense of unity. In order to establish such a network, the "information infrastructure" of Third World countries should be improved, for example, by placing small satellite dishes on such a scale that everyone has the possibility to seek, receive, and impart information and ideas through electronic media, regardless of frontiers. Therefore, proponents of this approach recommend the use of development aid to this purpose.

Other participants in this discussion emphasize the dangers of electronic networks. The digital behavior of each member might also be controlled by electronic means; without guarantees that this will not be done by governments, or by private companies, they fear a "Brave New World on the Net." Of course, safeguards must be provided against potential misuse of a world network. But this is a normal course in any technological process and does not affect the principle of creating connections between people all over the world that are suited to a technological system on behalf of mutual understanding. Another criticism emphasizes that networks can only function effectively if the participants already share moral norms. I suggest that this could be met by first installing a global network for *medical* information, bodily health being a universal value.

We have seen what the main problem was with Lundberg's scientific humanism: the question of how to reach agreement between different people with different opinions. Yet Lundberg came remarkably close to a solution when he saw man as a "symbolic animal": he was concerned with "the development of his power of communion, communication, imagination, sympathy and empathy," as a result of "man's capacity of symbolic behavior."[16] To this purpose, he drew attention to a "new science of semiosis, dealing with the nature of symbolic behavior,"[17] and this I take to imply that Lundberg's "scientific approach" must be modified for and extended to a new type of research: communication studies. The improvement of the technological information infrastructure is only a necessary condition for successful communication. According to Colin Cherry,[18] Aristotle already saw that communication does not necessarily bring people together; it can equally well drive them apart. Therefore it is high time that recent research on communication models, extended to pictorial exchanges of information, focuses on the so-called world flow of information. In other words, what is needed is not only "hard," but also "soft" technology, with the emphasis on "technology." The ethical component of the latter discipline has to be stressed.

It is certainly possible that the design of technological media leads to a "consumer-oriented," "manipulative," *world information system* that conditions "false desires and needs." But there is also room for research that is directed at the development of an electronic *world communication network* that is supported by, and supports, sympathy and empathy between human beings all over the world. To this purpose, two hypotheses suggest themselves for further testing.

One hypothesis is that sympathy and empathy arise primarily through exchange of "direct" information between individuals about the way they live and think. The other hypothesis is that *virtual* instead of *real* communication does not contribute to mutual solidarity, but tends to isolate people in an anonymous identity.[19] Recent history has shown the effects of isolating human beings, not only on themselves, but also on others. It is also known that tolerance emerged in *open* societies. Modern information technology may make the earth one open society, with one global community, and thereby lay the foundation for saving us from catastrophe. For without a sense of unity in humanity, agreement on important questions will forever remain illusory.

Notes

1. Compare the English translation of the Hippocratic Oath in Stephen J. Hadfield, *Law and Ethics for Doctors* (London: Eyre & Spottiswoode, 1958).

2. Compare modern editions of Francis Bacon, *The Advancement of Learning*.

3. Compare [D'Alembert], *Mélanges de Littérature d'Histoire et de Philosophie*, vol. 1 (Amsterdam: Aux dépens de la Compagnie, Nouvelle édition, 1760). There are several later editions and translations.

4. Compare Victor C. Ferkiss, *Technological Man: The Myth and the Reality* (London: Heineman), ch. 2.

5. Compare Herbert Feigl, "Ethics, Religion, and Scientific Humanism," *The Humanist* 28 (1968): 21–25.

6. George A. Lundberg, *Can Science Save Us?* 2nd ed. (New York: David McKay, 1961).

7. Compare Dennis Razis, this volume, "Opening Remarks."

8. Compare Lundberg, *Can Science Save Us?* p. 94.

9. Ibid., p. 17.

10. Ibid., p. 107.

11. Compare William K. Clifford, *The Ethics of Belief and Other Essays* (London: Watts & Co., 1947), pp. 28–69.

12. Lundberg, *Can Science Save Us?* p. 115.

13. Margaret Mead, "The Challenge of Automation to Education for Human Values," in John Diebold, *The World of the Computer* (New York: Random House, 1973), p. 347.

14. Ibid., p. 348.

15. Compare Colin Cherry, *The Age of Access* (London: Croom Helm, 1985).

16. Lundberg, *Can Science Save Us?* p. 115.

17. Ibid., p. 72.

18. Cherry, *The Age of Access*, p. 47.

19. Compare Francis Fukuyama, *Trust: The Social Virtues and the Creation of Prosperity* (New York: The Free Press, 1995).

16

Science and the Drama of Mankind: The Responsibility of Scientists and Intellectuals

Dušan T. Kanazir

First of all I would like to take this opportunity to thank Professor Dennis V. Razis and the Organizing Committee of the International Conference on Human Behavior and the Meaning of Modern Humanism for having kindly invited me to attend this so important conference. With one foot in the East and one foot in the West our colleagues on the Organizing Committee will, like a bridge, unify and synthesize our concerns into an integral picture of the most complex problems originating from the deepest socioeconomic crisis of the present civilization.

The aim of our gathering is to analyze the questions of survival and further evolution of our civilization. It is a good time to scientifically analyze the past and present errors and to think about the twenty-first century in the best way and to create necessary conditions to fulfill the aspirations of humankind to attain a new perception of humanism.

193

During the last decades growing scientific, social, and philosophical concerns about life, the future of man and bioenvironment, technological progress, and world conflicts (local wars) were and still are the main interest of politics, science, biosociology, and the human mind in general. The future of life and even the human species on our planet seems to be in question due to human behavior. Is the threat to survival a real one? It seems to me that all present threats are very real. Therefore we need a new meaning of humanism, grounded in bioethics, culture, education, science, human rights, and the wisdom for survival. We need knowledge on how to use the latest advancements in science and technology for the cultural, scientific, and economic prosperity of humanity. Today, the search for wisdom has new importance, because the survival of human beings and life can no longer be taken for granted. The ethical values and behavior of human beings must be tested in terms of survival, quality of life, and human rights.

The most serious obstacle on the road to further development of the present civilization, of its ethical values and humanism, is the division of the present world into unreconciled camps: one represented by very rapidly technologically and culturally developing nations, and another consisting of under- and nondeveloped countries living in scientific, technological, and cultural backwardness, in economic and social misery. The globe is not integrated; more than 50 percent of the human population, not yet literate, is dying from hunger. The world as a whole faces acute problems, such as social conflicts and disintegration of the Eastern Bloc, pollution and disintegration of the environment, waste of natural resources, recession, political and military threats, local wars, organized crime, and terrorism. The drama of contemporary civilization is the result of a deep moral crisis, of religious and ideological differences, of a misuse of power, knowledge, and technology.

The problem of problems is that the international economic

framework, based on greed and competition, has reached the final stage of unworkability. Can such complex socioeconomic and cultural conditions generate a new humanism? That is the most important but very probably a utopian goal, due to the biology of human beings, to their selfish genes and egoistic instincts developed during biological evolution.

Gene selfishness usually leads to egoism, greed, and selfishness in human behavior. We presently need to answer numerous questions: Is the human being a gene machine, responding to stimuli from the environment, programmed to preserve its individual existence? Which genes are they, how many of them are there, and how do they respond to endogenous (hormones, neurotransmitters, ions) and environmental stresses affecting the human brain and man's behavior? Do the faults in human behavior lie outside ourselves, in socioeconomic conditions? If this is the case, then the answers should be found in sociology, but if the causes of human behavior lie predominantly in the genome of the human brain, then the answers should be searched for in neurogenetics. The phenomena of human existence and experience are always simultaneously biological-genetic and social, and the explanation of human behavior must involve both of them.

The building of a new humanism, including a society in which individuals will cooperate generously and unselfishly towards a common goal and progress, cannot be expected from the biological nature of man, from his neurogenetic determinant and his brain. There are arguments, perhaps very simple, indicating a proximate causal relationship between genes and behavior. Mutations in genes coding the receptors for neurotransmitters and steroids may cause deep changes in human behavior. The genes are very slowly modified by mutations through evolution, whereas the world is changing much faster than the genes in our brain. Furthermore, our civilization as a selective mechanism favors selfishness, egoism, aggression, and violence. If that is the case, then a fundamental question follows. If the human being is among animals uniquely dominated by culture, how then can the culture and education influence the gene expression and human behavior? Can man "teach his genes" to become generous and altruistic? What would be the role of education and culture in the attempt to build new humanism?

The analogy between cultural and genetic evolution has frequently been pointed out. Cultural transmission seems to be analogous to genetic transmission in that it can lead to a form of evolution. The present scientific progress is the result of genes selected by natural and social selective mechanisms during evolution. The individual brain is shaped by natural selection and represents a unique combination of genes. Can we rebel against and free ourselves from the tyranny of the selfish genes that are the main obstacle in the attempt to build a new model of humanism for the twenty-first century?

Knowledge means and will always mean power. In the hands of men, this power is obviously misused. When political decisions are made in ignorance of biological knowledge and the genetics of man, at the level of poor ethical values and standards, they jeopardize man's future and the future of our globe. Rapid development of science and technology, rush for profit, lack of knowledge on neurogenetics as determinants, on human behavior, and especially stagnation in the evolution of human ethics and culture (that fact that 50 percent of the human population is illiterate) are the main factors causing ideological, religious, economic, social, and national conflicts and wars. Only Europe, owing to two great wars in this century, has paved the way with its blood for misguided ambitions, ideological disputes, and the rush for profit. Many intellectuals of the past played important parts in plunging the world into many difficulties. Well-educated, well-intentioned, and psycho-mentally integrated intellectuals also have the responsibility to find today a way to survival, peace, and prosperity for all people living on our globe. Our problems are obviously global and they should be approached in a global and scientific way.

It has finally become obvious that the obstacle to the survival and further harmonious progress of mankind is man himself. We ourselves, our genes, are the enemy of our prosperous future! The fate of the life of the community does not depend only on overt human assaults upon the environment but also upon the human systems and institutions in general—political governance, legal and social structures, cultural and educational institutions, economic and trade arrangements, as well as increased interaction of nations with each other. These problems should be solved in order to build the ultimate security, on the basis of political stability and preservation and improvement of the environment. To reach these goals the world needs a "Global Accord" that would serve as a basis for integral, global international political, social, national, cultural, and economic relations, a global approach to the preservation of biological characteristics and varieties and their improvement by new techniques of genetic engineering, as well as global attempts to enrich the environment in the twenty-first century. The main question is, therefore, whether the present world and national institutions, world policy-making and legal structures are intellectually mature and ready to respond to the present planetwide crisis? And what is the role of scientists in coping with it?

Ethical Issues, Dilemmas, and the Responsibility of Scientists

Science has produced knowledge that is being used for both good and bad purposes. Knowledge means possibility and power. Science resounds so loudly with claims of ethical purity, objectivity, and social responsibility, but in the rush for glory, wealth, and corporate power some scientists, leaders of fast applications of new technologies, have contributed to the present social and political crisis of the world.

To survive, the first rule is to force the researchers and scientists to reflect about the consequences of new knowledge applications and to foresee, if possible, not only economic, but social and ethical consequences in a longer perspective. Precisely at the stage of decisionmaking for the application of knowledge do the ethical questions arise. Scientists' ethical responsibilities have always been under undesirable religious, ideological, political, and military pressures. The applications of new basic knowledge gave rise and promoted the development of technology, the goals of which have been formulated by politicians, state administrators, the military, big multinational companies, and other parascientific factors. The consequences of such a policy were the total irresponsibility of scientists and their refusal to accept any moral liability for the use and abuse of new knowledge.

Morality in science has always been regarded as an area of subjectivity and relativity. It should be mentioned that technology in our century, besides gross benefits to the progress of our civilization, has also produced serious threats to the environment and further survival of mankind.

The consequences of this abuse of new technology are nuclear weapons, destruction of the environment, polluted food and water, and so on. In the attempt to conquer nature and achieve a comfortable life, quantitative material wealth, and progress, man and only man caused the present drama of our civilization. It is therefore obvious that without stable moral standards and values in the scientific community the dramatic crisis of our civilization cannot be solved.

Homo academicus, with his knowledge and new technologies, who at the same time is a human being, and a particular combination of genes, far from being purely spiritual and free from profane interests, is following the rules and laws of the economic market, including highly priced capital, competition, and the fight for power and hierarchy.

The question is how science, financed by governments, political establishments, military powers, and big multinational companies, can be and remain neutral, objective, and free. Scientific endeavors are so contaminated by parascientific interests that the following question might be raised: Could we at present foresee and evaluate the future of mankind and could we now, at the end of the twentieth century, imagine the contours of modern humanism, bearing in mind the human behavior connected with *Homo academicus*?

A new humanism would probably mean placing freedom, peace, social justice, solidarity, tolerance, equality, and truth as the basic values of human life. The next civilization should reaffirm, recognize, and affect them with a very high degree of worldwide consensus. It is obvious that certain new ethical, political, and socioeconomic conditions and new ethical values of scientists will be necessary for the survival, improvement, and development of our civilization.

The scientific ground of this urgent Global Accord on survival and development of mind will emerge from bioethics, from the responsibility of all social institutions and all individuals, from science and technology. Endeavors and results of scientists and technologists should not violate the life and health of human beings and other living organisms on our planet.

Can we in the present man-created hell foresee the future and the proper course for orientation? What criteria should be employed to choose the optimum of future possibilities presented by new knowledge?

It can very probably be achieved in the society if both policymakers and scientists become more and more conscious of the ethical problems of their nations and mankind. The ethical problems of science and technology have grown rapidly in the past decades as very important questions in almost all kinds of research. The responsibility of individual researchers has thus become increasingly stressed.

The moral and responsibility problems arise only with technological applications of new knowledge and with decisionmaking. Decisions are usually made on the basis of insufficient knowledge. Moreover, scientists find it very difficult to predict the long-range consequences of the application of the results of their research. The main characteristic of our civilization is particularly the speed with which technology collects new knowledge and transmits it to practice and application in unpredictable ways. This enormous psychological pressure upon scientists causes the greatest dilemma of their morality and responsibility, since their role in policymaking and in application of their new knowledge and high technology projects is nowadays practically negligible.

Decisions of individual researchers on ethical questions are further complicated by the fact that the harmful consequences of research are almost unpredictable. Today society leaves responsibility to politicians, administrators, military forces, big multinational companies, and sometimes even to organized crime associations. There are increasing efforts to eliminate scientists from influencing decisions on matters of extensive policies in technology, caring not about social consequences. The irresponsibility of policymakers, passively supported by numerous groups of scientists, has lead us to the present dramatic, socioeconomic crisis in the world.

How to increase ethical consciousness? Will it be possible to make scientists more aware of their ethical responsibility?

The quantity of knowledge is immense and is continuously forcing narrow specialization, in turn prodding one-dimensional thinking, narrow-mindedness, and a simplistic view of life and the philosophy of living. Such a restrained mind affects ethical values, emotions, and human behavior.

To achieve the above-mentioned goal, to increase individual responsibility and awareness of the scope of the present social and economic drama, the best means would probably be to educate and enlighten mankind, to promote and increase the levels of interdisciplinary education, and to include ethics, and bioethics in the first place, in the courses on technology. All this has to be done in order to increase the awareness of the need for comprehensive understanding of the issues linked with the man-bioenvironment interaction. Unfortunately, bioethics has not been treated so far within the exclusive domain of any one scientific discipline or profession. Consequently, open international dialogues on education, science, technology, bioethics, and the responsibility of scientists and professionals could become a new incentive in the effort to reach a Global Accord on how to create new political, social, and scientific conditions that will generate peace, cultural and scientific progress, wealth, and a new perception of humanism. Another problem is whether a rational, objective, and global response can be obtained. In that connection the most important question is: Do independent, free scientists and intellectuals exist in the modern world? If so, what is their real influence upon political and social life, and to what extent can they influence policymaking in science, culture, education, and especially in technological development? Whether and how can they take part in shaping and formulating the ethical values of our civilization? The questions are too complex, too vague and urgent, but appropriate answers are still absent.

There are totally independent writers, highly successful artists, and some relatively free scientists as exceptions. They exercise a certain but not a strong influence upon public life. The majority of scientists and intellectuals are semi-independent. Their limited influence upon policymakers depends on the cultural background and political institutions (parliaments) of their respective societies. Let us remember that decisions on nuclear and biological weapons, their production and experimental testing, are not made by nuclear physi-

cists, biologists, geneticists, sociologists, and the like, but by powerful state administrators and generals. However, some scientists
have been, willingly or not, involved in these immoral operations in
spite of their awareness of the social and biological consequences of
the application of their knowledge. For obvious reasons they will
never tell the truth about why they behaved in such an immoral way.

Conclusion

Scientists cannot leave responsibility to administrators, entrepre-
neurs, and politicians. Societies (parliaments) should demand today
that scientists take over their part of responsibility for the application
of new knowledge and research results. It would be necessary in a future perspective to look upon ethical issues as the most essential precondition for science, the whole society and mankind. Teaching systems and education, including ethics and morality at all levels, will
increase the awareness of this responsibility. There must be, using
mass media, open, objective, and continuous discussions by scientists
and policymakers on ethical issues in the application of science.

All these steps in education could minimize the misuse of new
knowledge, especially in the domain of genetic intervention at the
level of the human genome and brain. Science and especially new
technologies, molecular biology and genetic engineering, provide
man, in addition to nuclear energy (weapons), with enormous power.
The risk from disastrous misuse of this new power is obvious to all
scientists. These threats strongly suggest that new moral values are
necessary to enter the new millennium.

To build a new humanism we need new ethical values and wisdom
in how to use new knowledge for the benefit and prosperity of all of
mankind. We should think in a holistic way in our attempts to improve
the life conditions of the majority of the population of our civilization.
To reach that goal, bioethics and morality should gradually be incorpo-

rated into science and the humanities. Bioethics is becoming increasingly important when science applications are taken into consideration.

Because of human genetic determinants scientists should be, if they can, less selfish and egoistic and more altruistic for the future of our offspring. The rush for profit of the great powers, as well as that for the wealth of scientists, has been responsible for the destruction of our planet. We should all think about what we could leave to our children. The main question is how to slow down the rush for profit, how to bring in accord the rush for wealth and the health of men with sound moral rules?

It is slowly becoming apparent that social problems and the future of mankind depend not only on social conditions but on the individual genetic program (combinations of genes) and its expression by way of the brain in interaction with the environment. The ethos of our civilization evolved from such complex interplays.

The most important paradox of humanity is that man is changing the world much more rapidly than the changes taking place in man's genome and in the genome of his brain cells. This paradox is the consequence of a rapid development of man's intelligence.

The survival of humanity and the humanism of the "new order" will, therefore, depend on further evolution of man's intelligence, wisdom, culture, and contemporary ethical principles. The problem of problems, related to the future of humanity, is the genetic program of every human being.

We are now entering the age of molecular biology and genetic manipulations. The current research in molecular biology and genetic engineering (recombinant DNA technology) and particularly in human genome mapping, screening, and cloning, therapy by gene transplantation, fertilization in vitro, and transplantation of foreign genes into fertilized animal or human egg and plant cells, presage a new scientific era. This fascinating progress of molecular biology raises ethical, cultural, religious, and scientific questions.

Man is reaching the stage similar to that of Goethe's Dr. Faust. Man is about to become "Lord and commander of the elements" and could be punished as Dr. Faust was for trying to identify himself with God. Faust said, "I had the impudence to act like God, to create as He has done, and I am now punished." I have a feeling that this is happening to us now. Man was selected to be the only species allowed to make choices, and distinctions between good and evil, and to have a potential for reasoning. He made the choice to open Pandora's Box of Knowledge and has now reached the stage when he can never close it again. In other words, man must continue the search forever, for the wisdom to cope with new knowledge. The search for wisdom has a new importance today, because the survival of humanity, and life in general, can no longer be taken for granted.

Bioethics must play the most important role in political decisions. Two components of bioethics are new biological knowledge about man and human ethical values. Therefore, to survive we need knowledge and wisdom. Wisdom is the knowledge of how to use new knowledge for survival, and for the benefit and prosperity of mankind.

Molecular biology is penetrating more and more into the studies of human conduct and behavior. Attempts will be made to understand, at the molecular level and the level of gene regulation, the intellectual, emotional, moral, and esthetic capacities of man and the human species. A great deal of information is encoded in our genes, and this information, partly expressed in our brain cells and brain structures, interacts with personal experience to give us our knowledge about the external world. It may be expected that in this biological era molecular biology will have a tremendous impact on sociology, ethics, and the philosophy of science.

Whether man tries to change it and to teach the genes to be more altruistic is an open question now.

17

Ulysses and the Sirens: Constitutional Precommitment as a Rational Way of Collective Self-Command

Carla M. Zoethout

"Patterns of Human Behavior and Paranoid Elements in Human History. From Glorious Achievements to Monstrosities. The Role of Decision Makers." Thus, the title of one of the workshops of the Delphi conference. Being a constitutional lawyer, I would like to consider this subject from a constitutionalist point of view. That means I will regard the question of what people in a society may do to avoid chaos (the paranoid situation, if you like), to avoid turmoil. In other words: How can human beings elevate themselves from the state of nature to a civilized society?

First, the subject of this paper will be introduced. Second, I will focus on the idea of a constitution as a means of precommitment of a people. (What should the constitution contain, if it is a device for collective self-command?) Third, I would like to draw attention to a major problem of constitutions and constitutionalism. If the basic function of a constitution is to remove certain decisions from the de-

mocratic process, to tie the community's hands, then constitutionalism is essentially antidemocratic. The question therefore, can be put
thus: Should constitutionalism and democracy be regarded as an
oxymoron, or is it possible to reconcile the two major concepts of
Western (and many other) political systems?

Then, finally, the paradox of constitutional precommitment. How
can we justify the idea of a people tying itself to an "entrenched"
constitution?

Ulysses and the Sirens

Being in Delphi, Greece, I cannot resist the temptation of beginning
with the famous legend of Ulysses, by way of an introduction to the
problem of constitutional precommitment. As you all know, on their
way home, Ulysses and his companions encountered the Sirens,
birdlike creatures with the heads of women, who drew sailors to their
death with their irresistible, magic songs. In order to pass safely by
the coast of the Sirens, Ulysses instructed his sailors to fill their ears
with wax, so that they should not hear the strains. Meanwhile, he
himself should be bound to the mast, and his companions were
strictly enjoined, whatever he might say or do, by no means to release him, till they should have passed the Sirens' island. As they approached the Sirens' island, the sea was calm, and over the waters
came the music so ravishing and attractive that Ulysses struggled to
get loose. By cries and signs to his people, he begged to be released;
but they, obedient to his previous orders, bound him even faster.
They held on their course, and the music grew fainter till it ceased
to be heard, when with joy Ulysses gave his companions the signal
to unseal their ears. Then, finally, they released him from his bonds.[1]

In constitutional theory, the tale of Ulysses is sometimes used as
an analogy to the idea of precommitment of a people to a constitution. Ulysses, by binding himself to the mast, was able to hear the

Sirens' music without being shipwrecked. In the same way, a group of people, by tying themselves to a constitution, is enabled to live peacefully together by laying down certain rules. These rules concern the organization of the state, procedures for decisionmaking, and individual rights and freedoms. In a way, we can compare a constitution with Ulysses' mast, writ large.

It is necessary however, to consider the "Ulysses analogy" a bit more elaborately. Comparing the story of Ulysses to that of a people tying themselves to a constitution is in a way somewhat deceptive. The problem is this: Ulysses' maneuver to thwart the Sirens was not his own invention. It was not an act of great human creativity, as I used to think. On the contrary, Ulysses was assisted by Circe, the daughter of the sun (alas for us humanists, inclined as we are to exalt human capacity).

But despite this small—though important—addition, the analogy still strikes us as adequate. The point is: constitutions have also been preceded by a higher phenomenon, that is, constitutions are the result of the ideal of constitutionalism. *Constitutionalism* refers to a certain view of government action: it expresses the necessity of limiting state power by means of the law; it is the conviction that no government should ever have unlimited power to do whatever it wants, because every government can lapse into arbitrary rule unless precautions are taken.[2]

So far I have tried to analyze the idea of precommitment, both on the individual level (Ulysses) and on the level of a collectivity (a people binding itself to a constitution). The notion of a people committed to a constitution is inspired by the idea of constitutionalism, or limited government. Only when a government—even a democratically elected government—is restrained by certain rules and procedures, is the political system prevented from deterioration. But then, the question is, what exactly does this mean, constitutionalism?

Constitutionalism as a Device for Collective Self-Command

The kind of government constitutionalism insists on is "limited government." Arbitrary rule, of course, is the very opposite of limited government. Predictability of action is the basic rule of constitutionalism, while capriciousness or unpredictability is the mark of tyranny or dictatorship.

But let me try to come to a more precise definition. What are the elements of the concept of constitutionalism? There are two ways whereby the belief that a government should not enjoy unlimited powers can be realized in practice. On the one hand, constitutional restraints aim at protecting individual rights and freedoms against governmental interference. We may call this the *substantial* aspect of constitutionalism. The second aspect concerns the *formal* constraints of constitutionalism, an aspect that refers to the organizational function of constitutionalism. W. G. Andrews has summed up the essence of constitutionalism as follows: "Power is proscribed and procedures prescribed."[3]

Constitutionalism pertains to two kinds of relationships: on the one hand, the relationship between government and citizen, and on the other, the relationship between different branches of government (legislative, executive, and judicial). This is not a clearcut dichotomy, but it is useful for the rest of our analysis to make this distinction. Which elements should we regard as being quintessential for constitutionalism, without reverting to essentialism?

First of all, constitutionalism presupposes the existence of "higher law," which often means a *constitution* (though not necessarily a written constitution). A constitution is a collection of rules, establishing and regulating the system of government in a state, thereby enabling decisionmakers to do their job.

In this constitution, we may discern a formal and a substantial aspect. The formal aspect of constitutionalism again contains several elements. Constitutionalism as I would define it includes the principles of the *rule of law.* That is to say, the rule of law is not regarded in the general sense of "government under law," but the notion is interpreted in the more specific sense of the embodiment of principles of good law or the internal morality of law (Fuller). That is to say, the rule of law includes principles like *nulla poena sine lege,* the rule that laws should be general, abstract, and future-directed, and so on.

A third element that is generally regarded as quintessential for the idea of constitutionalism is the notion of the *separation of powers.* This notion has two aspects: a separation between the different branches of government (in combination with a system of checks and balances) and a separation between different levels of authority (federalism).

Fourthly, an element that is related to the principle of the separation of powers: the *courts* should (1) be *independent* of the other branches of government and (2) be able to *review legislative acts in the light of the constitution.*

Finally, in every political system worthy to be labeled constitutionalist, *individual rights and freedoms should find protection.*

These elements are widely accepted as the epitome of constitutionalism. That is not to say, however, that a political system which does not fulfill all of these elements is not to be considered a constitutional system. A political system may not wholly conform to the doctrine of the separation of powers or may lack a system of judicial review of legislation without being referred to the realm of unconstitutional systems.[4] Constitutionalism should be regarded as a continuum: political systems that draw near the left pole are less constitutional and political systems that tend to the right pole should be considered as being more constitutional. It seems advisable to proclaim that a political system in which individual rights and freedoms are not being protected is *eo ipso* unconstitutional.

Until now, I have presented an outline of the idea of constitutionalism as one of the leading ideals of Western political systems. There is, however, one serious paradox in the idea of limiting governmental power. I am referring to the so-called countermajoritarian dilemma, the tension between constitutionalism and democracy, the other substantive notion of Western political systems. The countermajoritarian dilemma alludes to the question of how to maintain the principle of decisionmaking by the majority while at the same time we try to bridle this power because of the conviction that unbridled power will lead to democratic absolutism.

Constitutionalism and Democracy: An Oxymoron?

One of the most concise formulations of the countermajoritarian dilemma—the discord between majoritarian politics and constitutionally anchored restraints—emanates from Lawrence Tribe: "In its most basic form, the question . . . is why a nation that rests legality on the consent of the governed would choose to constitute its political life in terms of commitments to an original agreement . . . deliberately structured so as to be difficult to change."[5] If the basic function of a constitution is to remove certain decisions from the democratic process, to tie the community's hands, then constitutionalism is essentially antidemocratic. A constitutional democracy is, from this perspective, a marriage of opposites, an oxymoron.

It is possible to reconcile the notions of constitutionalism and democracy, to regard them as correlative concepts, the one supplementary to the other. Democracy is not an essentially contested concept, as far as its meaning concerns. It is, however, if we shoot a glance at the ideas about how such rule is to be achieved.[6]

In my opinion, the definition of democracy that has been proposed by Barry Holden is a good point of reference for an analysis of constitutional democracy.[7] Holden defines democracy as a political system "in which the people, positively or negatively, make, and are entitled to make, the basic determining decisions on matters of public policy."[8] In this definition, we may distinguish between a procedural element and a substantial element. The procedural element concerns the following questions: Who is entitled to make decisions, about what subjects, and how can individual decisions be turned into a collective will? The substantial element of this concept of democracy embodies the political rights that are inherent to this conception of democracy.

First, the problem of who is to make decisions. Since the twentieth century, the dominant meaning of "the people" in the definition of democracy includes all, or virtually all, the adult population.[9] The next question is what the people can make decisions about. Holden speaks of being entitled to make decisions, thereby referring to a constitution or some system of fundamental values, according to which the people are authorized to make decisions on matters of public policy. The question remains, however: How do the people make the decisions, if there is a large group of people with a plurality of opinions? In general, the answer is that the will of the majority should prevail, because the will of the majority is counted as the will of the electorate.[10] In other words, a majoritarian decision is valid, a unanimous decision is even better. As a matter of fact, the rule of the majority is a choice for the least dangerous method. Abraham Lincoln expressed this conviction in his first inaugural address, when he underlined that democrats had no other choice than rule by majority:

A majority, held in restraint by constitutional checks and limitations, and always changing easily with deliberate changes of popular opinions and sentiments, is the only true sovereign of the people. Unanimity is impossible; the rule of a minority as a permanent arrangement is wholly inadmissible; so that, rejecting the majority principle, anarchy or despotism in some form is all that is left.[11]

In Barry Holden's concept of democracy, the procedural aspect concerns the question of who is to make decisions, about what—about certain matters of public policy—and according to which procedures.[12] The substantial aspect in his definition pertains to the fact that the making of decisions should be authorized by a constitution (in the broad sense of the term, of course).

In Norberto Bobbio's definition of democracy, the substantial aspect bears much more emphasis. Like Holden, Bobbio stresses the largely procedural character of this political system. In *The Future of Democracy,* he demonstrates that the only way a meaningful discussion on democracy is possible is to consider it as characterized by a set of rules (primary or basic) which establish who is authorized to take collective decisions and which procedures are to be applied."[13] However, this is not enough. Those called upon to make decisions—or to elect the representatives who are to make decisions—must be offered real alternatives and be in a position to choose between these alternatives. For this condition to be realized, Bobbio asserts, those called upon to make decisions must be guaranteed the so-called basic rights: freedom of opinion, of expression, of speech, of assembly, of association, and the like.

> These are the rights on which the liberal state has been founded since its inception, giving rise to the doctrine of the Rechtsstaat, or juridical state, in the full sense of the term, i.e., the state which not only exercises power *sub lege,* but exercises it within limits derived from the constitutional recognition of the so-called "inviolable" rights of the individual.[14]

According to Bobbio, from this follows that the liberal state is not only the historical but the legal premise of the democratic state.

Both Holden and Bobbio connect the existence of fundamental rights and freedoms to the liberal state and subsequently combine the liberal state and democracy. All the same, some questions remain unanswered. Is Bobbio right in asserting that in a democracy, there are alternatives for those who are to make the decisions concerning the public interest? In my opinion, we should rather assert that in every true democracy, fundamental rights and freedoms—especially political rights—ought to be guaranteed. After all, a democratic political system presupposes that individuals can express themselves, that they can exercise their right to vote, to demonstrate, to associate, and so on, in order to prevent the momentary majority from forcing its will upon dissidents and lapse into tyranny. The quintessential democracy presumes the existence of people with differing opinions: minorities. In other words, in every democracy the positive freedom of the individual is guaranteed by way of individual freedoms which allow for people to participate in the political system (the same holds true for the group). The individual (and the group) should have the opportunity to express herself and to unite, to assemble, with others for a common purpose. In that case only, the minority of today can become the majority of tomorrow. Only when individual rights and freedoms—which are presupposed in a democracy—are constitutionally entrenched can individuals really claim these rights. We should keep in mind, however, that the individual is playing different roles in diverse situations; employee, voter, concert lover, and so on. Because of this, she will be a member of another minority every time she accepts another role. Democracy, from this point of view, is not a static concept, but is in fact made up of constantly changing majorities and minorities.

Clearly, the perspective on democracy that I will take as a point of reference is constitutional democracy. Only when the decisions of the majority are also limited can democracy as such exist. Not only is there the obligation to respect individual rights and freedoms, but there are also other notions included in the idea of constitutionalism: the idea that all governmental power, even democratically legitimated power, should be limited by law. In this notion, the negative aspect of freedom emerges; the individual is free to do whatever she wants, that is, she will not be thwarted by others.

In other words, constitutional democracy presupposes a negative view of human beings: the essence of constitutional precommitment is that the individual (in a community) should be guarded against herself. However, when human beings tie their hands to a constitution, they are able to govern themselves. From this point of view, constitutional democracy also expresses a positive view of mankind. We may regard the notion as a combination of correlative concepts rather than a conjunction of apparent contradictions.

So far, I have tried to analyze the concepts of constitutionalism and constitutional democracy. Next I will focus on the question of how to justify constitutional precommitment.

How to Justify Constitutional Precommitment

Since the time of the founding fathers up to now, constitutional scientists have tried to justify the idea of a people tying itself to an "entrenched" constitution (a constitution that can only be amended by a supermajority, like the American constitution). James Madison, one of the founding fathers of the American constitution, denounced the idea that the constitution was a dead barrier. Bonds are not necessarily a form of bondage, he said. Constraints can even promote freedom. According to Madison, the process of amending the Constitution should be complicated and time-consuming; the democratic process of bargaining would be beneficial for the knowledge of both parties.[15]

The contemporary philosopher Stephen Holmes has elaborated upon the ideas of Madison and has strengthened the positive aspects of constitutionalism. According to Holmes, a constitution should be considered as *enabling* rather than *disabling*. By tying herself to a constitution, a human being (a people) is competent to self-government, instead of being hindered from it. An "inherited" constitution leads, from this perspective, to stabilizing and reinforcing democracy.

To comprehend this point of view, let us return to the story of Ulysses and the Sirens. Only by being tied to the mast was Ulysses able to sail along the cliffs and resist the temptations of these creatures. Thus, by committing himself to being tied to the mast, Ulysses anticipated the moment he would be less sensible and make the wrong decisions. In the same way, a constitutionally restrained democracy guarantees that the political process will not yield easily to the voice of the momentary majority (the injudicious moment), but will always respect the rights of the minority (the prudent moment).

In conclusion, I would like to return to the level of individual human beings. Possibly the best explanation of the function of constitutions emanates from the American economist and constitutional scientist, Friedrich Hayek. Hayek has a rather gloomy view of human beings. Human capacity is only restricted, he says. The immediate purposes of human beings will always loom large, and as a rule we tend to sacrifice long-term advantages to direct purposes. However, Hayek says, in individual as in social conduct we can approach a measure of rationality . . . in making particular decisions only by submitting to general principles, no matter our momentary needs.[16] In the same way, the long-term rules of the constitution protect us from giving in too easily to the momentary majority and forgetting about the rights of the minority altogether. I think this rational choice for self-binding as a means of self-command will surely appeal to humanists.

Notes

1. T. Bulfinch, *Myths of Greece and Rome* (Harmondsworth, England: Penguin, 1979), p. 274, and J. Hall, *Dictionary of Subjects and Symbols in Art,* rev. ed. (London: John Murray Publishers, 1986), pp. 315–16.

2. Arbitrary rule, of course, is the very opposite of limited government. The basic rule of constitutionalism is predictability of action, while capriciousness or unpredictability is the mark of tyranny or dictatorship.

3. W. G. Andrews, *Constitutions and Constitutionalism,* 2nd ed. (Princeton, N.J.: D. van Nostrand Co., 1963), p. 13.

4. An example of this is the Netherlands. Article 120 of the Dutch constitution reads that the constitutionality of statutes and treaties shall not be reviewed by the courts. (However, since 1953 the courts are empowered to leave aside a provision of Dutch constitutional law on the grounds that it is incompatible with self-executing international law. In that case, the judiciary is even directed not to apply a Dutch constitutional provision.)

5. L. Tribe, *American Constitutional Law* (Mineola, N.Y.: Foundation Press, 1978), p. 9.

6. Compare B. Holden, *Understanding Liberal Democracy,* 2nd ed. (New York: Harvester, Wheatsheaf, 1993), p. 3.

7. "A democracy is a political system in which the whole people, positively or negatively, make, and are entitled to make, the basic determining decisions on important matters of public policy," Holden, *Understanding Liberal Democracy,* p. 8.

8. Ibid.

9. Ibid., p. 15.

10. Ibid., pp. 43–44. See also N. Bobbio, *The Future of Democracy: A Defense of the Rules of the Game* (originally published as *Il Futuro della democrazia*) (Cambridge: Polity Press, 1987), p. 24.

11. A. Lincoln, "First Inaugural Address," March 4, 1861, in Abraham Lincoln, *Great Speeches* (Toronto: Dover Thrift Editions, 1991), p. 58. Lincoln's statement demonstrates that a decision by the majority cannot be equated with a decision of the whole people, Holden, *Understanding Lib-*

eral Democracy, p. 44.

12. However, this last aspect cannot be inferred from his definition of democracy.

13. Bobbio, *The Future of Democracy,* p. 24.

14. Ibid., p. 25.

15. S. Holmes, "Precommitment and the Paradox of Democracy," in *Constitutionalism and Democracy*, J. Elster and R. Slagstad, eds. (Cambridge: Cambridge University Press, 1989), pp. 216–18.

16. F. Hayek, *The Constitution of Liberty* (London: Routledge, 1960), p. 179.

18

A Businessman's Viewpoint

George P. Larounis

I assume my role here is to bring a businessman's approach or viewpoint into the deliberations taking place. Let me start by saying that neither business nor anyone else with some perception for that matter is unaware of the mess into which we have gotten our planet, nor of the clear and present danger involved, nor that something needs to be done about it quickly. Business, and quite justifiably too, prides itself on a "get things done" attitude. We praise ourselves for our ability to anticipate problems (no ostrich-like evasion for us) and to face them head on, deciding quickly and vigorously the tough measures that may be needed and implementing them just as quickly and vigorously, whether it be plant investments or closures, write-offs, and so on. In that regard we compare ourselves favorably with government, educational institutions, and the like, whom we tend to dismiss as slow, bureaucratic, and worse.

Yet, here, in the face of, without hyperbole, the greatest problem facing mankind, our very existence, one can almost discount business as a driving force in arriving at a remedy. My effort here will be to try to explain why and to propose a possible solution, since not to use the immense talents and resources of business in this effort would be a shame. Why this problem with business? Well, all you have to do is look at the letter from our president, Dennis Razis, in the preliminary program brochure to find the answer. He says, "Factors to be considered include the rapid development of the sciences and technology in sharp contrast to the stagnation in the evolution of human ethics; patterns of human behavior which have remained unchanged through history." Or, citing Lynn Margulis "To survive the ecological and social crisis we have caused, we may be forced into dramatically new kinds of cooperative ventures. We may even be pushed together toward a unity that has only previously been imagined by religion."

But success in business is founded on utilizing, even maximizing, or at the very best harnessing, these patterns of human behavior which we are being asked to change. We grow up thriving on competition, on marshalling resources and then managing them in the most effective way to produce a quality product efficiently and economically. In doing this, we take great pleasure in beating the competition, in expanding, often worldwide, in rewarding our employees and of course ourselves. Within this environment, we use the criteria of price, quality, availability, and not necessarily renewability, in choosing the resources we use, whether they be natural or artificial, energy, raw material, machinery, plant, and so on. And all this time we're looking at the marketplace and the competition. These are our control points and points of reference.

Believe me, this business world of ours can be very rewarding and stimulating and I don't mean simply from a monetary point of view, but also because it does rely on human behavior, which is gratifying to a competitive, "get things done" type of personality.

There is, however, here no incentive toward the type of behavior to which Dennis Razis and Lynn Margulis refer. This, of course, is not all bad. It results in the production of immense numbers of top-quality products at affordable paces. Many of these products are necessary, many useful, many a luxury, and many admittedly the result of a created need.

Now I don't want to convey the image that this world to which I am referring is completely without any recognition of other factors, such as social responsibility and environmental considerations, but it would be naive to argue that these latter concepts are basic motivators. Rather they are taken into consideration because of "enlightened self-interest," when imposed by customer pressure, when legislated, and, most importantly, when they do not give the competition an advantage.

Effectively then business is saying "Look, we're doing our job the best we can; it is a tough one, in a tough world environment, with tough competition, and we are playing by the rules of the game as given to us by society, by our governments, and by our traditions. It is a full-time job. Don't expect much more of us, and for God's sake don't try to change the basic motivators . . . look what happened to productivity and quality and the ecology when communism tried to do just that."

So what can we expect of business ?

My first conclusion. You cannot change business patterns of behavior without destroying the very fiber that makes business so vibrant and productive. Simply stated, as concerns the business world we know today, the Razis and Margulis proposals, as laudable as they are, don't stand a chance.

Yes, but say you, and quite correctly, this manner of proceeding is going to ruin us all. What good does it do to have a tremendously productive society, showering us with material goods, if in the process we are destroying the very resources that provide us with the goods, and the environment in which we have and which we need to permit us to enjoy these goods?

So let me rephrase my conclusion. There is no way you are going to get today's businessman to voluntarily change his patterns of behavior, nor, I submit, do you want to. But what you can do is to change his entire working environment in such a way as to permit him to expend his best efforts within a set of ground rules applicable to all, and which permit him at the same time to operate as a constructive world citizen in the effort which is the subject of this conference.

The analogy I like to make, because I love the game, is tennis. The players are required by the rules to hit the ball over a net of a determined height, within the confines of a court of a certain dimension, all overseen by a referee to ensure compliance, and this whether they are playing in Europe, Asia, Australia, Africa, or the Americas. Within these limits, competition is ferocious, each player practicing and honing his talents and doing his best to beat the other.

You might argue that trying to apply such rules to the business world is utopian—too big a job, business owners will never comply. Well, I'm not saying that it is going to be easy. But don't overlook the fact that we've come a long way since the days of untrammeled competition. The business world today does not operate in a completely undisciplined fashion. There is a whole body of law out there with which we are required to comply. Antitrust laws, employment regulations, social security, and, yes, environmental regulations.

But for business to comply, there is one absolute cardinal requirement—that we can the level playing field. Just as in the game of tennis, the rules must be applied to everyone and to be enforced for everyone. If one country of a region is excepted, then forget it, because it will give a reason for noncompliance by the others, who are not prepared to give away an unfair competitive advantage.

I'm afraid I haven't given business much credit for good ethics and morality, thereby giving you hope for change through voluntary compliance for the good of all. But, let us not sell business short. They are just as aware as you are of the problems facing our earth and just as worried, and they want to contribute to a solution to these problems. But they cannot do it voluntarily, or they will be eaten up by the competition. If given a "level playing field" where all play by the same rules, I'm sure that they can and will be a major contributor to the effort.

19

The Role of Global Corporations in Human Survival and Development: A Meliorist View

A. G. Kefalas

Business enterprises are the central agents in the process of the creation of material wealth. By combining the basic factors of production, namely, people, capital, resources, and equipment, into economically and technologically feasible endeavors, business enterprises produce the products and services which are so vitally necessary for human physical survival and economic and social well-being. This important function of business corporations, when combined with sound ethical and socially desirable political and economic value systems, can provide an environment conducive to human growth and happiness.

When a business corporation performs the above-stated functions in more than one nation it acquires the characteristic of a global corporation (GC). Conventional international trade and economic thinking has implicitly assumed that international business activities are desirable for all parties involved. However, recent world events—for example, the environmental crisis, the energy crisis, the food crisis, expropriations, nationalizations, executive kidnappings, oil embargoes, ad infinitum—have sparked a new examination of the relations among the nations of the world. The epicenter of this world-wide earthquake seems to be the GC. While some (primarily industrialized countries) revere GCs as the heroes in the human struggle for survival, others ostracize them as the villains.

As humanity's inquisitive searchlights, with the passage of time, have gradually focused away from the preindustrial era's preoccupation with the terrestrial globe to the contemporary postindustrial global village, it is becoming increasingly evident that if the desired goal of global survival is to be achieved, intellectual, scientific, and political forces must grant the GC a protagonist's role. Intellectual, political, and scientific dreams can only attain fruition if institutional leaders and decisionmakers intelligently plan future strategies and make the necessary decisions for implementing them in such a way as to complement and supplement visionary political, scientific, and intellectual thinking.

It is the main thesis of this work that just as conventional, intellectual, scientific, and political thinking has traditionally been dominated by provincial (discipline, field, or nation-state) attitudes, conventional GC managers have been trained to think and operate in a piecemeal manner, visualizing the world as a fragmented agglutination of small, unrelated nations which they can manipulate to their corporation's advantage.

The purpose of this paper is to provide a conceptual framework for GC design and management which incorporates the new thinking of global survival into conventional managerial decisionmaking processes. This framework will satisfy the basic conditions for a sustainable material equilibrium, as proposed by, for example, the Club of Rome's 1972 *The Limits to Growth* and 1994 *Beyond the Limit*, while still fulfilling the main goals of a private business corporation which strives for the profitable allocation of scarce economic, human, and material resources.

The Conceptual Framework

BASIC NOTIONS

A rudimentary review of GC literature will easily convince one that the appearance and growth of modern global corporations posed a great challenge and even threat to both conventional economics and traditional politics. Such traditional "laws" as demand and supply, comparative advantages, global price and wage equalization, increase in economic welfare, and increased economic development for all parties engaged in international economic relations are becoming, when viewed through the prism of the twentieth-century postindustrial era, to say the least, sheer generalizations void of any true relevance. In the international finance camp, post–World War II multinational business activities have rendered the once sound and valid regulations of the Bretton Wood agreements completely meaningless. The substitute system devised in 1971 to deal with the inadequacies of the previous system created more problems for countries and private institutions than it actually solved.

In international politics, the once viable concept of the sovereign state seems to be losing its political status. The nation-state finds itself in a dilemma where, in order to provide for the economic welfare of its citizenry, it is faced with a "Faustian bargain," where it must sell its political and social autonomy in order to assure some gains in economic development. Thus, the issue of territorial and political integrity ultimately must bow to the needs for economic sufficiency and development.

As with many other important issues, inquisitive thinkers and researchers often enlist themselves in one of two camps: the pessimists vs. the optimists. The pessimists, extrapolating their thinking as distilled from past experiences and past developments, see the malignant effects of GC evolution prevailing over the benevolent. They assert, for instance, that GCs, in the pursuit of their conventional goals, would cause greater inequality of wealth and destruction of the physical environment, which would, most likely, breed conflict between those who managed to secure a greater slice of the economic pie and those who were constrained to distribute their smaller slices to a larger population. In addition, they foresee a greater centralization in strategic decisionmaking and goal-setting, which would facilitate GC dominance over the nation-state. Finally, they prophesy that the diminution of the role of the nation-state would lead to a new corporate feudalism which would serve and benefit the "center" at the expense of the "periphery."

At the other end of the continuum are the optimists, who see the GC functioning as a unifying force in the world. In doing so the GC would shift the process of the creation of wealth through industrial production toward the poorer parts of the globe; it would transfer technology and managerial resources from the so-called overdeveloped countries to the less-developed countries and thereby solve most human and environmental problems; and it would promote greater regional and economic integration. With this accomplished the GC itself would evolve into a new and flexible form of functional international organization.

The present author is inclined to agree with the optimists with the proviso that GCs would have to adopt a completely new philosophy and devise a novel framework within which corporate goal-setting, decisionmaking and operations would have to be accomplished with an eye on "global interdependence," which would necessitate efforts toward increasing the size of the global economic pie rather than increasing the size of the individual's GC slice. The necessity for this kind of thinking is not intuitively obvious, even to the most astute corporate GC managers, particularly when their record of success thus far has been completely unprecedented and when he or she has been eulogized by some as "the earth manager."

The basic assumption underlying this work is that the GC's organizational structure and function provide the greatest potential, the "best tool," to use P. Drucker's expression,[1] for global sustainable material equilibrium, if for no other reason than the undeniable fact that a GC represents a global economy and cuts across national boundaries.

THE CONVENTIONAL GC MANAGEMENT MINDSET AND THE NEW WORLD REALITIES

Managers of a GC are human beings and as such are committed to operating in the world in terms of their conceptual understanding of the world—their own *Weltanschauung* as the German philosophers termed it, or their "model" or mindset as we today have christened it. The model intervenes between the manager and the "real world" in the same manner as corrective lenses intervene between the human eye and the "real object": the right corrective lenses will restore reality; wrong corrective lenses will distort reality. The model which distorts reality is called the *surrogate*. Through the distorting lenses of the surrogate the GC manager perceives the world as being characterized by Podsnappery, Divisio, Machiavellianism, and Allometry.

In summary, the surrogate envisions the GC manager's world as one that considers the activities, philosophies, and values of others as misguided, conceives of others as being extremely slow in learning, and views the world as divided by political ideologies and legal systems which are in need of GC manipulation. Under these conditions GCs can grow indefinitely along a path of undifferentiated growth characterized by replications of some "ideal" form of organization.

THE NEW WORLD REALITIES: SAME GAMES, NEW RULES

It is fairly obvious from the preceding brief description of the four basic pillars of the surrogate that, on the surface, the "model" as a whole appears to be logical, convenient, and workable. A closer look, however, will reveal that the apparent logic and workability is destroyed when viewed through tomorrow's rather than through yesterday's glasses. A rudimentary review of the literature on what has come to be known as "world problematique" will reveal that the contemporary world picture is being completed by the emergence of certain new, diverging and converging phenomena, some of which are the following:

Globalism—Nationalism
Abundance—Scarcity
Overdevelopment—Survival
Growth—No-Growth

A brief survey of the new world realities points to a number of discontinuities: (1) *World outlook.* Some First World countries are reversing their world outlook from globalism toward regionalism and even nationalism while most of the Third World is moving away from nationalism toward regionalism aimed at a united front that encompasses some 80 percent of the world's population. At the same time, however, there is an encouraging trend toward First and Third World cooperation as well as First and Second World cooperation (for example, EU, NAFTA, OPEC). (2) *Existence of resources and material wealth.* The physical existence of resources is becoming a more decisive criterion for determining their availability. According to this criterion most of the First World will be resource-poor. (3) *Economic development.* There is strong suspicion, and considerable documented evidence, that the First World has reached its limits to growth, whereas most of the Third World needs and would substantially benefit from economic growth.

The Systemic Model: A Systems Approach to GC Management

If the GC is to survive, and if its functions are to be made congruent with the desired sustainable material global equilibrium, the GC manager's philosophy and practices must be guided by the following "philosophical principles," and "operational principles":

PHILOSOPHICAL PRINCIPLES

Managers manage their corporate affairs through models. The process of abstracting from reality pertinent events and organizing them into a coherent and manageable whole (modeling), is governed by the modeler's view of the world. By choosing from among many alternative models and by experimenting with a few of them (simulation), the manager formulates the company's vision, mission, and main policies, which then become, as they are diffused throughout the organization, specific objectives, goals, and standards, or targets, for specific individuals. It is then obvious that the corporate philosophy has a much larger impact upon the individual corporate member's behavior than is commonly believed. The new managerial philosophy consists of the following four principles:

(1) *Adaptation and learning.* All organic systems, in an effort to reach and maintain a goal, engage in behavior which is referred to as "trial and error." The chief characteristic of this behavior is that the number of trials is, with time, reduced by a process of the communication of feedback information containing a measure of the deviation between the goal and the actual performance. Through this negative feedback information the system eventually minimizes the number of

trials required. This process is called learning and adaptation. In contemplating the design and strategies of their organizations, GC managers should keep in mind that the collective intelligence of the organization must detect learning potentials and attempt to implement them rather than to suppress them. Any attempt at suppression will conflict with the organic system's basic need to learn.

(2) *Holism.* Organic systems are wholes with irreducible properties. The divided world of the "fifties and sixties" represented a natural phase in human economic and sociocultural evolution that seems to be reaching an end. The number of trials and errors have begun to diminish with each new United Nations or Group of Seven conference and other world conferences. The "wholes" created by the formation of the Group of 7, OPEC, EU, NAFTA, ASEAN, and other regional agreements, are exhibiting a tremendous capability for learning and a desire to preserve their wholeness. The *division* of the past is today an instrument which has lost its effectiveness. Managers are again advised to look at their organization, and especially at themselves, as Janus-faced entities, who, looking inward, see themselves as self-contained, unique wholes, looking outward as dependent parts. Just as a company cannot be divided into arbitrary parts without destroying its effectiveness, likewise the world of today must be viewed in the same manner. The holistic properties of the GC's environment can be expected to strengthen rather than weaken in the near future. Managerial philosophy, if it is to remain relevant in the future, must accept this trend as a natural property of systemic behavior rather than as an anomaly.

(3) *Cooperation.* As indicated earlier, the traditional antagonism among the many nations of the Third World has been replaced with a strong desire for cooperative behavior. What is more significant, however, is the cooperative mood shared by some of the First World nations and the entire Third World. Of particular importance is the cooperative agreement between the European Union countries and the Third World

known as the Lomé Convention. This represents a first step toward world cooperation that no manager, and especially no global corporation manager, can afford to ignore. Since he or she will be asked to implement these schemes, it is important that the organizational structure and strategies he or she devises be cooperative in nature.

(4) *Organic growth.* Managers will be greatly tempted to endeavor to repeat the allometric growth pattern with which they are so familiar from their experiences of the last two decades. This temptation will be intensified even more by the similar eagerness of the leaders of the Third World, anxious to recover and to make up for lost opportunities. However, the temptation must be resisted by all means. The Sirens of the Third World Titan, seductively calling for exponential growth, must be resisted by the Odysseus of the GCs, for they must realize that the success of their endeavors will be endangered, and ultimately terminated, should they allow themselves to succumb to them. There are several pragmatic reasons why this would happen. For one thing, there is increased awareness in the world that our resources are finite, and this awareness is accompanied by the desire to prolong their existence. For another, the continued exponential growth of economic activity hinges upon substantial growth in the developed world, which will absorb any excess production. With the downward trend in the First World, the odds that an African refrigerator will find a place under the saturated sun of the West are very small.

OPERATIONAL PRINCIPLES

The above philosophical principles provide an outline of the GC manager's thinking horizon. They constitute, in other words, the four major pillars of a managerial ethos. In addition to that, however, managers need some practical guidelines which will enable them to carry out their long-range planning and day-to-day operations. The last section of this inquiry is devoted to outlining the operational principles which the author considers most important.

(1) *Investment principle.* The need for corporate growth stands out as being the most important criterion in deciding to "go international." Once this need has been established then the decision as to whether and where to invest usually depends on the rate of return on investment. Thus, regions or nations of the world which promise a high rate of return on investment receive the lion's share of direct foreign investment while those regions which do not offer this prospect are bypassed. Of course, the entire process is considerably more complicated than this, but most executives will admit that "when the chips are down, that's what counts."[2]

If the philosophy of the systemic model is adopted, then the allocation of economic resources and managerial talent will be initiated and stimulated by the need of a particular niche of the ecosystem rather than by the needs and wants of the GC. Given the current preference for private investment in lieu of public aid, the GC manager will be expected to invent "low rate of return" projects which will contribute toward the economic development of the recipient region. Obviously, the customary rates of return (10 to 20 percent) will be incompatible with the objective of the aid.[3]

(2) *Technological and production principle.* The quest for high rates of return on investment, coupled with certain unique conditions of "growth societies," such as a large, affluent market, tight supply of labor, and so on, has greatly influenced managerial decisions regarding the kind and extent of technology utilization and production processes. Operating under the once sound premises of the surrogate, managers devised production technologies geared toward producing large quantities via a continuous process of substitution of machine power for "muscle power." The GC of the future will have to abandon both large-scale production for the large and prosperous market and the high-capital and technology-intensive production processes

which minimize the need for human participation. More specifically, the so-called technology diffusion inside the Third World will have to be of a different kind than that which has made the First World rich. The most important, and the most abundant, resource of the Third World is its people. It makes perfect economic sense to utilize this abundant and renewable "resource." There is a technology which is designed to do just that. Schumacher gave it the name "intermediate technology," defined as "a nonviolent technology, based on small units, that lends itself for use by people who are not very sophisticated or very rich and powerful."[4]

(3) *Environmental acceptability principle.* Until recently there was an inherent bias against any sort of ecological consideration in investment decisions, whether domestic or international. In most business and industrial engineering schools the manager has traditionally been educated to make decisions by carefully investigating the economic and technological feasibility of the proposed project. Any warnings about the finiteness of the earth, as a reservoir of resources and as a sink for the deposit of the economically nonreprocessable residues of production, were dismissed as nonsense lacking a basic understanding of the price mechanism and the potentials of the twentieth-century *deus ex machina* megamachine.[5]

Global managers have, thus far, had little to worry about with respect to environmental considerations, especially if their corporation had branches in the Third World. However, the temporary lack of any environmental controls in these "pollution havens" of the Third World should not be considered to be a permanent condition, despite assurances by political leaders and Chamber of Commerce representatives. It is absolutely essential that GC managers realize this fact of life and build ecologically acceptable plants from the very beginning. To fall into the trap set by the con artist consultant that, "The poor need jobs more than they need clean air," will be like falling into a lobster trap; it is easy to get in but impossible to get out.

(4) *Conservation principle.* It is becoming increasingly clear that the physical availability or lack of resources is the invariant in the calculus of demand and supply. However, this idea of using nonmonetary equivalents in planning and managing organizational resources is as foreign to the manager as the idea of employing the price mechanism is to the ecologist. If a nonmonetary evaluation system for organizational resources is adopted, then the conventional attitude of "doing more with less" becomes questionable. There seem to be strong hints that a transition towards "doing less with less" is unavoidable.

(5) *The physical or geographic horizon principle.* With the First World's increasing decline in economic activity, with its increased dependence on the Third World for raw materials and resources, and with its moral commitment to help the Third World develop, the conventional planning horizon of the GC manager, which was more or less limited to the First World, must now be expanded to include the vast number of peoples in the Third World. If the excess capacity of the industrial establishment that "growthmania" has created is to be utilized, the decision to "go LDC" (invest in less-developed countries) is no longer an alternative, but rather, a necessity, if massive relocations of humans are to be avoided.

(6) *The size of the adventure principle.* It has long been suspected and it has recently been documented that after a certain point the size of the firm begins to become a disadvantage. Since most GCs have reached gigantic dimensions, Schumacher's "small is beautiful" seems not only aesthetically sound, but it also makes excellent economic sense. In "going LDC," existing GCs must plan and manage their operations in the Third World as "mini-multis." This kind of size strategy is indeed most appropriate, given the substantial fear that the gigantic size of the GC will dominate the nation-state or, for that matter, render it obsolete.

(7) *Ownership principle.* More and more GCs are abandoning

the once-preferred strategy of 100 percent ownership. In relinquishing part of its assets, the GC must attempt to avoid the most common pitfall of joint ventures, which is putting control of the locally owned portion in the hands of a few rich nationals. Such unorthodox plans as employee ownership must become more and more common. The wealth of the firm must be shared by those who need it most: the marginal worker and clerk, not the already rich landowner and affluent native.

(8) *Type of arrangement principle.* More and more of the actual production and marketing of the GC should be performed by native forces. The role of the GC must be more or less that of technology supplier, management consultant, and capital supplier. Such unusual strategies as project coordinator, turnkey projects, and other innovative, contractual arrangements[6] would enable the GC to avoid massive deinvesting of its most expensive and precious investment: human capital. By the same token, this scheme would save the Third World the substantial amount of money that would have had to be invested in rediscovering ideas that can be adapted with a minimum of expenditure.[7]

(9) *Location and personnel principle.* The conventional industrialization of the Third World by GCs has led to massive and inhumane urbanization in these countries. The GC's decision to invest in the city is interpreted as a new ray of hope for the rural population, their longed-for El Dorado. But once these hopefuls move into the city, a terrible process of misery ensues. The GCs of the future must follow Schumacher's advice and attempt to create an "agro-industrial structure in the rural and small town areas." The process of the integration of nationals into the managerial ranks of the GC hierarchy has been extremely slow. The Japanese are notoriously slow to integrate non-Japanese into their management. IBM is usually cited as the most notable exception to this rule. Obviously this discrimination against the "thinkers" of the Third World is no longer feasi-

ble nor desirable. Upward mobility within an organizational hierarchy should be as much a motivating factor for nationals as it is for "expatriates."[8]

(10) *Ethical principle*. If there has ever been a troublesome concept in most GC executives' minds it must be "ethics." While their legal staff and consultants conceive of ethics as a legal concept, namely, compliance with the law, congressional investigators and business and social critics all over the world, motivated by the massive uncoverings and voluntary disclosures of corporate bribes and political contributions of corporate funds, have shown considerable doubt about this narrow conception of ethics.

Ethics—as the branch of philosophy dealing with values relating to human conduct, with respect to rightness and wrongness of certain actions and to the goodness and badness of the motives and ends of such actions—goes beyond the questions of legality and legitimacy of managerial decisionmaking. The GC manager who aspires to contribute toward the goals of the new world order should know that ethics consists of a set of rules of conduct recognized in respect to a particular class of human actions or a particular group.[9] The group with which managers are affiliated is not only their own stockholders, superiors, and subordinates, but all of these plus the entire social and political environment.

Conclusion: A Meliorist Look into the Corporate World

Is there any evidence that a transformation of the type described in this paper could be conceived of as anything short of a utopia? Are there instances where GC executives have shown, indicated, or even hinted at changes in corporate philosophies, policies, objectives, or managerial practices which may be construed as the beginning of a new era of transformation? There is no one single answer to these questions. Hard-core evidence of a shift of corporate orientation away from the surrogate and toward the systemic model is meager. There exists, however, considerable evidence in the form of public statements made by high-ranking executives of some of the largest GCs hinting at a true "change of heart" in corporate boardrooms. Although most concerned scholars would interpret these statements as purely "cosmetic colorings," we believe that the stature and sincerity of the people who made these statements cannot be taken too lightly.

At the most general level there exists considerable evidence of transformation along the philosophical and operating principles outlined above. Today one sees, for example, a common code of conduct for all GCs operating within the twenty-four OECD members. Although the code has been viewed by the Third World as an attempt to tell the host countries to grant more and not less freedom to the GC, a more serious look into the code will indeed reveal some encouraging rays of hope. To this one could perhaps add the thousands of self-publicized codes of conduct which followed the U.S. congressional hearings on multinationals in 1975. GCs that have signed and indeed observe the Sullivan Code, which aims at completely eliminating racial discrimination and human exploitation in South Africa, contributed toward the realization of the current state in that part of the world. Elsewhere we have provided some examples of a few corporate responses to and indeed anticipation of most of the changes described under the ten operating principles.[10] In conclusion, here is how Walter B. Wriston, the chief of Citicorp and Citibank, described future GC managers and the GC's role in the new world order in 1976:

> The development of the world corporation into a truly multinational organization has produced a group of managers of many nationalities whose perception of the needs and wants of the human race knows no boundaries. They really believe in one world. They

understand with great clarity that the payrolls and jobs furnished by the world corporation exceed profits by a factor of 20 to 1. They know that there can be no truly profitable markets where poverty is the rule of life. They are a group which recognizes no distinction because of color or sex, since they understand with the clarity born of experience that talent is the commodity in shortest supply in the world. They are managers who are against the partitioning of the world, not only on a political or theoretical basis, but on the pragmatic ground that the planet has become too small, that our fate has become too interwoven to engage in the old nationalistic games which have so long diluted the talent, misused the resources, and dissipated the energy of mankind. The world corporation has become a new weight in an old balance. It must play a constructive role in moving the world toward the freer exchange of both ideas and the means of production so that the people of our planet may one day enjoy the fruits of a truly global society.

Notes

1. P. F. Drucker, "Multinationals and Developing Countries: Myths and Realities," *Foreign Affairs* 53 (1974).

2. United Nations, *World Investment Report: An Executive Summary* (New York: United Nations, 1993), p. 1; *Transnational Corporations in World Development* (New York: United Nations, 1988), p. 16; *Draft International Code of Conduct on the Transfer of Technology* (New York, United Nations, 1981), p. 3; and A. Rubner, *The Might of the Multinationals* (Westport, Conn.: Quorum Books, 1990).

3. H. Okuzumi, "Taisei Corporation Plans for the Year 2000," *Long Range Planning* (1990): 53–65; and W. E. Halal, "Global Strategic Management in a New World Order," *Business Horizons* (November-December 1993): 5-10.

4. E. F. Schumacher, *Small Is Beautiful: A Study in Economics as if People Mattered* (London: Blond and Briggs, 1973).

5. A. G. Kefalas, "The Global Corporation's Role in the New World

Order," *Forum* (1992): 26–30; *Global Business Strategy: A Systems Approach* (Cincinnati, Ohio: Southwestern Publishing Company, 1990); "Goals for Multinational Corporations," in *Goals for Mankind: A Report to the Club of Rome on the New Horizons for the Global Community* (New York: E. P. Dutton, 1977); and "The Environmental Imperative: The Death of Surrogates," *General Systems* 19 (1974): 155–63.

6. Kefalas, *Global Business Strategy*.

7. G. Hamel, Y. L. Doz, and C. K. Prahalad, "Collaborate with Your Competitors—and Win," *Harvard Business Review* 67 (1989): 133–39; J. N. Behrman, "Transnational Corporations in the New International Economic Order," *Journal of International Business Studies* 12 (1981): 29–42; L. S. Welch and A. Pacifico, "Management Contracts: A Role in Internationalization?" *International Marketing Review* 7 (1990): 64–74; and Skelly, Yankelovich, and White, Inc., *Collaborative Ventures: A Pragmatic Approach to Business Expansion in the Eighties* (New York: Coopers and Lybrand, 1984), p. 10.

8. C. K. Prahalad, *The Multinational Mission: Balancing Local and Global Vision* (New York: The Free Press, 1987), and F. A. Maljers, "Inside Unilever: The Evolving Transnational Company," *Harvard Business Review* (1992): 46–52.

9. W. C. Frederick, "The Moral Authority of Transnational Corporations," *Journal of Business Ethics* (1991): 165–78; J. M. Kline, *International Codes and Multinational Business: Setting Guidelines for International Business Operations* (Westport, Conn.: Quorum Books, 1985); United Nations, *World Investment Report, Transnational Corporations,* and *Draft International Code*; and "Church Group Gnashes Colgate-Palmolive," *Advertising Age* (1986): 46.

10. Kefalas, "The Global Corporation's Role" and "Goals."

20

What Is an Ideology and Do We Need It?

P. B. Cliteur

In his opening address to the Delphi conference Dr. Razis pointed at one of the aims of the conference: to develop a holistic point of view towards global problems. The desired result of the conference was described as the definition of modern humanism, the development of strategies to prevent a global catastrophe, and the establishment of an international society dedicated to the survival of the human species. Razis was well aware, however, that this undertaking sounds rather idealistic. And yet it is necessary. We may perhaps even be pushed together toward a unity that has only previously been imagined by religions. The message for the future is, Razis tells us, "cooperate or perish."

In this article I will not address the problems of our time directly. I will not talk about the population explosion, the deterioration of the ecosystem, and other developments which might render our planet uninhabitable. I will try to reflect on our attempt to tackle world problems in general. This will be a "metaperspective."

One of the aims of this conference is to develop a *comprehensive approach to social and political problems.* The presupposition is that by combining various scientific insights it is possible to develop a comprehensive approach to problems. However, this way of thinking has come under attack nowadays. Many important thinkers challenge the pretension to develop a comprehensive approach to global problems. A discussion has been going on for some time about the end of ideology, the end of life- and worldviews, the end of all comprehensive thinking. According to postmodernist thinkers like Jean François Lyotard[1] and other influential political philosophers such as Francis Fukuyama, we are now in a specific phase or condition of development that can be characterized as the end of ideology, the end of history, or the end of the grand narratives. That brings us to a rather paradoxical position. On the one hand, one of the most prominent elements of our present predicament is that we need a collective, comprehensive, and global approach. On the other hand, leading intellectuals stress the prevalence of individualism, fragmentation, and the futility of attempts to use theoretical reasoning to develop a consistent sets of ideas to solve our problems.

The most clear thinker in this tradition of "endism" is, in my opinion, Fukuyama. He states that we are at the end of ideology. Socialism, fascism, and communism have had their day. There are no rivals left for liberalism to compete with.[2] That would point in the direction of *one* ideology as the sole victor of ideological strife, but because ideology is only possible in contrast to competing ideologies, the end of ideology is in a certain sense also the end of the ideology of liberalism.

Although these general traits of the end-of-ideology debate are clear, there is still much that remains to be clarified. Neither Lyotard nor other proponents of the end of ideology give us a very clear idea of the implications of their stance. Should every general idea of what we stand for from now on be rejected as illusory? Should every attempt to justify our actions from the perspective of a general framework of ideas be cast aside as stillborn? That would be an impoverishment of the human condition, and one of the most important aims of the Delphi Society, to wit, to develop a general framework for the solutions of global problems, would be barren. I would like to challenge those postmodern and otherwise nihilistic trends in modern culture and make a new case for developing ideologies that may help us to overcome our present problems.

In this commentary, I will outline three conceptions of ideology. Only after this semantic propaedeutic work can we tackle some other relevant questions such as: (1) Is it indeed true that ideology in the sense outlined is at an end? and (2) Is it *desirable* that ideology will be exhausted? The result of my analysis is that ideology in the third sense, ideology as the coherent presentation of our political convictions, has to be revitalized. As a matter of fact, one of the aims of the Delphi Society is to develop a new ideology to save us from global catastrophe.

Ideology as the Veil of Interests

The first concept of ideology I want to address is ideology as the veil of interests. This is the concept of ideology as it has been used by Karl Marx, and that by means of his work exerted an enormous influence on social and political thought in the twentieth century.

The reasoning of those who use this concept of ideology is not difficult to understand. The quintessence of their approach to the social order is the concept of *power.* Like Hobbes, they say that every human being and every group of humans yearns for power. The oppressor can suppress those subjected to his power by physical means. But no government can ever be based merely on physical power, because even the most powerful tyrant still has to sleep. In that situation, at least, the palace guard has to accept power as based on other grounds than the exertion of physical power. This line of reasoning brought David Hume to the idea that in the end power is always based on opinion: the voluntary subjection of people to the authority of others.[3] We can also put the matter as follows: power must be transformed into *authority* to be effective in the long run.

The intriguing question then is: How can somebody with power attain authority? How does he make the suppressed *believe* his power is legitimate? Now the notion of ideology appears on the scene. The suppressor uses the idea of "ideology": a sophistic assemblage of reasoning that has the sole end of consoling people about their fate.

In the history of political thought very few people have been prepared to defend ideology in this sense. Most of the great political thinkers have been critics of this type of ideology. The most famous such critic was, of course, Karl Marx.

Another question is: *Will* ideology in the sense of the veil of interests disappear? It is possible that one *hopes* it will vanish but at the same time be pessimistic about the chances of this happening. People will always invent new ideologies to justify their privileges. Ideology will be with us until we are in the utopian situation that there is no inequality between people, that is, in heaven.

This is the pessimistic view. The more optimistic vision is that of the Enlightenment. In his well-known essay "Beantwortung der Frage: Was Ist Aufklärung?" Immanuel Kant epitomized the ideals of the Enlightenment with the Horatian adage, "Aude sapere."[4] By critically using our intellectual capacities, man can free himself of superstition and take the lead of his own life.

Ideology as Illusory Speculation

A second concept of ideology we have to discuss is the use of the word in another derogatory sense: ideology as the accumulation of idealistic, pretentious principles, thought out by philosophers in their ivory towers, without relevance for practical-minded politicians and other well-thinking people. In this sense the word was coined by Napoleon.

The meaning of the word in the sense Napoleon used it is still in vogue. The concept of ideology first appeared in the work of the French philosopher Antoine Destutt de Tracy (1754-1836), who used the word "ideology" in 1796 to mean a science of ideas, a program of reductive semantic analysis that would lead to institutional reforms, beginning with a sweeping reform of French schools. Napoleon was initially sympathetic to the ideas of Destutt de Tracy and his circle, but later he became estranged from their work and dismissed the "ideologues" as impractical visionaries.[5]

Although Marx adopted the Napoleonic fashion of using "ideology" as a term of contempt, there is a significant difference in the way Napoleon uses the word and the way Marx would later use it. For Napoleon ideology was the idle speculation of the powerless against those who wield power, whereas according to Marx it was mainly the powerful that used ideology to suppress the weak. However, both agreed on rejecting ideology as misleading.

Ideology as Coherent Presentation of Our Political Conviction

Finally, I will treat a third conception of ideology. This time it is the concept in a neutral, a nonderogatory sense. It is ideology as the *comprehensive, systematized, and coherent presentation of our political convictions.* In this sense the word is used in the titles of books on political ideologies. When John Gray writes about *Liberalism,*[6] Bernard Crick on *Socialism,*[7] or Ted Honderich on *Conservatism,*[8] these writers are not engaged in presenting liberalism as false consciousness or socialism as an assemblage of useless speculation. They present us a more-or-less neutral (although in some ways critical) presentation of what those political ideologies stand for. I favor this last semantic approach of the word "ideology."

That means that it is very important to distinguish this last conception of ideology sharply from the other two. One can be vehemently opposed to ideology in the first two senses, but still be enthusiastic about ideology in the third sense. Actually, that is the stance I would venture to defend in this article. That defense has two dimensions. I will contend, first, the normative claim that developing an ideology as a global perspective in the third sense is a valuable human enterprise and, second, that ideology as the coherent presentation of our political convictions will never vanish.

The first thesis entails the task of refuting the much-advanced claim that ideology in the third sense necessarily leads to ideology in one of the first two senses. But let us first try to frame a more elaborate idea of what ideology in the third sense can be. First, it is a *total* vision of political reality. It tries to develop a concept of society as a whole, at least from the perspective of political thought. It brings also a certain *coherence* to our political ideas and tries to give a *justification* for them.[9] Political ideology in the nonderogatory sense is concerned with questions such as the following: What is the proper ambit of state activity? How do we visualize the relation of the individual to the state? Does society rest on an overlapping consensus of values? Do individuals have any natural rights?

Characteristic of ideology in the third sense is that we try to bring our conviction A in relation to conviction B. We do not feel satisfied with a chaotic mass of atomistic ideas and feelings toward political and social problems, but we try to see some unity, some conceptual framework, in our ideas. One of the aims of the Delphi Society has to do with this specific striving.

Most people hesitate to assert that they have an ideology. They consider themselves to be concerned with concrete and pragmatic questions, not with such philosophical activities as developing a vision of reality as a whole. Many people will even envisage this as a somewhat pompous affair, and some as superfluous. Yet, when they are confronted with some shocking events they are usually less hesitant in presenting their reasons for their indignation. When pressed further, they even give a justification for their anger, bringing those reasons in harmony with each other. What happens is that gradually something of a coherent set of ideas comes to the fore. Step by step the person in question is presenting her coherent and systematized set of ideas and explaining the relation of these ideas towards each other.

Take the case of Salman Rushdie. When he was sentenced to death by Iranian fanatics, a wave of indignation spread across the Western world about this fundamentalist medievalism. Demonstrations were held, discussions organized, petitions of adherence presented, and so on. What was especially striking was that people who had never thought about the right of free speech suddenly felt themselves obliged to stand for it, in deeds as well as for the justification of this important democratic principle. Cultural relativism is usually at a low ebb in those kinds of confrontations. People suddenly realize that their ideas are not contingent facts of life and that principles such as free speech (or for that matter freedom of religion) are not the arbitrary makeup of this liberal society, but that these principles have a justification and that people can be asked to justify their principles.

I do not hesitate to say that in the face of our current problems we will develop new schemes, new global approaches, and that we will reject the postmodern, nihilistic tendencies of contemporary thought.

Notes

1. Compare Jean-François Lyotard, *La condition postmoderne* (Paris: Les Editions de Minuit, 1979), and *Le Postmoderne expliqué aux enfants* (Paris: Éditions Galiée, 1988), pp. 35ff.

2. Francis Fukuyama, "The End of History?" *The National Interest,*

(Summer 1989), and *The End of History and the Last Man* (New York: The Free Press, 1992).

3. Compare the commentary in A.V. Dicey, *An Introduction to the Study of the Law of the Constitution* (London 1987 [1885]), p. 77.

4. Immanuel Kant, *Schriften zur Anthropologie, Geschichtsphilosophie, Politik und Pädagogik I,* vol. 11 (Frankfurt am Main: Wilhelm Weischedel, Suhrkamp, 1964), pp. 53ff.

5. Compare David Braybrooke, "Ideology," in *The Encyclopedia of Philosophy,* Paul Edwards, ed., vol. 4 (New York: Macmillan, 1967), p. 127.

6. John Gray, *Liberalism* (Open University Press, Milton Keynes, 1986).

7. Bernard Crick, *Socialism* (Open University Press, Milton Keynes, 1987).

8. Ted Honderich, *Conservatism* (Harmondsworth, England: Penguin Books, 1991 [1990]).

9. Compare Stephen Macedo, *Liberal Virtues: Citizenship, Virtue, and Community in Liberal Constitutionalism* (Oxford: Clarendon Press, 1991), pp. 39 ff.

21

The Negative Role of Religions

Antony G. N. Flew

There have in different times and places been innumerable different systems of religious belief and practice. Most of these often extremely unsystematic systems presumably possessed both some positive and some negative as well no doubt as some neutral role or roles. But if we are to find any role, or roles, whether positive or negative or neutral, which characterizes, or which characterize, all religions it will surely have to be one, or it will have to be those, which necessarily characterizes, or characterize, all religions as such. But, before proceeding to that more philosophical inquiry, I will first simply mention in passing the most important negative role played by any system of religious belief during our twentieth century and will follow that with a similar mention of my own favorite example of a positive role.

This most important negative role is that played by the Roman Catholic church in its total opposition to what it insists upon describing as artificial contraception. (The permitted, supposedly natural alternative is that described by Polish wits as "Vatican roulette.") That church has of course from time to time been joined in this campaign by various, sometimes surprisingly different allies.[1] The main but by no means the only reason for accounting this total opposition as importantly negative is that, without such effective checks upon population increase, it must remain practically impossible to abolish real, absolute, Third World poverty (as opposed, that is, to the very different, not to say factitious, relative, First World variety). (For instance: of the approximately 20 percent of the population of the United Kingdom recognized as thus relatively poor, over 40 percent possess both color television sets and video recorders.)

Suppose, for instance, a population is rising at 3 percent a year. The whole economy will then have to expand at that same rate if the average standard of living is not actually to decline. The amount by which economic growth exceeds the population growth rate constitutes the only surplus available to finance improvements in anyone's standard of living. Since population growth rates of 3 percent or more are today common in Third World countries, and indeed in some such scarcely Third World countries as Syria and Jordan, it should be obvious that and why in such countries investments in effective birth control programs are the investments most likely to yield the greatest and the most sustainable improvements in average living standards.

It would be unfair and unbalanced not to give that same Roman Catholic church due credit for the part played by Catholicism in bringing about the collapse of the Soviet empire. Had it not been for the fact that the vast majority of the Polish people are exceptionally devoted Catholics, and that their Catholicism is so closely identified with their Polish nationalism, Poland would surely not have been the least tractable of the Soviet quasicolonies and the first to emancipate itself.[2] In its final stages the process was, of course, substantially advanced by the election and subsequent activities of a remarkable Polish pope.

So much for what I see as the chief contemporary negative and positive roles of one major religion. Now for the more universal, philosophical question of the negative role of religion as such. The first move must be to ask what are the defining characteristics of religious belief. I suggest that, at least for present purposes, there are two and only two essentials. The first is that a religion involves belief in the existence of one or more supernatural beings. The second is that a religion involves the belief that these supernatural beings either require something from us humans and/or can be persuaded to do something for us. The gods of Epicurus, who were neither interested nor participants in human affairs, must be disqualified as gods of religion on the second count. The God of Spinoza, of the Spinozist Einstein,[3] must be similarly disqualified on both counts: a God identified with Nature (*Deus sive Natura*) cannot be either a supernatural being or—*a fortiori*—a supernatural partisan participant in human affairs.

It is, surely, obvious that beliefs in supernatural beings which do have some concern with human affairs can and do have substantial effects both positive and negative on human conduct. That they were originally invented and introduced for that purpose was, it would seem, first, and perhaps I should add, mistakenly, maintained by Plato's uncle Critias, the leader of the Thirty Tyrants who seized and for a time maintained despotic power over Athens after the disastrous defeat in the Peloponnesian War.[4] The religious beliefs in this case were, of course, beliefs in the existence and activities of the Olympians. Plato himself was later to advocate systematic censorship of the bad examples so often set by these gods.[5] It is remarkable that Plato's concern was throughout more with the likely behavioral effects of believing various religious doctrines than with their truth or falsity.

He, surely, would have found it difficult to dissent from Freud's contention that religious doctrines are, one and all, illusions. Freud begins by pointing out that they "tell one something that one has not oneself discovered and . . . claim that one should give [these dogmas] credence."[6] But, since the evidence for their truth is so inadequate if not altogether lacking, we should recognize them as illusions. "An illusion," however, "is not the same as an error, it is indeed not necessarily an error."[7] Freud would have us speak of "a belief as an illusion when wish-fulfillment is a prominent factor in its motivation."[8]

We need here to make a fundamental distinction between two kinds of reason, two senses of the word "reason." In one sense, the evidencing sense, a reason is something which is designed to show, or to help to show, that some proposition is in fact true. In the other sense, the motivating sense, a reason is something which provides people with a motive for believing or for pretending to believe or for trying to induce themselves to believe, that some proposition is in fact true.

The classical argument to which this fundamental distinction can most illuminatingly be applied is that of what has traditionally been labeled Pascal's Wager.[9] Pascal begins by insisting that reason—by which he means what we would distinguish as evidencing reason—"can decide nothing here." He then attempts to reveal to unbelievers that we have an overwhelmingly strong motivating reason to induce ourselves to believe that the doctrines of the Roman Catholic church are true. We should, Pascal, argues, be madly imprudent not to do so. The fatal fault in this argument is, given that no evidencing reasons are available to probabilify any of the infinite array of theoretically possible alternatives upon one of which individuals have to bet their lives, Pascal is not warranted to assume that there are only two: Roman Catholicism and atheist naturalism. Today the most widely urged of these theoretically possible alternatives is Islam, which threatens all unbelievers, and specifically all Christians, with an eternity of torture.[10]

Given the fundamental distinction between kinds of reason, senses of the word "reason," we can appreciate Freud's contention as being that there are no sufficient evidencing reasons to believe that any religious doctrines are true, and that the origin and continuation of such beliefs is to be explained by reference solely to motivating reasons. Religious dogmas, he wrote, "are not the residue of experience or the final result of reflection; they are illusions, fulfillments of the oldest, strongest and most insistent wishes of mankind; the secret of their strength is the strength of these wishes."[11]

We may well accept the first of these contentions—about the lack of sufficient evidencing reasons for believing—without accepting the second, the contention about the sufficient explanation for the origin and continuation of religious beliefs. For it is surely manifest that many believers—however mistakenly—do still believe, as most believers in the past presumably believed, that they do have sufficient evidencing reasons for holding the religious beliefs which they do hold. Indeed, what must now be called the First Vatican Council proclaimed as defined dogmata of the Roman Catholic church: not only "that the one and true God our creator and Lord can be known through the creation by the natural light of human reason,"[12] but also that, "If anyone shall say, that miracles cannot happen . . . or that the divine origin of the Christian religion cannot properly be proved by them: let him be anathema."[13]

Taking for granted his contention about the lack of sufficient evidencing reasons for holding any positive religious beliefs, Freud proceeds to argue that most of us could and should dispense with all religious illusions. This means restricting our belief to those propositions which we have the best available evidencing reason to believe to be true. For, as Freud insists in conclusion, "Science is no illusion. But it would be an illusion to suppose that we could get anywhere else what it cannot give us."[14]

If once it is or were to be granted that religious beliefs are all illusions, in the sense that they are beliefs which there is no sufficient evidencing reason for holding to be true beliefs, then it surely follows that the negative role of religions is that they necessarily represent as true what there is at best no sufficient evidencing reason to believe to be in fact true. This is not the occasion nor is there space here to develop a systematic case for the crucial contention that religious beliefs do indeed lack adequate evidential foundation. But there is room and it may perhaps be illuminating to indicate the lines on which scientifically well-informed persons, unprejudiced by their upbringing among what Islam knows as "the peoples of the book," might be expected to approach the questions of the existence and activities of the God about whom they have been informed or misinformed by generations of rabbis, priests, and imams.

Such persons could have no reason even to entertain the possibility of a revelation until and unless they were able to provide themselves or were provided with a persuasive natural theology. For without a natural theology strong enough to probabilify the supernatural vouchsafing of some supplementary revelation, such scientifically minded enquirers would have to argue that the very fact that the stories of miraculously endorsed supposed revelations were stories of miraculous occurrences was a sufficient reason for dismissing them as untrue.[15] They would have, therefore, to start from the findings of natural science. But, since these findings include the achievements of Darwin, they could scarcely see organisms as premises for an argument to design. In seeking a cause for the beginning of the universe they would turn to the cosmologists and expect, if they were given any cause for the Big Bang, to be given a cause of the inorganic and impersonal kind which constitutes the stock in trade of a physicist.

If, *per impossible*, any of these inquirers did put forward the bold, not to say reckless, conjecture that the universe is created and maintained by an omnipotent and omniscient personal being, then it would surely never occur to them to suggest that such a being might be somehow acting as a partisan participant in human conflicts within it. It would appear obvious to such unprejudiced inquirers that everything which occurs or does not occur within a universe so created must, by the hypothesis, be precisely and only what its omnipotent and omniscient creator wants either to occur or not to occur. For what scope could there be for creatures really to defy the will of their creator? What room even for a concept of such defiance? So for such a creator to punish creatures for what, by the hypothesis, he necessarily and as such ultimately causes them to do would be the most monstrous, perverse, and sadistic of performances.[16] Such a creator would most naturally be conceived—as, I am told, some Indian thinkers describe their God—to be "beyond good and evil."

The step from the existence of a creator to the conclusion that the creator is indeed any sort of partisan in the created universe is as big as it is crucial. Because they have taken absolutely for granted a prejudicial conception of a creator, assuming that anything possessing any of the elements of that conception must necessarily possess them all, many even of the greatest thinkers have made this step without noticing, and in consequence without anxiously seeking some justification for, the making of it. Joseph Butler, who held the senior see of Durham in days when a Christian commitment was still a precondition for securing such appointments, was certainly one of the two finest philosophical minds ever to adorn the Church of England's bench of bishops. Yet even he, having in his *Analogy of Religion* deployed what he considered a sufficient natural theology, stated his "Conclusion" to be that:

> There is no need of abstruse reasonings and distinctions, to convince an unprejudiced understanding, that there is a God who made and governs the world, *and will judge it in righteousness* . . . to an unprejudiced mind ten thousand instances of design cannot but prove a designer.[17] [Emphasis added]

To Butler it thus seemed utterly obvious that a proof of a designer and maker of the universe must at the same time be a proof that that designer and maker will also be a righteous judge, rewarding and punishing. Yet earlier in that same work of natural theology Butler had himself confessed that the natural world provided no warrant for that conclusion:

> Upon supposition that God exercises a moral government over the world, the analogy of this natural government suggests and makes it credible that this moral government must be a scheme quite beyond our comprehension; and that this affords a general answer to all objections against the justice and goodness of it.[18]

In this perspective we can gain a greater appreciation of the world-historical achievement of the children of Israel: namely, the transformation of a one-among-many tribal god into the unique, omniscient, omnipotent, creator God of "the peoples of the book." It is entirely natural to conceive tribal gods as being devoted to the values and interests of the tribe, endorsing its established norms and providing support in its wars. That, after all, is what such gods are for. But how could anyone who was open-mindedly and for the first time entertaining the idea of an omnipotent and omniscient creator, and who was not prejudiced by influences deriving from that book, ever possibly think of such a being as a partisan in conflicts within creation? Such ideas have no place within a natural theology, and there can be no evidencing as opposed to motivating reasons for introducing them there.

I cannot end more appropriately than by quoting from the concluding words of one of the great series of Gifford lectures, Sir Charles Sherrington's *Man on His Nature*. They well express his—and my—positive reaction to the negative role of religions:

If you will man's situation is left bleaker . . . compared with a situation in which the human mind . . . had higher mind and higher personality . . . to learn and to take counsel from, this other situation where it has no appeal and no resort beyond itself, has . . . an element of tragedy and pathos. To set against that, it is a situation which transforms the human task . . . to one of loftier responsibility. . . . We have, because human, an inalienable prerogative of responsibility which we cannot devolve, no, not as once was thought, even upon the stars. We can share it only with each other.[19]

Notes

1. For instance, at the World Population Conference held in Rome in 1954, delegates from Roman Catholic countries were constantly found in holy-unholy alliance with delegates from Communist countries. They were together committed to denying that there were or could be problems of overpopulation. The Communists no doubt remembered how in his 1844 *Outline of a Critique of Political Economy* Engels had abused Malthus for producing his "vile, infamous theory, this revolting blasphemy against nature and mankind." What a pity that no one then seems to have noticed the much later letter to Kautsky (February 1, 1881) in which Engels claimed that, if and when population problems did arise, a Communist society would be best qualified to solve them.

2. This is not the place to deploy evidence for this contention. But I will not resist the temptation to tell of the atheist Polish academic who, during my first visit to Poland in 1966, wryly and mischievously asked for sympathy for his predicament: "I have now to attend mass lest people should think I am a Communist."

3. For a statement of Einstein's reasons for being in this understanding an atheist, see Albert Einstein, *Out of My Later Years* (London: Thames and Hudson, 1950), pp. 26–27. For most of these later years Einstein was an honorary associate of the Rationalist Press Association.

4. H. Diel, *Die Fragmente der Vorschratiker,* W. Kranz, ed. (5th and

later editions, Berlin, 1934–54), fragment 25. For a critique of such pre-social scientific speculations, see Antony Flew, *Thinking about Social Thinking* (London: HarperCollins, 1991), ch. 5.

5. Plato, *The Republic,* pp. 376Eff.

6. Sigmund Freud, *The Future of an Illusion,* W. D. Robson-Scott, trans. (London: Hogarth, 1928), p. 43.

7. Ibid., p. 53.

8. Ibid., pp. 54–55.

9. For a more thorough treatment of this argument, which, in a form offering Islam as the alternative to atheist unbelief, is to be found first in the Muslim writer Al Ghazali, see Antony Flew, *An Introduction to Western Philosophy: Ideas and Argument from Plato to Popper,* rev. ed. (London: Thames and Hudson, 1989), pp. 218–21.

10. See, for instance, Paul Kurtz, ed., *Challenges to the Enlightenment: In Defense of Reason and Science* (Amherst, N.Y.: Prometheus Books, 1994), ch. 20.

11. Freud, *The Future of an Illusion,* p. 52.

12. Heinrich Denzinger, *Enchiridion Symbolorum,* 29th ed. (Freiberg i-Breisgau: Herder, 1953), sec. 1806.

13. Ibid., sec. 1813.

14. Freud, *The Future of an Illusion,* p. 98.

15. For a neo-Humian argument to this conclusion see, for instance, Antony Flew, *Atheistic Humanism* (Amherst, N.Y.: Prometheus Books), ch. 3.

16. Yet precisely this is the cosmic vision presented by the Koran. See, for instance, Kurtz, *Challenges to the Enlightenment,* ch. 20, especially pp. 276–79 and attached notes.

17. Joseph Butler, *Butler's Works,* W. E. Gladstone, ed., vol. 1 (Oxford: Oxford University Press, 1896), p. 371.

18. Ibid., p. 162.

19. Sir Charles Sherrington, *Man on His Nature* (Cambridge: Cambridge University Press, 1940), p. 404.

22

Neurobiological Bases of Modern Humanism

José M. R. Delgado

At the Tenth Humanist Congress held in Buffalo, New York, in August 1988, speakers emphasized the need to build a world community for the twenty-first century based on freedom, interdependence, science, reason, and global ethics.

Since all these elements depend on the functioning of the human brain, knowledge of neuronal structures and their activities is essential for the understanding of human manifestations of intelligence and personality.

In agreement with Eibl-Ebesfeldt, Hirsch, Kupfermann and Weiss, and many other investigators,[1] behavior is related to two, and only two, elements: our genes and the sensory inputs received from the environment. Heredity determines much of our structure as *Homo sapiens*. We are born with innate programs which control reflex activities, such as blinking, swallowing, and coughing, without the need of learning. Their neurological mechanisms are related to specific driving neurons which activate groups of neurons and muscles to perform complex motor functions.[2] Perhaps there are commands to trigger these pre-established neuronal mechanisms. Only man has the capacity to speak, yet we do not have some abilities that other animals possess. While we lack sensors to recognize the presence of magnetic fields, ultrasound, infrared light, cosmic rays, and many other stimuli, we can detect them with transducers invented by man. Our innate intelligence, however, has biological limits and we have little understanding of a variety of subjects of crucial importance, including infinity, eternity, reasons for existence of the universe, and the purpose of human life.

The second element essential for our development is stimuli from our surroundings. There is a similarity between baby food chosen by parents and the early sensory inputs which are provided to each child by chance or by parental care. In both cases, the individual is a passive recipient: initially an infant cannot choose or modify his environment because his neuronal networks are still very immature. Food will be digested, absorbed in the intestines, and metabolized to develop the bones, muscles, and body of each growing baby. Information penetrates through the senses, circulates within the nervous system and influences the growth of dendrites and neurons which are the bases for developing mental activities, systems of values, intelligence, and behavioral reactivity.

These mechanisms of learning, storing of experiences, and evaluation of reality are essential for the process of humanization and for the structuring of personal identity. The individual mind is formed by extracerebral elements of information and experience which enter the brain through the portals of the senses and then are circulated, combined, and stored intracerebrally, eliciting external manifestations of behavior. Reception and decodification of incoming signals require referential systems which are not contained in the information but evolve gradually during the process of learning. One objective of education should be to give each individual a better understanding of his behavioral and mental potential, clarifying biological and cultural determinants in order to obtain a greater degree of personal freedom and diminish possible manipulation by the elites who monopolize power and knowledge.

Due to anatomical and physiological limitations, our brain can never be in direct contact with reality, only with its symbolic representations which penetrate through the senses and circulate within the neuronal networks in the form of electrical, chemical, and microanatomical phenomena.[3] Sensory receptors transduce external stimuli, codifying them as spatiotemporal patterns of neuronal discharges. The perfume of a rose is transmitted by molecules which reach our nostrils and activate olfactory sensors to initiate electrical activity circulating inside the brain, affecting specific areas of the limbic system to produce a pleasant sensation.

While reductionism and materialism should be avoided, we must recognize our dependence on supporting neuronal mechanisms for the existence of sensations, emotions, and humanism. Neuronal and mental activities should be considered as two integral aspects of our biological unity, with semantic, instrumental, and intellectual limits which must be investigated separately within each organism.[4]

One similarity between computers and brains concerns the processing of information because, in both cases, the outside world can only circulate inside as codes. The essential difference is that unlike the computer, the brain has a mysterious inner sensitivity enabling it to "feel" sensations and to react emotionally. Where is the decodifying mechanism? How do we learn to decipher the meaning of the circulating signals? We do know that learning is totally necessary in order to comprehend: previous experiences stored in the referential system of memory allow us to compare the present with the past. The meaning of symbols is not transmitted by genes. Similar messages may be expressed in English, Spanish, Arabic, or in any other idiom with very different sounds and written symbols. The meaning of humanism is interpreted in different ways by each culture and this affects each individual. Some universal values depend on the anatomical and physiological structuring of the brain. We are at the beginning of a new era which may be considered mental and neuro-biological, with consequences more transcendental than the past industrial and technological revolutions, because we have the potential to influence the spiritual conditions of human beings, their own self-realization and happiness, the humanization of man, and to diminish individual and collective violence. These goals may be considered difficult and utopic, but every attempt at a local level should be encouraged and can ultimately affect human society.

While genetic evolution is slow and may take millennia, cultural evolution is very fast and may be accomplished in only one or two generations. With the aid of present knowledge and technologies, the future evolution of man does not depend on blind natural destiny, as in the past, but on human intelligence and cooperation to establish aims and strategies. The evolution of the species can be affected by these plans, which should be developed to optimize human potential in agreement with the biology of all individuals, integrating races, cultures, and philosophies.

Until recently, cerebral manifestations were beyond scientific reach because the brain was well protected by teguments and skull and no suitable technologies had been developed. Now we can study the depth of the brain with invasive as well as noninvasive methods, relating neuronal activities with specific sensations and behavioral manifestations. The essence of our humanity resides within the brain and depends on chemical and electrical neuronal activity, which are the essential material support for all physiological and mental manifestations.

We should not identify material mechanisms with the mind, while accepting their importance for the maintenance of life. In the absence of oxygen, glucose, blood circulation, and other elements and functions, obviously we could not think or love. Memory is related to the synthesis of proteins; early sensory stimulation is decisive for the establishment of dendritic connections. Introduction within the brain of minute amounts of neurotransmitters such as serotonin, acetylcholine, amino acids, and other substances, may produce spectacular effects, increasing or decreasing aggressiveness, sleep, appetite, sexuality, and other behavioral activities. Our growing ability to investigate and modify the physiological mechanisms of the mind is improving our understanding of humanity, including our biological, emotional, and intellectual potential. We may now begin to explore the fundamentals of personal identity, education, and even the purpose of human life. These possibilities represent a tremendous responsibility and power, new in the history of civilization, to influence the biological structuring and behavioral manifestations of man and to establish the functional bases of modern humanism. We must decide what kinds of human qualities and attributes we would like to encourage, why and how. Who is going to propose suitable plans, what will be their purpose, how will these plans be accomplished, which techniques should be used, and what risks should be recognized and avoided?

We have begun to develop technologies to influence neuronal and mental activities. It is therefore imperative to reach common agreement concerning ethical bases of behavior. Humanism should play a decisive role in this endeavor.

A plan for the future action of humanism should take in consideration the following:

1. The brain is shaped by only two elements: genes and sensory inputs. We may investigate the mechanisms of each and should use this knowledge intelligently and ethically.

2. The human personality, with all its good and bad characteristics, develops according to the physical and cultural environment provided.

3. The present is very different from the past due to technological revolutions. General education should use anticipatory thinking in order to foresee and prevent future problems, and should also encourage participatory activities in finding original solutions. Some aspects of traditional philosophies and beliefs should be recognized as outmoded.

4. There is a *biological unity* of all human beings determined by the similarities of their anatomy and functions. This reality should be the basis for unifying mankind.

5. Many aspects of the civilized world have been created not by Nature but by the inventions of our working brains. We must know and ethically use this artificiality.

6. Personality is shaped by the frames of reference inculcated in children's brains without their knowledge or consent. This fact represents a strong initial limitation of personal freedom.

7. The brain has specific structures for the perception of pleasure and pain. Pleasure areas are stimulated with greater intensity by spiritual and artistic inputs than by materialistic satisfactions. A new direction of education, drives, and motivation is necessary.

8. Teaching of facts is an essential part of education, but we should also teach critical evaluation, including how to think and how to be happy.

9. Humanization of man should be the most important task for future generations.

Notes

1. I. Eibl-Eibesfeldt, *Ethology: The Biology of Behavior* (New York: Holt, Rinehart and Winston, 1970); J. Hirsch, ed., *Behavior-Genetic Analysis* (New York: McGraw Hill, 1967); and I. Kupfermann and K. R. Weiss, "The Command Neuron Concept," *Behavioral and Brain Sciences* 1 (1978): 3–39.

2. C. A. G. Wiersma, "Function of the Giant Fibers of the Central Nervous System of the Crayfish," *Proceedings of the Society of Experimental Biology and Medicine* 38 (1938): 661–68.

3. J. M. R. Delgado, *Physical Control of the Mind: Toward a Psychocivilized Society* (New York: Harper & Row, 1969).

4. J. M. R. Delgado, "Triunism: A Transmaterial Brain-Mind Theory," in *Brain and Mind,* Ciba Foundation Symp. 69, new series (Amsterdam: Excerpta Medica, 1979), pp. 369–96.

23

Models of Human Brain Functions and Dysfunctional Elements in Human History: A Close Relation

Martha Koukkou and Dietrich Lehmann

This contribution presents an integrative, systems theory–oriented model of the functions of the human brain. Based on this model[1] we discuss (1) the functions of the human brain which mediate human survival and psychobiological health and well-being, that is, human wisdom, and (2) the factors which cause deviations of these brain functions and thus may result in the dramatically dysfunctional relationships of humans to themselves and to the earth: the paranoid elements in human history.

The model emerged as synthesis of data and theories from a broad spectrum of neuroscience disciplines concerned with functions of the human brain and with the relationships between brain functions and behavior. The basic message which comes from this *synthesis of data and theories* is the following: The main cause of the dysfunctional relationships of humans to themselves, to their own children, and to their physical environment has to be sought in a basic philosophical error, in other words, in a sum of false scientific and philosophical assumptions that humans have made in their historical efforts to explain their own nature, the organizing principles and the aims of their behavior as well as the meaning of their relationships to the earth. *These false assumptions produce their negative effects through the brain functions with which humans internalize their culture, mainly during development.*

Examples of what is meant by false assumptions about human nature and its organizing principles are proposals such as the following: human destructive behavior is the result of a fault in the biological evolution of mankind; or, the human neocortex is poorly coordinated with phylogenetically older structures of the human nervous system that are supposed to produce innate human aggression; or, the concept of dualism, and the endless discussions about separation between brain and mind, intellect and physical world, rational and emotional processes, and nature and nurture in development. *The common characteristic of such false assumptions is the misunderstanding of the brain processes which underlie the genesis of the dimensions of human existence that have been called "mind."* This corresponds to the misunderstanding of the functions of the human neocortex. We are glad to be able to refer to other authors who also explicitly or implicitly proposed that such concepts about human nature are erroneous.[2]

Thus, most of these false assumptions have been questioned and this leads to some important revisions. These revisions, however, have not yet reached the broader family of neuroscientists, the decisionmakers, and the general public. Thus, humanity continues to use archaic ideas about human nature and about humanity's needs in order to decide about health and disease, human rights, and peace and war; peace and war with ourselves, with other parts of humanity, or with the earth itself.

There is no space to discuss why such false assumptions may

have developed. We concentrate on *how* and *why* false, verbalized philosophical or scientific assumptions not only produce dysfunctional behavior, but also dysfunctional results in applications of some otherwise ingenious scientific human achievements aiming to shape their relationships to themselves and to the earth.

The Model of the Functions of the Human Brain

THE THEORETICAL FRAMEWORK: THE SYSTEMS THEORY APPROACH

Systems theory is concerned with problems of organized complexity. Life is a phenomenon of organized complexity. The dynamics of human brain-behavior relationships have been studied within the framework of systems theory.[3] From the perspectives of this theory a system is a "whole" composed of a set of parts (subsystems) and at the same time is a subsystem of bigger and more complex systems. The behavior of each system *presupposes* and *emerges out of* the continuous and dynamic interaction between systems and subsystems. A given degree of cooperative interaction between systems and subsystems is the prerequisite for keeping the balance between the interactive systems on a functional level. Thus, each system's behavior is studied in terms of relations and interactions, in terms of goals and aims of these interactions, and in terms of organizing principles. False basic scientific assumptions about human behavior concern its aims and its organizing principles.

Within the framework of our model, human behavior presupposes and emerges out of the continuous, dynamic, and parallel interactions of the individual with his/her external (social and physical) and internal environments. A human's internal environment is (1) the functions of the different organs, for example, the heart, muscles, brain, and the like, and (2) the sum of the knowledge that has been created in the individual's brain as result of the interactions.

This knowledge is about the social and physical realities in which the individual is born and lives, about the self, and about the qualities and consequences of the interactions between the self and reality. Thus, human behavior emerges out of a continuous, dynamic, and parallel interaction of the individual (the living system "human being") with his/her acquired knowledge, his/her body functions (the functions of the subsystems = the organs, including the brain) and his/her social and physical environment. The aims of these continuous interactions are: (1) the perception of the messages which continuously reach the brain from the internal and external realities; (2) the acquisition of knowledge about the informational significance of the momentary configurations of these messages for the psychobiological health of the individual; and (3) the knowledge-implemented (memory-driven) functional adaptation of all aspects of behavior to this significance.

Thus, human behavior can be defined in terms of a continuous and dynamic interaction of the individual with his/her internal and external realities, and in terms of a continuous knowledge-dependent, knowledge-implemented, and knowledge-reflecting psychobiological adaptation to the informational significance of the messages which come from the realities. The basic argument is that behavior, thus defined, is initially always purposeful and well-adaptive. The goals of behavior are primarily the maintenance of the psychobiological health of the individual within his/her often unpredictably changing environments, and secondarily the creation of knowledge which enables the maintenance and/or restoration of the psychobiological health or the avoidance, reduction, removal, and so on, of obstacles to this goal. *Humans are seen as self-organizing living systems that are oriented towards survival, psychobiological health, growth, differentiation and autonomy, and that are knowledge-dependent and knowledge-implementing.*

HUMAN BEHAVIOR AND THE HUMAN BRAIN

The evidence integrated into the model shows that (1) human behavior is a multifactorially defined and multidimensionally manifested psychobiological phenomenon; (2) the brain, and specifically the neocortex, is the organ which generates and coordinates all dimensions of human behavior (emotions, thoughts, actions, decisions, plans, and so on); (3) knowledge acquired and created in the individual's brain is the internal organizing principle, the locus of generation, coordination, and control of well- or maladaptive human behavior by the brain; and (4) humans are born with a basic set of continuously recycling, highly complex, multifactorially defined, multiply and multilevel feedback-controlled and interdependent psychobiological operations (*the cycle of human communication*), with which they start their postnatal lives in dynamic interaction with their internal and external environments. With these operations, humans cumulatively acquire and create in their brains knowledge about their realities, and continuously update, enlarge, and use this knowledge for the organization of all dimensions of their present and future behavior.

Thus, knowledge acquired and created in the individual's brain as a result of the interactions with the internal and external realities in turn shapes the realities which can be perceived, felt, remembered, thought, planned, imagined, and the like. This knowledge also shapes the recognition of the meaning of the messages which come from these realities as well as the decisions humans make. These decisions shape the quality of human actions and thus the relationships of humans to themselves and to the world around them.[4]

Accordingly, there can be no innate aggressive human "drive" which causes maladaptive and catastrophic behavior. The main determinant of the quality of human interactions with the realities and of therewith emerging behavior, be it well- or maladaptive, be it co-

operative with the earth or catastrophic, and so on, is the quality of
the created knowledge in the human brain. The human brain is considered to be a knowledge-creating system, which organizes itself
and the individual's well- or maladaptive behavior on the basis of its
biography.

PSYCHOBIOLOGICAL DEVELOPMENT

The evidence integrated in this model shows that already at birth
healthy infants have at their disposal all the brain functions necessary
to start their postnatal life in a given physical environment as active
members of their social group.[5] Basic innate knowledge enables the
newborn (1) to use the operations of the cycle of communication in
order to explore and evaluate the messages from the internal and external realities in regard to their effects on the organism's well-functioning; (2) to respond to these messages with response patterns
which keep the organism well-functioning or restore its inbalances;
and (3) to call upon the caregivers (the social environment) to get involved and take care of the well-functioning of the organism when
the innate response patterns do not suffice.

The prerequisite of postnatal survival is active interaction with
the caregivers and their active involvement. The quality of this involvement, that is, the way with which mothers, fathers, pediatri-
cians, or other caregivers, and, later, teachers, psychologists, priests,
and so on, interact with the child and take care of the child's priorities and needs (psychobiological health), depends on the facts, cultural assumptions, and beliefs known to them about the nature and
needs of human beings, the aims and meanings of interactions with
children, the aims and ways of education, what is "normal" or "ab-
normal," what is "good" or "bad," the meaning of interactions with
the earth, and so on, and on their biography.

Infants have at birth no knowledge about the characteristics of the physical environment, socioeconomic status, physical condition, and the like, as well as the beliefs, values, habits, national and religious dogmas, and so on, of the social reality into which they are born. Via the interactions with this social reality and with the physical environment, children cumulatively acquire and create in their brains knowledge about themselves and their realities, and use this knowledge to form behavior.

In other words, from the moment of birth, children (future decisionmakers) are in constant interaction with adults who seek directly or indirectly to shape the children on the basis of their own biography and historically accumulated beliefs on meanings and ways of behavior in their culture. These unavoidable interactions shape the knowledge which is created in the child's brain (in the brains of the next generation) and thereby shape the psychobiological development of the individual and the behavior of the next generations.

Knowledge acquired and created in the individual's brain as a result of cooperative interactions with the social realities leads to creation of knowledge, which results in a well-adaptive behavior. The cooperative interactions parallel the keeping of the balance between interacting systems on a functional level. Contrarywise, knowledge created in the individual's brain as a result of conflicting interactions with the social realities results in "paranoiac" relations of humans to the world and to themselves. Thus, creation of knowledge does not automatically mean intelligence and wisdom. It means the creation of a complex code of communication which mediates and modifies intrapersonal communication and the communication between individuals, generations, and social, national, and religious groups as well as the relationships of humans to the earth.

In other words, the basic determinant of the quality of human behavior, measured by humanity's psychobiological health and effects on the earth (be they intelligent and wise or maladaptive and catastrophic), is the quality of the knowledge which is created in the individual's brain, especially during development, through the inter-actions with the cultural values of the social environment. *This is the fundamental proposal of the theories and data synthesized in this model.*

Accordingly, the question arises: If our cultural beliefs include indeed false assumptions about the meaning of basic aspects of life, like the meaning of psychobiological health and the ways to achieve it, or the meaning of interactions with the earth, or the nature of human emotions, and so on, the result is that these false assumptions will be "inherited" by the next generation not via genes but via un-avoidable interactions. *Acquired knowledge of false assumptions leads to false perceptions, false understandings, and false interpre-tations of interactions, that is, to misunderstandings. Misunder-standings lead to dysfunctional interactions.*

The exponential growth of communication in our times expo-nentially multiplies the possibility that false assumptions are widely disseminated.

Conclusions

A neuroscience approach to the genesis of well-adaptive or dys-functional and destructive human behavior is presented in the form of a systems theory–oriented, integrative model of the functions of the human brain. This model emerged out of the theories and data in the neurosciences concerned with human brain-behavior relation-ships.

This synthesis showed that human behavior is generated and co-ordinated by the mnemonic functions of the human brain. With these functions, humans assimilate and use information from their internal and external environments in order to create retrievable symbolic representations of the outcome of the interactions with the environ-ments, as well as in order to (1) create individual knowledge about emotions, thoughts, plans, coping, and problem-solving cognitive-emotional strategies, skills, and the like; (2) coordinate behavior within their realities; and (3) manipulate the world around them, aiming primarily at keeping the interactions on a functional level. This knowledge has lead to the formulation of the various philosophical and scientific assumptions, as well as the cultural rules and beliefs of humankind.

The sum of the thus-acquired knowledge enables us at the end of the twentieth century to affect our world to such a degree that we must realize that we have become co-architects of the very future of the earth and of its inhabitants, including ourselves.

We met in Delphi because we realize that we may not always have done a good job scrutinizing our cultural beliefs and scientific decisions as to their adequacy for constructing a safe and sane future. We now ask ourselves why this is so, and how can we stop this negative development.

The data and theories integrated in our model of the functions of the human brain indicate that this poor job is not the result of a fault in the biological evolution of mankind. Thus, our destructive behavior is neither inevitable nor unalterable. The evidence shows that the basic causes of the dysfunctional relations of humans to themselves and to the earth result from a misunderstanding of the very meaning of human nature and specifically of brain-behavior relationships. However, as long as we keep misunderstanding the real nature of our problems, our efforts to find solutions cannot be successful. Hippocrates said, "Humans should not only try to find the causes of a phenomenon, but mainly the beginning of the causes of the phenomenon." Thus, more than ever before it is of vital importance that all kinds of thinkers become aware of two things: firstly, that there are false philosophical and scientific assumptions in our brains, and secondly, that the false internalized assumptions influence the way we perceive and evaluate the external world and ourselves and thereby influence the quality of our behavior as manifested in our dysfunctional interactions with ourselves, with our own children, and with the world.

The challenge to the neurosciences is to try to understand the way in which internalized false assumptions affect the brain's creative functions, and to realize that in order to participate efficiently in the effort to understand human destructive behavior one has to stop misunderstanding the human brain. In other words, the challenge to neuroscience is to recognize that the same creative brain functions which led to the scientific discoveries that have shaped the world in a functional or in a destructive way can be used to discover ways to stop this destruction.

The key issue is the task to rethink our own nature. This rethinking will enable us to realize that our destructive behavior is not due to some inherited evil in us or to some evil around us which we have to fight. Our destructive behavior results from our intensive but sometimes erroneous efforts to find solutions to problems whose causes we misunderstand. The hope is that once the causes are correctly understood, we will be able to trust again the creative functions of our brains and to use them to produce functional interventions, and thus produce well-being for the earth and its inhabitants, including ourselves. In doing this, we will live up to our creative potential and thus display wisdom.

Notes

1. M. Koukkou and D. Lehmann, "A Model of Dreaming and of Its Functional Significance: The State-Shift Hypothesis," in *The Functions of Dreaming*, A. Moffitt, M. Kramer, and R. Hoffmann, eds. (Albany, N.Y.: State University of New York Press, 1993), pp. 51–118; "An Information-Processing Perspective of Psychophysiological Measurements," *Journal of Psychophysiology* 1 (1987): 109–12; and "Dreaming: The Functional

State-Shift Hypothesis. A Neuropsychophysiological Model," *British Journal of Psychiatry* 142 (1983): 221–31; D. Lehmann, "Fluctuations of Functional State: EEG Patterns and Perceptual and Cognitive Strategies," in *Functional States of the Brain: Their Determinants*, M. Koukkou, D. Lehmann, and J. Angst, eds. (Amsterdam: Elsevier, 1980), pp. 189–202; and D. Lehmann and M. Koukkou, "Brain States of Visual Imagery and Dream Generation," in *The Psychophysiology of Mental Imagery: Theory, Research and Applications*, R. G. Kunzendorf and A. A. Sheikh, eds. (Amityville, N.Y.: Baywood, 1990), pp. 109–31.

2. See, for example, G. Baumgartner, "Organization and Function of the Neocortex," *Neuro-Ophthalmology* 3 (1983): 1–14; D. Bindra, *The Brain's Mind: A Neuroscience Perspective on the Mind-Body Problem* (New York: Gardner, 1980); G. M. Edelman, *Neural Darwinism: The Theory of Neuronal Group Selection* (New York: Basic Books, 1987); A. Gore, *Earth in the Balance* (New York: Penguin, 1993); P. Karli, *Animal and Human Aggression* (Oxford: Oxford University Press, 1991); J. Konorsky, *Integrative Activity of the Brain* (Chicago: University of Chicago Press, 1967); K. H. Pribram, *Languages of the Brain* (Englewood Cliffs, N.J.: Prentice Hall, 1971); and J. Szentagothai, "The Brain-Mind Relationship," in *The Brain-Mind Problem: Philosophical and Neurophysiological Approaches*, B. Gulyas, ed. (Assen/Maastricht: Leuven University Press, 1987), pp. 61–78.

3. L. Bertalanffy, "General System Theory and Psychiatry," in *American Handbook of Psychiatry*, vol. 3, S. Arieti, ed. (New York: Basic Books, 1974), pp. 705–21; and J. G. Miller, *Living Systems* (New York: McGraw-Hill, 1978).

4. L. Goldstein, "Brain Functions and Behavior: On the Origin and Evolution of Their Relationships," *Advances in Biological Psychiatry* 13 (1983): 75–79; J. Groebel and R. A. Hinde, eds. *Aggression and War: Their Biological and Social Bases* (Cambridge: Cambridge University Press, 1989); S. Grossberg, ed., *The Adaptive Brain I: Cognition, Learning, Reenforcement, and Rhythm* (Amsterdam: Elsevier, 1987), and *The Adaptive Brain II: Vision, Speech, Language, and Motor Control* (Amsterdam: Elsevier, 1987); E. R. Kandel and J. H. Schwartz, *Principles of*

Neural Science (New York: Elsevier, 1981); P. Karli, *Animal and Human Aggression*; J. Klama, *Aggression: Conflict in Animals and Humans Reconsidered* (Harlow, Essex: Longman, 1988); and D. Lehmann and M. Koukkou, "Brain States of Visual Imagery."

    5. G. Dawson and K. W. Fisher, eds., *Human Behavior and the Developing Brain* (London: Guilford, 1994); and S. Oyama, *The Ontogeny of Information* (Cambridge: Cambridge University Press, 1985).

24

Where to Humanism?

Joel Wilbush

It goes without saying that I am deeply grateful to the organizing committee and Dr. Razis for having invited me here and the honor they gave me of being the closing speaker. My only fear is that, having listened to me for forty minutes, you would not fully share my sentiments! This is our last day together. This is the last address of our meeting here at Delphi. It behooves me to speak of our determination to work for a better world, our resolve to make every effort to help humanity, of our hopes for the future. All this, while I still feel as if caught in a relentless march of events, a predestined course which cannot be changed: as if I were but a bit player in an ancient Greek tragedy.

And yet, I believe, it can be done: there is a way out, fate, the moirai, can be circumvented. I have, like all of you, considered numerous options, deliberated long over our position, sought some solution—but have come up with little more than a few questionable proposals, plans which are certain to be unpopular, projects sure to be rejected; with almost nothing which may even sound inspiring. But I still have one more suggestion: Let me put it before you and hope you find it interesting.

Humanity's "Paranoid" Behavior

However horrifying, it is not the tales of destruction or the predictions of woe which have depressed me. We have been hearing these for years; in fact, people have become so inured to them that, we are told, they no longer listen. And we have not come here to repeat these stories: others are doing it, and with much greater skill. Besides, the world has heard it all; everyone must by now know what is happening.

Much as I find people's growing indifference, nay callousness, disturbing, I am more appalled by the almost universal tendency to ignore it all, by the growing mood of denial. If the facts are well known, and they obviously are, if their consequences are understood, and by now they must be, then why are people, their institutions, the authorities, behaving the way they do? Why are the facts dismissed, warnings ignored, research predictions doubted? Why are the governing bodies of nations, world organizations, religious authorities behaving as if the data, the scientific conclusions, are no more than the ravings of a millenarian lunatic, hoisting his placards and shouting on a street corner, proclaiming the imminence of the Day of Judgment, the end of the world?

It is this illogical behavior, this impossible response, which is so difficult to understand; and, as the title of this conference declares, it is this which is the main reason for our being here.

During the last few days we heard many explanations, many attempts at understanding this almost general, "paranoid" behavior. Most speakers pointed to psychological, ideological, and political factors, to religious or cultural convictions, as the main reasons for this attitude. Not only do emotional states, strong convictions, or powerful beliefs prevent people from fully understanding the situation or interfere with their comprehension of the data and their significance, but they may actually induce reactions against all outside efforts at explanation, even rouse some to regard such actions as an attack on cherished beliefs. Indeed, it is not rare for such ideas so to dominate people's minds that they become overoptimistic, trusting in providence or other external power to save them and the world.

Some speakers, however, attempted to implicate organic rather than cultural factors as the main causes for this behavioral oddity. Some pointed to genetic factors, others suggested that the failure of the palaeocephalon, the older, physiological brain, to keep pace with the human, expanding neocephalon may be at the root of this problem. I have also added my voice to the organicist camp, a side I seldom support, arguing that much deeper, biological forces are involved, and call for their examination.

Basic Biological Factors

My arguments are very simple. The gross similarity between the behavioral patterns and developmental course of human and animal, even plant, social groups, make only one conclusion possible: the incomprehensible cause for humanity's behavior in the present crisis must lie, as that of animals undoubtedly does, in the biological, rather than idiosyncratic cultural, aspects of man. This behavior seems "paranoid," incomprehensible, only because it is biological, not logical, human.

But I had better explain matters in more detail, especially as it would directly lead us to the main subject of this address. Now: don't be too alarmed. I find myself in the position of a British stand-up comic, whose name I have forgotten, who, having noted the look on his audience's faces when he announced he was going to recite Shakespeare, promptly calmed them saying he had simplified the words of the bard—until he understood them himself.

The Growth and Decay of Human Communities

An impartial, unimpassioned observation of human patterns of settlement shows little difference between them and those of other species, especially species not subject to much predation. Making the most of available resources, people multiply, increase in numbers, and flourish, often spreading to other lands. The continuing exploitation of the environment, at an increased tempo, dictated by the greater needs of the enlarging community, however, finally destroys the very basis of the community's success. The polis which exceeds the limits set by philosophers nearly two and a half millennia ago is then faced with a number of choices. It may develop other resources, part with a great number of its citizens as they emigrate, or continue its existence at a very much reduced standard of living. Historically, however, solutions were often forced by war, as neighbors took advantage of the community's weakness.

These patterns of rise and fall, in their main outlines, have been repeated throughout history, in small, circumscribed island/oasis settlements as in great empires. Some of the best examples are recorded in the history of Hellas, its islands and peninsulae, which, denuded of their tree cover, soon eroded to their skeletal rocks, forcing their inhabitants to leave for other lands. They are even more starkly visible where little subsequent occupation followed, as in Copan in Central America or Easter Island in the Pacific. They can, moreover, be observed among other species or even experimentally reproduced in animal communities.

Growth and Adaptation to Seasonal Cyclicity

Growth, increase in bulk and increase in numbers, is one of the most basic characteristics of living matter. Dependent, in the last analysis, on the chemical, or physicochemical, cellular process of mitosis, when DNA molecules split, chromosomes divide and a single cell becomes two, it is influenced, like all chemical processes, by the environment. Growth takes place only when conditions are right; it slows when they deteriorate and completely stops as they worsen. Unprotected living matter, in these adverse circumstances, is quickly destroyed unless rendered dormant and enclosed in special covering. More complex organisms, drawing on their physiological resources, can maintain a more or less adequate *milieu intérieur* to avoid a shutdown. The more advanced forms of life, all of which exist only in social groupings, can, through cultural applications, ensure not only protection from fairly severe adverse conditions, but continued growth. This, however, depends on the cultural traditions of each group and their members' acceptance of their obligations toward it.

The most common examples are adaptations to seasonal variations, more so in subtropical and temperate climates, to aridity of deserts and biting cold of northern winters, and are usually accompanied by cyclical fluctuation of the growth and fertility of the plants and animals of these regions. Immediate exploitation, rapid increase in size, and, more so, numbers during times of plenty proved an evolutionarily successful trait, selected by many unrelated species. Large numbers of young helped survival when subject to predation or harsh environments, whether encapsulated, covered, kept inside the bodies, or protected in the society of adults. Once the seasons changed growth could be resumed and all life flourish.

When this did not happen, when cosmic events interrupted the planetary succession of the seasons, mass extinctions followed. Many of these recurred at approximate intervals of twenty-six million years. Others, of particular species or groups of species, limited to one area or another, when not secondary to local geophysical factors, were as often due to disease or predation as to the destruction of the environment, largely by the very species which died as a result of it.

Patterns of Improvident Exploitation

These generalities, most of which equally apply to man as to animals, are only too evident all around us. Plants cannot move; they must make do with the often limited patch of land on which they are rooted. Many species continue vegetative growth until stressed, if by nothing else but seasonal changes, to flower and fruit, their descendants repeating the cycle on fresh soil. Many animals, from insects to vertebrates, similarly quickly exploit the resources round them, grow and multiply. When their immediate environment can no longer support them, animals, unlike plants, can seek fresh fields. Locusts move with the wind but birds follow fixed routes; smaller forms, like insects, rarely cover any distance, but lay eggs which can withstand adverse conditions, or become dormant for the winter.

Maggots may rapidly consume an animal carcass, pupate, and, when conditions are difficult, can remain dormant, their imagos emerging when it is again suitable to start new broods. Tadpoles in a desert pool grow fast and, as the water evaporates, the larger turn cannibal, eat the smaller and reach the point of metamorphosis, to form the next generation. In some isolated areas along the North American Arctic coast lemmings quickly multiply until, having overgrazed the land, most starve and die. When the land returns to its former state the few survivors attack the fresh meadows and multiply again, establishing four-year cycles of growth and decline. European lemmings migrate until, according to the accepted story, they reach the sea and "commit suicide."

However improvident when judged by hindsight, the seemingly "paranoid" adaptation for unlimited growth and increase in numbers as long as food is available, proved, as already noted, a successful evolutionary stratagem. It has therefore been incorporated in the genetic template of most animals, including, as Malthus already realized, man. And it is this hereditary trait which is responsible for man's incomprehensible "paranoid" behavior.

Though no experimental proof is really needed, an unintentional experiment, performed some two centuries ago, may be of interest. This involved the sequelae of release of goats on uninhabited Pacific islands as living "food stores" for shipwrecked sailors. Like the lemmings, the goats multiplied. When they consumed everything most died of starvation; the island recovered but was denuded afresh by the surviving goats, and the cycle repeated. The introduction of exotic species into "virgin" territory which contains no natural predators follows the same patterns, at least in its initial steps of multiplication, growth, and destruction of the environment, though the latter is, in most instances, cut short when man interferes. Such intervention does not, of course, occur when man himself, or his domestic animals, are the exotic species.

The Relation Between Biological Factors and Emotive or Intellectual Activity

Though the resemblance between the "improvident" growth and inevitable decline of biological species and those of historical human communities is so very strong, it would be a mistake to adopt too strong an organicist view and blame all on biological factors. Man's behavior is inextricably bound with his culture; and even if the prime cause of the behavior and actions we are now considering is almost certainly biological, it is strongly influenced and obviously expressed in cultural terms.

Yet, it is precisely this which raises new anxieties. The realization that these elemental biological forces can influence us not only "externally," in what, without being aware of their influence, we do, but also "internally," affecting our emotional and intellectual life, is, to say the least, extremely alarming.

Observing plants and animals we take for granted that they are not conscious of such emotions as "urges to multiply"—though devoted care of the young, in insects, fish, birds, or mammals, makes it at times difficult to deny. We know we feel these emotions, and it is quite legitimate to ask to what extent these feelings are the expressions of biological forces acting upon us. Indeed, it is more than urgent that analytical examination is not limited to these deep primary emotions, like protection of the young, but extends to our beliefs, ideologies, religious creeds, or codes of morals, and includes the possibility that at least some are strongly influenced by these primeval biological edicts, are only blind urges masquerading as lofty principles.

May I here, in an aside, point out that this is more than feasible. For, once we realize the artificiality of body-mind dichotomy we can accept that such "urges" can be as much a part of the genetic template as the shape of one's nose.

Not long ago, while discussing a related subject, a biologist friend started vigorously attacking one culturally "sacred" principle after another. On defense, I found it difficult to ward off his assault on romantic love, in any case out of fashion today, with film heroines, much to the disgust of my wife, jumping into bed with men they have just met. But, while conceding that, indeed, it is often but a euphemism for the primeval urge to multiply, I argued that just as often it partakes of the best in human mutuality. Neither was it easy to disagree with the claim that cultural, and especially racial, intolerance bore an unmistakable resemblance to biological rejection: the rejection of foreign tissue on a cellular level, or of those which differ in smell, form, or behavior on the level of organisms. Nor, frankly, did I wish to press the point that human intolerance had a malevolence all of its own.

I became somewhat uncomfortable when my friend turned his attention to motives behind the reverence for, and sanctity of, human life. Though, I must confess, I could not help but appreciate the irony of his contention that the real force behind the protests of pro-lifers was not the sanctity of developing life but the expansionist demands of what Dawkins called "the selfish gene," I still could not agree with his main arguments. Respect for human life might, I conceded, have its remote origin in genetic "calculations," but it is the very cohesion of community, which these supposedly support, which itself generates forces of its own. Even if, as such biological theories suggest, human beings are only a genetic "convenience," having come into existence, they have, through their mutuality, created remarkable cultures with their own values.

It was then that, all of a sudden, I understood the source of my premonitions of doom, the sense that, as I have put it, I was just a bit player in a Greek tragedy. How can we, I asked myself, oppose this primeval energy of life? Constantly influenced, often dominated by this force, how can we fight its expansionist biological activities? How can we be ourselves?

Man in Evolution

Man is a product of the evolutionary process. According to some views he, like other complex organisms, came into being primarily as a means of spreading the genetic material of which he is composed and which he carries in the form of gametes. This, judging by the burgeoning multitudes of mankind, he has done with great success. However, man, in contrast to other, equally successful organisms, has, apparently by accident, acquired in the course of his evolution other, rather remarkable, characteristics. These gave him not only the ability to adapt, the capacity to understand and plan, the skills to build and create, but, above all, the faculty of self-conscience, the intellectual power to ask questions.

Evolution is going on; however remarkable man is, however exceptional his culture, he is but a transient form. What has come into existence by chance can disappear by accident; there is no guarantee man will survive; there is no guarantee evolution will replace him by some better organism.

We, however, believe man is worth saving.

And may I here, again, depart from the text. Man has probably regarded himself as special since the emergence of consciousness. Egocentric tendencies continued as ethnocentric prejudices to be only partially converted into anthropocentric convictions. These have been elevated by religious and ideological movements to the image of "the crown of creation" with a "manifest destiny."

How come, having disregarded all such claims, I still consider man as something special? I do so largely because of mathematical considerations. The genome of a hominoid, a member of the superfamily which includes the apes and man, contains thousands of millions (six billion) of units. Just imagine the permutations in which these may appear! Accident has resulted in a most remarkable permutation possessed by man. It would be a catastrophe should it be interfered with. After all—a deviation of only 2 percent results in a chimpanzee!

Possible Evolving Future

Evolution is not a mysterious process; the manifestation of the actions initiated by organic compounds, which constantly increase in number, its character is determined by the unending permutations of these compounds, which ensure that, within limits, no environment interferes with their activity. Yet, though no higher intelligence, no directive power, is involved, once started, evolution, like the activity which it expresses, has an almost unstoppable inertia. It goes on, becoming more complex as it creates more complex forms, which, in their turn, goad it on. Man, as yet the most complex, has, however, surpassed them all, expanding the processes of evolution itself through the emergence of aggressive human cultural evolution. Together, biological and cultural evolution have greatly gathered speed, changing the planet and still continuing to change it. It is impossible to predict the future, it is impossible to say where we are being taken. It is only possible to ponder, examine the possibilities, and guess.

Cultural evolutionary activity may yet drive the disparate human communities to abandon individual paths, join and agglomerate into a megasociety. This has been envisioned as a process similar to that of insect supersocieties, but involving the whole planet. It has also been pointed out that while attempts were made to do so already several thousands of years ago, never have they been so compelling, never have they had the communication technology of today, nor have they ever been so general, as in contemporary plural societies and supranational organizations. On the other hand, conscious of the many disruptive forces, doubters wonder whether the genetically based rejection of foreign elements would allow such a society to form.

Neither cultural nor religious traditions are strangers to prophesies of the extinction of human life, the end of the world. Both science and human history tell us of the death of whole orders of beings, the dissolution of great nations, the destruction of their cultures. There is no assurance this will not happen to the family of man and his culture.

Though surrounded by evolutionary flux, some plants, animals, even human communities, survive with little change—provided their environment remains untouched—often becoming living fossils. Though the main body of humanity is sure to change radically, some communities, though few compared with those in the past, may, by chance, find themselves "out of the race" and survive unchanged. Present-day culture may, alternatively, also survive in an "encapsulated," seedlike form. And it would not be the first time a culture thus survived, for it happened several times, most notably when classical culture was reborn in the Renaissance among the barbarian tribes of Western Europe.

Many scientists feel that since contemporary social systems have largely eliminated natural selection little future change of man's physical attributes is to be expected. Biological evolution has, however, never stopped; the mixing of populations and improvements in health and urbanization have resulted in new, successful genotypes, while the demands and stresses of modern culture have given advantage to the fittest. The losers have unfortunately been marginalized, posing grave social problems.

More radical physical and other changes may follow the development of physiological and allied technology and concurrently, or somewhat later, that of bioengineering. A wide selection of capabilities may become available with the manufacture of appliances which may, in addition to replacing diseased or injured organs, allow humans to work in polluted, toxic, or other hostile environments, including those on other planets. Bioengineering may offer similar abilities to a select few, which through manipulation of the gametes may become hereditary. The almost inevitable advent of artificial intelligence may, in time, lead to science-fiction mixed communities of biogenic and nonorganic individuals. A further semi- or fully independent evolution of the latter is also a possibility.

Opting Out

Whatever happens, whichever change is to come, whenever it happens, the future seems to hold neither role nor hope for present-day humanity and its culture. A transient link in the chain of evolution, man seems doomed to disappear. And he may disappear—for evolution cannot be stopped—it is *the* future. We cannot fight it, but we can circumvent it.

We can "get off," opt out of the evolutionary process.

As much as I find this choice exciting, I also find it extremely troublesome. This is not so much because of "logistic" reasons, for the evolutionary processes are taking place within the global human society, but, even more, because of emotional, ideological, even "spiritual" reasons. The evolutionary process is the future; "opting out," we relinquish all claims to any possible future role, we become marginal.

A Parallel Course

This is not, however, the whole truth. Though "getting out of the race," giving up on any competitive enterprise, may, in social terms, mean defeat, it is not so in a struggle to preserve our identity, to retain an exceptional character which is, otherwise, sure to be destroyed. Though, judging from the fate of species which were "left out" of the race, it involves a risk of stagnation, a danger of physical and intellectual inactivity, these may be minimized by insistence on a constant relationship with the rest of mankind, members of the new evolving entity.

This act also obviously does not entail a "branching off" from a "main stem," even if it is, just as plainly, a parting of the ways. The clidistic tree is a scientific, human construct, based on hindsight; branch and main stem can only be determined after the fact. We shall be judged by posterity. Indeed, following palaeontological clidistics humans can only trace their ancestry through a number of "branch lines" prior to attaining their recent taxonomic eminence.

It is not the hope of ultimate crowning as "main stem" that

should motivate shunting into a parallel track, but our concern to preserve humanism, to keep this exceptional stage of human development, this rare permutation of genes, from destruction by the forces of time and change.

I find myself again in a situation, but described by another comic, Jerry Lewis, a North American, who cried, "Stop the planet, I want to get off!"

Summary

My thesis is simple. Since both the "paranoid" behavior we constantly witness and the environmental changes we face have their origin in the deepest elements of living matter and the very processes of evolution, we cannot fight them directly. No frontal opposition, no argument, no education, can defeat these blind, powerful forces. However, they can and should be circumvented.

We have the intelligence, the foresight, the means and motive to do so—and do so we must.

Once we opt out of the evolutionary process, immunize ourselves against its influence, we can, as an independent force, live beside the developing new entity—with the hope of perhaps being able, later, to divert its course to less threatening, more humanistic, channels. Honest analysis of the situation and our own motives is an imperative first step. A constant relationship with those who do not join us is essential. Enthusiasm is vital, energy a must, and some luck may also help.

Humanism still has a chance.

25

The Delphi Declaration

August 1995

This Declaration derives from an International Multidisciplinary Conference on "Human Behavior and the Meaning of Modern Humanism," which was held at Delphi, Greece, from June 14–17, 1995. The participants, from many fields of Science and the Humanities, pondered the human predicament. In a four-day intensive scientific exploration, participants from a wide range of disciplines* debated the dominant issues of the existence of the human species. This was the first occasion on which such an intellectually diverse group has approached the subject of human existence holistically and from so many different perspectives. A consensus was reached on the six issues below:

---

*Anthropologists, Sociologists, Biologists, Neurobiologists, Physicians, Physicists, Astrophysicists, Chaos Theorists, Environmentalists, Economists, Management Experts, Writers, Artists, Theologians, Clergy, Philosophers, Humanists, Businessmen, Journalists, and Politicians.

296 THE HUMAN PREDICAMENT

(1) Human population growth is of grave concern as a potential source of unprecedented human and natural catastrophe. Every nation must unite in the effort to determine planetary capacity.

(2) The abundance of resources in the developed world and the poverty in the developing countries is threatening political tension, mass migration, and violent confrontation. This problem, addressed until now with policies of "sustainable development," must be approached anew with rational and scientific methods.

(3) Human-made modifications of the planetary ecosystem ("environment") threaten to produce irreversible and catastrophic changes.

(4) Wars, and the dangers inherent in the use of weapons of mass destruction, threaten the survival of many forms of life, including human.

(5) Ongoing advances in science, technology, and biology are changing the world dramatically. However, the basic characteristics of human behavior and the central principles of ethics remain unchanged. Though these have, through the centuries, inspired humankind's most glorious achievements, they have also been responsible for the most terrible monstrosities in human history. The development and implementation of a new global Ethic and Philosophy, to face the challenges of the emerging new world, is therefore vital for human existence.

(6) Survival of the human species also makes it absolutely necessary that the study of human behavior be intensified. This study should be holistic in character and integrate findings from biological, neurophysiological, cultural, philosophical, and other sources.

These issues are the most important in the world today. The future of humankind depends on resolving them. We cannot confront these issues with archaic philosophical, religious, and biological thinking. Such thinking explains the difficulties encountered at the recent International Conference on Environment and Human Population

Growth. We need a new approach and a new organization. This conference has therefore unanimously decided to create the Delphi Society. This new society will approach the problems of human existence and the future of humankind holistically and from a multidisciplinary point of view with a unifying concept based on the patterns of human behavior. An understanding of human behavior is absolutely necessary if we are to explain how we came to our present plight. The study of patterns of human behavior will be a long-lasting project for the society, so that the action of the society today will have to be guided by an approximate understanding of human behavior.

The broad goal of the society will be to contribute to the greatest issues that humanity is facing today:

- Prevention of global catastrophe
- Creation of an environment supportive of peace and progress for all human beings
- Prevention of a sixth mass extinction of life on the planet, and preservation of the human species.

The society will undertake the enormous task of translating these precepts into practical action. A plan of action will be designed based on objectives that might act as catalysts for global change. These objectives include the new concepts of "population health," and "a new role for medicine" for a sustained balance of reproduction and optimization of the environment.

To promote these goals effectively, we will cooperate with governmental and nongovernmental agencies, business and industry, mass media, environmentalists and conservationists, and advocates of allied causes.

The Society has the ambition to succeed where all the religions and all the ideologies throughout the centuries have been largely unsuccessful, i.e., to define a way that will unite the human species.